THE RELEVANCE OF
METAETHICS
TO ETHICS

ACTA UNIVERSITATIS STOCKHOLMIENSIS

STOCKHOLM STUDIES IN PHILOSOPHY 5

TORBJÖRN TÄNNSJÖ

THE RELEVANCE OF METAETHICS TO ETHICS

ALMQVIST & WIKSELL INTERNATIONAL

STOCKHOLM

© Torbjörn Tännsjö

ISBN 91-22-00068-2

Printed in Sweden by

Almqvist & Wiksell, Uppsala 1976

PREFACE

The question I raise in this study was originally put to me by my students when I lectured on the moral philosophy of Stevenson: is metaethics relevant to normative ethics? Their reason for asking it, was their scepticism about the fruitfulness of metaethical studies. This was in 1968 and it was at a time when the dominating interest among students of philosophy in Stockholm lay in political questions.

When trying to answer the question, I had to make a wide variety of interpretations of it. I had to distinguish between various kinds of metaethical studies and I had to define various concepts of relevance. I had to discuss actual metaethical theories as well as possible ones.

Although I feel a bit more certain about the answer to the question whether metaethics is relevant to ethics, I have to admit that the rationale of this question, viz. the problem whether metaethics is a fruitful field of investigation for moral philosophy, has not yet been definitely solved. My study is relevant to the settlement of this question but it is not itself the answer to it.

I am indebted to several friends for helpful criticism of earlier versions of this book, in particular to Lars Bergström, Gunnar Andrén, Lars O. Ericsson, Harald Ofstad and Giuliano Pontara.

Ia Hallberg, Eva Liss and Maj-Britt Tolstad have helped me with the typing of my manuscript. Stephen Theron and Craig McKay have checked my English. I am very grateful to all of them.

Torbjörn Tännsjö

Stockholm February 1976

CONTENTS

Chapter One: THE PROBLEM 9
1. Background 9
2. The Significance of the Question: Is Metaethics Relevant to Ethics? . 12
3. The Meaning of "Metaethics" Made More Precise 16
4. The Meaning of "Relevant to Ethics" Made More Precise 20
5. The Plan of This Study 27
6. Some Central Theses of this Study 28
7. Some Terminological Remarks 28

Chapter Two: COULD MY PROBLEM BE TRIVIALLY SOLVED? . . . 30
1. Background 30
2. A. Gewirth on Ethical Non-neutrality 31
3. L. Bergström on the Question Whether Metaethical Theories Imply
   Ethical Statements 40

Chapter Three: THE RELEVANCE TO ETHICS OF R. BRANDT'S
NATURALISM 44
1. Background 44
2. R. Brandt's Concept of Naturalism 45
3. R. Brandt's Concept of Synonymy 47
4. Further Problems With the Concept of Synonymy 49
5. Is Linguistic Naturalism Relevant to Ethics? 51
6. Summary of the Chapter 55

Chapter Four: THE RELEVANCE TO ETHICS OF C. L. STEVEN-
SON'S EMOTIVISM 57
1. Background 57
2. Emotivism and the Justification of Ethical Statements 58
3. Stevenson's Arguments in Support of His Sceptical Theses 60
4. Do the Alleged Consequences of Emotivism for the Possibilities of
   Rational Justification in Ethics Prove Emotivism Relevant to Ethics? 87
5. F. A. Olafson in Defence of the View that Emotivism has a Sort of
   Pragmatic Relevance to Ethics 96
6. The Chapter Concluded 106

Chapter Five: THE RELEVANCE TO ETHICS OF R. M. HARE'S
UNIVERSAL PRESCRIPTIVISM 108
1. Background 108
2. Does "Ought" Imply "Can?" 108

3. Does Hare's Universalism Make the Distinction between Act- and Rule-Utilitarianism Collapse? 118
4. Ethical Argumentation and Deliberation in the Light of Universal Prescriptivism 125
5. A Brief Summary of the Chapter 136

Chapter Six: GENERAL CONCLUSIONS 138
1. Background 138
2. What is Metaethics? 139
3. Conclusions About the Logical Relevance to Ethics of Metaethics . . 146
4. Conclusions About the Relevance to Ethics in an Ethical System of Metaethics 172
5. Conclusions About the Pragmatic Relevance to Ethics of Metaethics 184
6. Is Metaethics Therapeutically Relevant to Ethics? 194
7. The Chapter Concluded 214

Annotated Bibliography 217

Bibliography Containing Books and Articles Referred to in this Study . . . 224

CHAPTER ONE

THE PROBLEM

1. Background

R. M. Hare has described[1] how, after the end of World War II, he returned to Britain and to civil life with a wish to study moral philosophy; these studies, he supposed, would lead him closer to the solution of substantial moral problems. It is not to be wondered at, then, that his reading of the following passage by C. D. Broad, in *Five Types of Ethical Theory,* gave him quite a shock:

> We can no more learn to act rightly by appealing to the ethical theory of right action than we can play golf well by appealing to the mathematical theory of the flight of the golf-ball. The interest of ethics is thus almost wholly theoretical, as is the interest of the mathematical theory of golf or of billiards. And yet it may have a certain slight practical application. It may lead us to look out for certain systematic faults which we should not otherwise have suspected; and, once we are on the look out for them, we may learn to correct them. But in the main the old saying is true: *Non in dialectica complacuit Deo salvum facere populum suum.* Not that this is any objection to dialectic. For salvation is not everything; and to try to understand in outline what one solves *ambulando* and in detail is quite good fun for those people who like that sort of thing. (p. 285)

Hare's feelings of dismay, founded as they were, on an apparent conflict between a keen interest in moral problems and the prospects for their solution which moral philosophy, according to Broad, could offer, reflect a problem for moral philosophy which would seem to be extremely important: what kind of relation holds between morality and moral philosophy; has moral philosophy any bearing on substantial moral problems?

The question whether moral philosophy has any relevance to substantial moral problems is seldom discussed by moral philosophers. All the same I think it possible to give a rough indication of how it has arisen, historically speaking. I think the problem of whether moral philosophy has ethical relevance arises at a certain point in the history

---

[1] In "Broad's Approach to Moral Philosophy".

of moral philosophy on account of a certain group of views on certain matters that becomes dominant at this point.

Moral philosophy deals, of course, with a *complex* of rather different problems. I think it wise to make some distinctions here. Roughly there are at least four main disciplines *within* moral philosophy. I distinguish between *normative* ethics, which deals with questions like 'What is intrinsically good?', or 'What normative principles are valid?', *descriptive* ethics, which deals with questions like 'What is considered good in Sudan?', moral *epistemology,* which deals with questions like 'What is moral knowledge?', 'What are the sources of ethical knowledge?', 'Is ethical knowledge possible?', and so forth, and *metaethics,* which deals with questions like 'What does the word "good" mean?', 'What is the function of the term "ought"?', and so forth.

I take normative ethics to be central to moral philosophy. Other parts of the subject may be of interest for their own sakes, metaethics for linguistics, descriptive ethics for anthropology, and so on, but I think it is because these subjects are presupposed to be relevant to normative ethics that they are studied by *moral philosophers*. My thesis is that the problem of whether moral philosophy has ethical relevance arises at precisely the point where the study of metaethics becomes dominant. And in this monograph I will question the presupposition that metaethics is relevant to normative ethics.

Generally speaking, I think the *problematic* character of metaethics regarding its relevance to normative ethics appears clear when one realizes how particular metaethical problems arise in moral philosophy, compared to the way in which other problems of moral philosophy have arisen.

Epistemological considerations naturally arise as one gets into difficulties when trying to reach a rational agreement about a certain question. When one thinker holds that the world is composed of atoms and the other asserts that it is composed of fire while both support their contention with some piece of evidence, both claiming to have *knowledge* of these mutually inconsistent propositions, then it is naturally asked what it *is* to know such a thing, what *sources* there are available for such kinds of knowledge, and so forth. Sometimes epistemological considerations may tell against scientific views. It may, for example, be pointed out by an empiricist that if the only evidence the atomist has for his views is what he has concluded purely from thinking, then he has no right to claim knowledge for his contention.

A parallel situation has often been held to obtain in ethics. Problems of ethical epistemology have arisen when agreement among rational people has been hard to achieve in ethical matters. But various views have been held about ethical epistemology. Naturalists in ethical epistemology (which is different from naturalism in metaethics) have held that there are no problems peculiar to ethical epistemology. Ethical knowledge is only one kind of empirical knowledge and what may be said about empirical knowledge may be adapted to ethical knowledge as well. The sources, the scope and limits, and so forth, are the same.

Intuitionism of, say, Moore's sort, has an epistemological aspect as well as a metaethical one. According to intuitionism, ethical knowledge is very different from empirical knowledge, it is knowledge about nonnatural facts and it is gained through very special sources, viz. intuition or rational insights. Yet, ethical "knowledge" in the sense of true, well-founded belief is possible, according to intuitionism. And of course the discussion about its sources, its scope, limits and so on, is of the utmost relevance to normative ethics.

In as far as "moral philosophy" is taken to be chiefly a matter of normative ethics and ethical epistemology, its relevance to normative problems and also its practical relevance is obvious. But the introduction of noncognitivism (or value-nihilism, emotivism, prescriptivism or whatever name one prefers to give this current group of ethical theories) produces problems on this very point. For according to these theories ethical statements, if there are such "statements" at all, lack truth values, and may perhaps not even be supported with reasons having any logical compulsion at all. Hence, no ethical knowledge is possible. All of a sudden quite a few problems just dissolve. The discussion about sources of ethical knowledge, or the scope and limits of ethical knowledge, or about criteria of ethical knowledge, and so forth, becomes idle.

At this point in the history of moral philosophy, which is of course not strictly speaking a point but an event streched out ever a long period of time, a crisis is produced. The object of moral philosophy is drastically changed. One has to study what is left to be studied, and this is ethical language, ethical communication, ethical thinking and feeling and such "positive" facts, besides the problems of normative ethics. In some places even the study of normative ethics itself becomes suspect. For what kind of science is it that deals with questions to which there are no answers that can be known?

Problems, say, about the meaning of ethical terms, were not quite foreign to earlier periods of the history of moral philosophy, for even intuitionists like Moore speculate about the meaning of the word "good"; but now it becomes dominant and the primary interest of many moral philosophers. And now the problem of the relevance to normative prob-

11

lems of moral philosophy becomes acute. For, if conceived of as metaethics, viz. the study *of* ethics rather than *in* ethics, to use Häger-ström's words, how is moral philosophy related to normative problems? What does it matter to a person who, primarily, wants to deal with practical problems about what to do and, secondarily, with normatively ethical problems about what principles of conduct are valid, what certain *words* mean?

This, I think, is a fairly true sketch of how metaethical problems have cropped up in moral philosophy and, also, a rough indication of how the problem of whether metaethical problems are relevant to moral philosophy has struck most modern moral philosophers. To put it polem-ically, what possible interest is there in problems that are investigated mainly because they are the only ones left now that certain other prob-lems which were once apparently of the utmost consequence have vanished? But the polemical form of the question must not tempt us to give a rash answer to it. For the genesis of a certain study is one thing, and its logical relations to a certain group of problems quite another thing. The question of what the relevance of metaethics to normative ethics is remains to be answered.

2. The Significance of the Question: Is Metaethics Relevant to Ethics

The importance of the question of the ethical relevance of metaethics is perhaps too obvious to need stressing. If for no other reason it may at least be discussed in order to clarify a philosophical debate which has taken place during the two last decades. Yet there is one aspect of this question which deserves further comment: could the answer to the question of the ethical relevance of metaethics be of importance to those who are concerned with the question whether it is legitimate from a normative point of view to pursue metaethical research? Could a better understanding of the relation between metaethics and normative ethics be of any help to those who wish to know how valuable or fruitful metaethical research is, apart from the fun involved? This view seems to be implicit in R. M. Hare's description of his dismay when getting to understand Broad's view of the relation in question, and it is implicit in a less "moralistic" way in the following quotation from W. Frankena's *Ethics:*

... we shall take ethics ... as being interested in meta-ethical questions mainly because it seems necessary to answer such questions before one can be entirely satisfied with one's normative theory (although ethics is also interested in meta-ethical questions for their own sakes). (p. 5)

Now, does the value or fruitfulness of metaethical research in any way depend on the relevance metaethical theories have for normative ethical questions? The answer to this question is in no way simple. Questions as to what kind of research ought to be pursued fall in part outside the realm of the science in question and this seems to be true even for moral philosophy, in this case because a definite answer to the question presupposes, among other things, far-reaching *empirical* investigations. We must know something about the *effects* of the research in question. All the same I think the problem could be simplified to some extent, provided one does not require too definite a solution.

In order to get a better understanding of the conditions for such a partial solution I shall draw a distinction between two kinds of possible effects of scientific research, viz. between rational and non-rational effects. This distinction must remain vague but it could be roughly characterized in the following manner.

When science is pursued, knowledge is reached (or not reached) as the result of a complex chain of actions and activities. These actions and activities have a vast number of consequences—too vast to be surveyed—relevant to a normative assessment of the actions and activities themselves. Among these consequences there are some which result from misunderstanding (people behave immorally because, say, they think Stevenson has proved that everything is permitted), some which are due to the fact that the scientist was doing research and therefore not engaged in some alternative activity (if all the radical scientists in the United States went into politics and fought against US imperialism perhaps it could be smashed) and many others of this sort. These kinds of consequences I shall call "non-rational", in contradistinction to "rational" ones. Rational consequences are those which obtain because some agent has based some of his actions on an understanding of and belief in the results of the science in question.

To a normative assessment of the legitimacy of a given kind of research, non-rational as well as rational effects are relevant. But, at the same time, it is very difficult to survey the non-rational effects and even the rational effects are inaccessible to a moral philosopher lacking empirical data. So the question of the moral legitimacy of metaethical research cannot here be definitely answered. But a partial solution of the problem is within reach. For there are good reasons, I think, to suspect, firstly that the normative status of metaethical research, assessed with due attention to all the relevant consequences, depends in most cases on the normative status of metaethical research, assessed with due attention only to the rational effects. (The reasonableness of this statement is dependent on which normative view is correct. Given a teleological view it is an empirical generalization but given a deontological view it is the consequence of a *prima facie* reasonable ethical principle, viz. special weight must be given to the rational effects from a moral point of view.) And, furthermore, the rational effects probably often depend for *their* worth on what kind of knowledge is the outcome of the research in question. Knowledge of a high degree of "practical relevance" is likely to give rise to important rational effects.

What then is practical relevance? One way of showing a piece of research to be practically relevant seems to be to show that it is necessary for some other kind of research which we consider to be indispensable for some practical purpose. A natural candidate in the case of metaethics would be, of course, normative ethics.

But here problems crop up. For, firstly, someone might retort that the one and only objective of the sciences is to "seek the truth", and so look askance at the "utility". Secondly, it might be contended that metaethics is relevant to other (than normative) problems of some importance. Thirdly, it is in fact doubtful whether normative ethical problems themselves are really of practical importance. I will examine these objections one by one.

The first objection is, I think, easy to meet. Scientific research *has* indeed important effects, rational as well as non-rational, and these *are* of practical importance (if perhaps not the *only* things that matter). This I believe to be self-evident. Moreover, "seeking the truth" is an insufficiently specific aim, even if a necessary aim of all science. You cannot gain access to *all* the truths (whatever this might mean) and there is no perfect "logical order" which tells you in which way to proceed. And then, what is more natural than making some choices, as to subject matter, because of practical considerations? To fail to do so, in my opinion, would not even be fun.

The other objection presents more difficulties. As a matter of fact it can only be answered after going through a complete list of all possible candidates, which means writing not one monograph but several. I can only express a vague feeling on this point. And my feeling is that such an examination would not lead to the discovery of independent reasons for metaethics. Most metaethical theories are devised to give us ethically relevant informations.

14

Even the third objection is not easily dismissed, although it is rather paradoxical. The point could be elaborated in the following manner. Today, from a practical point of view, we know enough about what constitutes the good society, about what is right and wrong and such like. Of course we disagree on a highly theoretical and abstract level, in philosophical papers, but when it comes to the most urgent moral problems, such as whether exploitation is permissible, imperialist wars can be defended, and so on, then all decent people agree, some because of teleological considerations, others because of deontological considerations. The most urgent problem of our time is not to get to know more about what is right, but to get people to do it, or at least, not to do what is obviously wrong. *Qua* moral philosophers we should seek solutions to problems that relate to this objective.

I am myself very much in sympathy with this argument, as regards its validity. I think it obvious that at least the oppressed in our society know fairly well what is wrong. Their main problem is that they lack optimism about the prospects of bringing about a change. All the same I am in doubt about the relevance of the argument. For even if it is true that the main problem today is to arouse the moral and political indignation of those who are oppressed, it is not unthinkable that this may be done partly through reflection on moral problems.

To sum up this section: It has sometimes been maintained that metaethical studies could only be morally defended with reference to the relevance to ethics which these studies may have. This claim is hard definitely to prove or disprove. It requires, to be rationally assessed, a knowledge of the rational as well as non-rational effects of very complex actions and activities. And that sort of knowledge could not be achieved without empirical investigations. But granted that normative ethical problems have practical relevance the claim seems reasonable at least to some degree. If so then the question of the extent to which metaethics is relevant to ethics seems to be of some importance for scholars faced with the problem whether to pursue metaethical research. Two kinds of complication remain, however. First of all it is possible that metaethical studies could be defended because of some kind of relevance other than ethical. And in that case a negative answer to my question would not be fatal. Secondly, it is possible that my empirical presuppositions in this chapter are wrong so that it would not do at all to show that metaethics is relevant to ethics in order to defend it. However this may be, a disproof of the claim that metaethics is relevant to normative ethics would at least be a disproof of *one* argument in defense of the view that metaethical research is legitimate from a moral point of view.

3. The Meaning of "Metaethics" Made more Precise

In order to make precise my question whether "metaethics is relevant to ethics" I shall try (in this section) to make more precise the meaning of "metaethics" and the meaning of "relevant to ethics" (in the next section). My ambition is not, however, to make explicit definitions— this will have to wait until Chapter VI—but to vaguely characterize the phenomena and to draw a demarcation line around certain kinds of studies and concepts that could easily be thought to be included unless I take these precautions.

The meaning of the term "metaethics" varies in a somewhat bewilder- ing way. Only some of its senses will be of interest for my purpose. Furthermore there are studies usually classified as "ethics", "analytical ethics", "critical ethics", "moral epistemology" etc. among which some *are* of interest for my purposes. Thus I shall not be satisfied with a "descriptive" definition of "metaethics".

As I am going to deal with the problem of characterizing metaethics I think it wise to state some conditions that a theory must satisfy to be "metaethical" in my sense. These conditions are intended to reflect my objective with this study. Having these conditions available I shall be able to proceed one step further towards a clearer conception; I will then roughly characterize the kinds of theories that are to be included in the denotation of the term "metaethics". Here some theories will be excluded which many would tend to call "metaethical". Finally in this section, three theories will be selected for a close examination of their ethical relevance; more however of the arrangement of my study in Sec- tion 5 of this chapter.

I consider that the following conditions roughly reflect my aims and reasons for the choice of the object of my study.

First, naturally, some condition of "descriptive reasonableness" must be met. It must not be an abuse of language to call the theories I pick out "metaethical"; at least there must be some person who in some situa- tion could accept my nomenclature. On the other hand this condition is not to be understood as stronger than this. It must not, for example, prevent theories which no one, not even the theorist himself, has actually called "metaethical" from being included or entail that all theories some- times classified as "metaethical" should be included ipso facto.

Secondly, a condition of "representativeness" must be met. The theories covered by my definition must be representative in relation to a good deal of what is produced by moral philosophers at universities who practise an "analytical" philosophical method. This condition is in line with my critical goal.

Thirdly, a condition of "fruitfulness" must be met. This is a condition to the effect that the meaning of "metaethics" must be so defined that the quest for ethical relevance for metaethics in its turn, at least *prima facie,* has some relevance to the question whether metaethics is worth studying in general and as a part of moral philosophy in particular. This means that I will not be satisfied with a definition of 'metaethics' which makes studies that are obviously devoid of any practical importance metaethical. Of course, this condition cannot be made sharp unless we know the meaning of "relevant to ethics". And its strength is dependent on the empirical facts I discussed in the foregoing section of this chapter.

Now, let us see what can be said to characterize a concept of metaethics within the limits set by these three conditions of (1) descriptive reasonableness, (2) representativeness and (3) fruitfulness, as well as by my aims in general within this study. Perhaps if we turn to the metaethical literature we shall get some ideas or hints about some alternative ways of defining the concept.

Among possible defining characteristics are the following.

Metaethical Statements

Metaethical statements should be ethically neutral. They should be statements about the meaning, function etc. of ethical terms, ethical language or ethical argumentation. Now and then, metaethical statements have been taken to be purely logical or analytical, but on other occasions they have been taken to be descriptive as well and even normative.

The Analogy with Meta-Science

A rough analogy has often been drawn between the relation between metaethics and ethics and the relation between the methodology of science and science itself. Metaethics has been conceived as a "second-order" study.

Metaethical Questions and Problems

There are, I think, roughly two ways of conceiving typical metaethical questions. There is a narrow conception that takes as "metaethical" only questions concerning the meaning and function of ethical language, concerning the nature of ethical concepts and statements, and so forth, and there is a wider conception which includes as well questions concerning explanations of ethical knowledge, concerning theories of ethical argumentation, concerning the correct view of the rationality or objectivity of ethical statements, concerning the clarification of the meaning of "praxeological" terms such as "action", "intention" etc.

Among the characteristics that I have mentioned, some are restrictions on the kind of object of metaethical studies, some on the methods used in these studies, and some on the problems discussed. It is rare for 'metaethics' to be defined in terms of the purpose behind the studies; sometimes, however, "ethical relevance" of some sort has been required.

It is not easy to assess more definitely these various proposals. Some of them are undoubtedly metaethically biased and hence of no use for my purposes. Others are even biased regarding the answer to my basic question whether metaethics is relevant to ethics. Yet there are some which seem to be a good point of departure.

To remain reasonable for my purposes, the demand for "ethical neutrality" must not be interpreted as a stronger requirement than to the effect that no *explicit* ethical statements should occur as an essential factor in a metaethical theory. The highly controversial question whether ethical statements are implied, must be left open. Besides this condition, no condition will be placed upon the methods used. Hence, descriptive statements as well as non-ethical evaluations will be allowed besides analytical and logical statements.

The current analogy with scientific methodology will not be used as a defining characteristic. This analogy, I think, is what has made the *term* "metaethics" so popular and it has, I think, also transferred some prestige to metaethics from the celebrated discipline of metalogic. Yet I consider the analogy as much too problematic (and even misleading, as will become clear later) to be of any use.

As for the restrictions on the problems that are "metaethical" in my sense, I shall make a decision that might seem somewhat unnatural. I shall draw my demarcation line in accordance with what I above called the "narrower" conception of metaethics. Only problems and questions about the meaning, function and so on, of ethical language, of uses of ethical language, of ways of using ethical language, of ethical concepts, of ethical statements, and of ethical argumentation, will here be considered metaethical. Thus questions concerning truth, objectivity, the rationality of ethics, valid ethical reasoning, "praxeological" concepts, ethical knowledge, and so forth, will be discounted as not being metaethical.

Now, this must not be *too* narrowly interpreted. Firstly, there are some theories of ethical argumentation that *are* included all the same, viz. those theories which are descriptions or analyses of what people accept as good reasons or valid reasons etc. Only theories *about*[2] valid reasoning are excluded; the same holds, *mutatis mutandis,* for truth, and knowledge Secondly, theories about validity, objectivity, rationality, etc., of morals, though excluded, may (and will) be discussed in this study all the same for they are in their turn often held to be implied (in some manner) by theories that I would be prepared to call "meta-ethical" and which seem herewith to gain relevance to ethics. Thirdly, statements to the effect that what is expressed by certain phrases in contexts typical of normative ethics is neither true, objective, nor accessible to rational argumentation, and so forth, *will* be included being not *about*[2] truth, objectivity or rational argumentation *but about ethical language* in ethical contexts. All the same it must be noticed that my conception of metaethics in this respect is narrower than at least one common conception. On the other hand my conception seems to be well in accordance with what has been the rule in the rare discussion about the relation between metaethics and normative ethics, cf. for example the annotated bibliography about this.

Some Theories to Examine

I am now in a position to choose some typical metaethical theories for examination. I intend to concentrate on the following three: R. Brandt's general view of naturalism, as it has been stated in *Ethical Theory,* C. L. Stevenson's emotivism, as it has been stated in *Ethics and Language* and, to some extent, in *Facts and Values,* and R. M. Hare's universal prescriptivism, as it has been stated in *Freedom and Reason* and in *The Language of Morals.* One could of course have picked out other theories as well, but simultaneously these three are, influential, thorough, and of different methodological types. I think further reasons for my selection would be unnecessary.

---

[2] The meaning of "about" is not quite sharp here. I will explain my use of it more clearly in Chapter VI Section 3, especially pp. 161–167. What I have in mind may be roughly indicated in the following way. When, on the one hand, it is asserted that there is moral truth this assertion is excluded from the denotation of "metaethics". The import of this assertion is, though not quite precise, that there exists some ethical fact. On the other hand when it is asserted that what is expressed in certain (ethical) contexts is true or false then this statement *is* included in the denotation of "metaethics". For this statement is (at least *prima facie*) a statement about ethical statements, not about fact. The same distinction may be indicated for ethical knowledge. The statement that there is ethical knowledge (implying that there is ethical truth) is excluded. But the statement that what is expressed in ethical contexts is a possible object of knowledge is included, being a statement about ethical statements and not *prima facie* about ethical fact.

From my conclusions about the concept of metaethics it follows that there are seldom any "homogeneous" metaethical theories to be investigated (many theories have metaethical as well as, say, normatively ethical "parts"). This will be obvious to anyone who considers my sample. When I discuss the relevance of these theories I am only considering one aspect of the theories. The authors all make statements that fall outside what I have called "metaethics", even in these writings which I have considered to be typical. This is important and should be kept in mind since the results I claim, are mainly critical. Hence, my general conclusions, even if true, only affect *one* part of the examined theories, what one could perhaps, with Professor Popper, call their "quest for definitions".

4. The Meaning of "Relevant to Ethics" Made more Precise

I shall now deal with the second part of my question of whether "metaethics is relevant to ethics" in order to make it more precise. What does "relevant to ethics" mean in this context?

Again, I shall try to state some conditions that must be satisfied by the concept in question. These conditions are intended to reflect my aims in this study. I shall then indicate some kinds of concepts of relevance; here, however, I postpone the details until I actually need the concepts in my examination of certain metaethical theories, viz. the theories of Brandt, Stevenson, and Hare. I shall also try to develop the concepts in a comprehensive way in Chapter VI.

The meaning of "ethics" will, with only a few exceptions, be taken as primitive, or "left to our intuitions". This, I think, will do no harm since my conclusions will, normally, be general, i.e. about normative or evaluative relevance in general. The exceptions to this rule are in Chapter VI where I will have something more to say about the concept of ethics; I will distinguish between "morals" and "ethics" (which are otherwise used synonymously in this study) and I will say something about various aspects of ethics (I will distinguish between ethical "observations", or "intuitions", ethical results, methods of ethics, and so forth.)

The conditions which any definition of the concept "relevance to ethics" must fulfill in order to be useful for my purpose, are the following.

First of all, some condition of "descriptive reasonableness" must be satisfied. It will be satisfied as soon as there is some person who, on considering the relation between metaethics and normative ethics, would be (or have been) willing to use the term "relevant to ethics" in the way I do.

Secondly, some condition of "fruitfulness" must be satisfied. Again I require that answers to the question of whether metaethics is "relevant to ethics" be, at least, of some *prima facie* relevance for the question whether metaethical studies are worthwile to deal with.

Thirdly, some condition of "specificity" must be satisfied. This condition is designed to comply with the idea that what is here to be examined, is whether metaethics has any *special* relevance for ethics, i.e. a relevance which it does not share with, for example, physics and chemistry. Hence, to mention one example, an affirmative answer to the question whether metaethics, like the study of latin, sharpens our thought, will not do as an answer to my question of whether metaethics is relevant to ethics.

The third condition in particular is very vaguely expressed. I shall try to sharpen it somewhat when I give an account of the various sorts of concepts of relevance to ethics. Here I will begin with an example. Let us imagine a person, P, making the following report about her intellectual development.

I used to be a supernaturalist. This was the result rather of my upbringing than of reflection. I simply took it for granted, unreflectingly, that ethical statements were to the effect that God approved of, disapproved of, or was indifferent to human motives, traits of character, and behavior in general. This forced me into moral positions against which my whole being protested. In particular I held the most stupid opinions about what it was proper for me, as a woman, to do. Then, all of a sudden, I began to read Hägerström. It was quite a revelation. I became an emotivist. I now saw that ethical language was nothing but a means by which emotions and feelings are expressed; I saw that ethical sentences did not describe any facts or express anything that was capable of being true or false. This was a period of great liberation, not only intellectual, but emotional and practical as well. Until then moral problems had resulted in controversies where my poor and superfluous knowledge of theology had been confronted with the thorough and superior understanding of various authorities on the subject. Now I realized that instead, what was on stake, was a confrontation between *my* feelings and emotions and *theirs*. It was now an easy thing to get rid of all my prejudices about the proper things for women to do. But at the same time I felt a bit uneasy. It was as though I had in some sense become 'irresponsible'. I could not take quite seriously my ethical deliberation, argumentation and thought, my 'ethical practice'. It is strange, but it was in a way as though ethical opinions were something that only 'happened' to me. I was 'taken' by a certain position. The moral view I held was only the 'result' of an 'equilibrium' of my self with all its contrary impulses. This made me care less about ethics. I began to study chemistry instead of the moral philosophy I had studied for some years, since I now found it difficult to deal scientifically with ethical problems. A science of ethics, it seemed to me, would have to be a science of human motivation. And what I had seen of psychoanalysis, behavioristic psychology, and so forth, did not seem to offer the prospects of any progress in those disciplines.

In this example it indeed appears as though a great many relations would hold between metaethics and normative ethics. Most of these appearances will prove to be deceptive, however, as we proceed, but at least they illustrate various ways of *conceiving* of the relevance to ethics of metaethics.

First of all it seems as though P had taken her supernaturalist metaethicist views to *imply* certain ethical statements. At least it seems as though she thought that together with certain statements of theology they would imply certain ethical statements about what it is proper for women to do. I shall call these two relations *logical* relations. I shall define them in more detail when I come to refer to them further.

Secondly, it might be wondered at how exactly P conceives of the step from her belief in certain norms to her view later that these had been only "prejudices". Are these norms really held by P to be implied by the supernaturalist metaethical theory (together with certain statements about the will of God?) Or, are there any other, suppressed premisses here? I can think of a relation between metaethics and ethics where it takes not only metaethical and empirical statements to deduce certain ethical conclusions but also *ethical,* or at least *normative* premisses as well. Some premisses about the "ethical importance" of findings about language or speech could have been implicitly involved here too. This would lead me to speak of a kind of "moral relevance" to ethics of metaethics; or, I would also use the term "relevant to ethics in an ethical system".

Thirdly, as one realizes how vague the suggestions about possible logical relations between metaethics and ethics are in the example, one may get the idea that the most important part of the story deals with a kind of what I shall call "pragmatic" relation between metaethics and ethics. As P *accepted* the emotive theory she *changed* her ethical views. Her belief in emotivism seems to have contributed to, or perhaps even "necessitated", in some sense, her belief in certain ethical views inconsistent with the views of her youth. And this concept of pragmatic relevance to ethics would, I think, be even more to the point if it were taken to apply also when a *change* of metaethical views contributed to the adoption of a certain new *attitude* towards ethical statements. Ethical statements were not accepted *in the same way* as before and, eventually, even a kind of *indifference* to ethics evolved. And was this perhaps not

22

so much the result of the simple acceptance of emotivism as a result of a change of metaethical beliefs, from supernaturalism to emotivism?

Fourthly, there are also signs of what I shall call "therapeutic" relations between (studies of) metaethics and normative ethics. I shall use this term for cases where studies, acceptance, etc. of metaethical theories contribute to a better or more effective ethical argumentation, deliberation, thought and so on. And in the example here there are signs of such effects. On the one hand negatively; the belief in emotivism caused a lack of interest in ethical problems. On the other hand positively; the belief in emotivism, or, perhaps rather, the disbelief in supernaturalism, made the rejection of certain ethical views easier, since ethical argumentation was exempted from theological considerations.

I have here indicated various lines of interpretation of the phrase "relevant to ethics". This concept may be conceived of as a logical concept, a moral concept, a pragmatic concept, or a therapeutic concept. Are all these lines of interpretation interesting from my point of view? Are there any other lines of interpretation which are of interest to my purposes although they are not illustrated in the example? These questions I shall try to answer by applying my conditions of adequacy for the concept of relevant to ethics to the concepts. I shall then discuss some concepts that satisfy some, but not all, conditions of adequacy and I shall show why they are inadequate.

Are My Concepts of Relevance Adequate to My Purposes?

As far as I can see, the logical relevance of metaethics to ethics is an obvious subject for my investigation. If metaethical statements, alone or in conjunction with empirical statements, imply ethical conclusions, this *is* a case of relevance to ethics. This relevance would be specific; no other discipline would share it, and this would, of course, also be a descriptively reasonable interpretation of the term "relevant to ethics". And, if metaethics possessed this kind of relevance, this would be at least *a* reason to study it, i.e. the concept would then be fruitful.

The moral relevance to ethics of metaethics, or, as I will sometimes prefer to call it, "relevance to ethics in an ethical system", is perhaps the *most* natural interpretation from a purely descriptive point of view of the term "relevant to ethics". When I hold that a fact is relevant to ethics I usually mean exactly that a statement of this fact, together with some valid ethical principle, yields some ethical statement logically (probably a statement about the very same object discussed in the statement tested for its moral relevance.) Whether this kind of relevance is specific or not, or which instances of it are, can only be settled after the condition of specificity has been made sharper. When I require that the moral relevance in question be specific, I require that the meta-ethical result be morally important not only because it indicates, say, some sociological fact such that a certain person has a certain ethical conviction, a fact incidentally which is itself morally relevant since some valid ethical principle is to the effect that if a person has *this* ethical conviction he should think twice about his ethical views. In addition the discovery must not be such that it could just as well have been made by some other discipline. On the other hand the ethical statement itself is not necessarily such that it could not have been known unless the metaethical finding were made. The ethical belief may of course have other sources as well.

Pragmatic relevance to ethics may be of various sorts. Not all of them, to be sure apply specifically to metaethics. The pragmatic concept of relevance applies when the acceptance of a metaethical theory, or a change of metaethical views, contributes to, or "necessitates", the acceptance of a certain ethical statement, or a certain attitude towards ethical statements. The condition of specificity must be handled with great care here so that interesting cases are not excluded. But on the other hand not *all* pragmatic effects are interesting from my point of view. I think it reasonable to require that the acceptance of the meta-ethical statement be "necessary" in order for the effect to obtain, in the sense only that *this* way of producing the effect is more *rational* than any alternative way. Even if studies of mathematics, as a matter of fact, would produce the same effects as the study of metaethics, but there would be some more point in acting in the relevant way differently (as regards one's acceptances) after having accepted the metaethical statements rather than after having accepted the mathematical ones, this change would be, in the intended sense, "specific". It is hard to tell at this stage of the investigation whether the pragmatic effects in the example above are specific. One has to know more about *why* they obtained before one can tell. The condition of fruitfulness is, I think, satisfied to a greater extent the more rational the pragmatic effects are, i.e. the better are the reasons for them which have brought them about. I shall handle this condition, and the former, however, with great care, since there is a risk that these conditions are somewhat in conflict with the condition of descriptive reasonableness. Pragmatic relations have often been taken as examples of "ethical relevance" in the rare discussion of this problem. I will therefore give an account of some instances of pragmatic relevance which are *not* very specific and where the "fruitfulness", in my sense, is dubious.

Therapeutic relevance is a kind of widening of the concept of pragmatic relevance by widening the second argument for the relation between metaethics and ethics. Here not only acceptances are discussed but possible effects on our total ethical "practice". Again there will be problems with the condition of specificity. And again I shall try to solve these by requiring that the effects on people's ethical practice, their way of conceiving moral problems, their capacity for reaching ethical conclusions, their sensitivity to ethical distinctions and so forth be at least as "rational" as the same effects produced by some other discipline. The condition of fruitfulness of the concept will, again, be better satisfied the more rational the effects are. The condition of descriptive reasonableness is unproblematic. Therapeutic relations have often been held to obtain in the discussion of the relevance of metaethics to ethics. Whether the weakened interest in ethical problems, or the more effective deliberation where theological considerations are eliminated, are specific effects as they obtain in the example above is, again, hard to tell. One has to know more about *why* these effects obtained.

These are the kinds of concepts of relevance to ethics that I will discuss in this study. I think there are no others that satisfy all my three conditions of adequacy to a reasonable degree. But there are certain concepts that satisfy some but not all conditions. Let us see why.

Some Inadequate Concepts of Relevance

It has sometimes been held that metaethical theories loosely "presuppose" ethical statements. Perhaps there is some relation of presupposition which satisfy my conditions of adequacy and which is neither a relation of logical, moral, pragmatic, nor therapeutic relevance? I think that there is not, but this view cannot, of course, be proved. In order to make it somewhat more plausible, however, I will discuss a few interpretations of the term "presupposition" and see how they square with my conditions of adequacy of the concept of relevance.

First of all, it has been held that a theory "presupposes" another theory whenever the former implies the latter. This concept is already subsumed under the concept of logical relevance.

Secondly, as has been the case with W. T. Blackstone in the article "Are Metaethical Theories Normatively Neutral?", metaethical theories may be taken to be entailed by ethical theories. This relation has been named as also a relation of "presupposition" by John T. Wilcox, in "Blackstone on Metaethical Neutrality." It is perhaps a reasonable interpretation of the term "relevant" in the contexts considered. But this concept is redundant, too, for less obvious reasons than the former. *If* a metaethical theory in this sense "presupposes" a normative theory there is also *another* metaethical theory, viz. the negation of the theory itself, which entails *another* ethical theory, viz. the negation of the ethical theory here discussed. So the concept of logical relevance to ethics will be sufficient for my purpose.

Thirdly, a common line of interpretation of the term "presupposition" could be phrased, I think, somewhat as follows: The statement *p* presupposes the statement *q* if, and only if, it is necessarily the case that, if *p* has sense, then *q* is true. And perhaps this kind of concept of presupposition is a reasonable interpretation of the term "relevant" in the contexts considered? Well, let us try to find out what the definition really amounts to.

One way of taking "has sense" would be to take it to mean *has a truthvalue*, i.e. *is true or false* (notice that sense here is a property of statements, not of sentences.) But now, provided we use a two-valued logic and interpret "negation" in an ordinary way, this concept is stronger than the concept of logical relevance and too strong to be of any interest at all. For, now, that *p* presupposes *q* is equivalent with the statement that it is necessarily the case that, if *p* then *q* and if not-*p* then *q*. But this means that all statements presuppose every tautology and no other statement.

Fourthly, there are a wide variety of possible *pragmatic* interpretations of the term "presupposition" that are interesting from my point of view. But they are most conveniently discussed *as* concepts of pragmatic relevance to ethics. I think Strawson's concept of weak implication in "On Referring", for example, is such a pragmatic concept which may be discussed as I discuss pragmatic relations between metaethics and ethics.

Fifthly, there is a great variety of relations of ethical "non-neutrality" which undoubtedly would be fruitful objects of investigation from my point of view but which are hardly cases of ethical "relevance". Take the following cases. It has now become a common-place to observe that there are many relations between science and society in general about which the scientist should be aware. The *effects* of research could be assessed from a moral or political point of view. The scientist's own moral views and political convictions may determine to some extent which the scientist should be aware. The *effects* of research could forth. But two reasons tell against counting such relations as relations of ethical relevance. First of all they are not specific enough. What is true about metaethics in this sense is true as well of other disciplines.

Secondly, the relations here mentioned are not really "relevance"-relations. It is not that metaethical knowledge is a part of, or aids us in our ethical investigations. The effects here are too "external" to count as instances of relevance to ethics.

5. The Plan of This Study

Having hopefully made the outline of my problem a bit sharper, I am now in a position to start solving it. This, however, will have to begin with an examination of a possible objection to this whole project. Someone might perhaps charge me, not with the impossibility of what I am attempting to do, but with the triviality of my problem. Perhaps there is someone prepared to answer that metaethical theories obviously are relevant to ethics simply because they entail ethical statements. If this objection were correct, and it is based on a rather commonly accepted view, my problem would be trivially solved. Then metaethics would be relevant to ethics.

After having dealt at least preliminarily with the question whether metaethical theories entail ethical statements and, hence, with some current views of the neutrality of metaethics, I begin my examination of my problem by a critical examination of the ethical relevance of the theories I picked out for this purpose in Section 3 of this chapter, viz. R. Brandt's naturalism, as put forward in *Ethical Theory*, which will be examined in Chapter III, C. L. Stevenson's emotivism, as put forward in *Ethics and Language* and *Facts and Values*, which will be examined in Chapter IV, and R. M. Hare's universal prescriptivism, as put forward in *The Language of Morals* and *Freedom and Reason*, which will be examined in Chapter V.

After these two parts there remains a further part of this study to be mentioned. The first part, which clarifies my problem and render an account of my objectives, and the second part, which examines actual metaethical theories, are to prepare the way for a more general assessment of the ethical relevance of metaethics. These general theses are dealt with in Chapter VI.

For the benefit of the reader it should be noted that the two latter parts of this study, Chapters III, IV and V on the one hand and Chapter VI on the other, are rather self-contained. They could be read separately, together with the introductory Chapters I and II.

6. Some Central Theses of this Study

The problem of the reasonableness or truth of the various metaethical statements which I am considering I will not attempt to solve. What concerns me here is only what would "follow" (in the various senses I have indicated) if those statements *were* true, or if they *were* accepted. My conclusions are intended to answer only the latter kind of questions.

My main conclusions fall into two separate groups; firstly I make some critical assertions about the theories of Brandt, Stevenson, and Hare: for none of their theories have I been able to find any relevance to ethics. Here, however, my conclusions are restricted in an important way. I have only examined such relations between metaethics and ethics that are suggested by these philosophers themselves or by philosophers who have examined their theories. Secondly, I make some general assertions about metaethics on the whole. Again my conclusions are mainly negative: no kinds of metaethical theories have logical or moral relevance to ethics. And no metaethical theories have very specific pragmatic or therapeutic relevance to ethics.

It should be noticed that this conclusion is partly dependent on my decision regarding the definition of "metaethics". It will turn out that a slight change of the definition, which would as a matter of fact, lead outside most of the metaethics *actually* practiced and, hence, violate my condition of adequacy for the concept of 'metaethics' (representativeness), would seem to invalidate my negative conclusion. This, of course, could be interpreted as a suggestion that the methods and aims of metaethics be changed accordingly.

Again I must warn, however, against too critical an interpretation of my conclusions; these are indeed of some relevance to the question whether the study of metaethics should be pursued but, of course, this question is far from answered even if my conclusions should turn out to be correct.

7. Some Terminological Remarks

Only a minimum of logical symbols will be used in this study and I will explain my use of them in the contexts where they appear. But there are some other terminological peculiarities that should be explained now.

I use the words "statement" and "proposition" in a somewhat technical sense. With these words I refer to the semantical content, to *what is expressed* by sentences. And I use these words in a wide and inclusive sense i.e. not only factual statements are included but also the semantic content of, say, imperatives—if there is any. This use of mine is without ontological committments, it is only a convenient way of dealing with theories that take for example commands into account (where commands are taken to be what is expressed by imperative sentences).

Quotations will be made in the following manner. I use simple quotation marks when I refer to intensional entities like concepts and statements, i.e. the phrase "'the book is blue'" refers to the statement that the book is blue. Instead of using simple quotation marks I will also sometimes refer to statements and concepts with phrases of the kind "the statement that ..." and "the concept of ..." Double quotation marks will be used in reference to *linguistic* entities like words and sentences. I will also use double quotation marks to indicate ironic distance.

When my own words are inserted into quotations, to explain the context, I put them between brackets of the following type "/.../"

The word "interpretation" I will use equivocally to denote statements assigned to sentences as well as the relation assigning statements to sentences. When I say that an interpretation is "descriptively reasonable" or "reasonable from a descriptive point of view" I intend to say, not that the statement itself is reasonable or valid or something of the sort but that it is reasonable to assume that the sentence in question really expresses the statement assigned to it. This may be reasonable for various reasons which will be obvious in the context. It may for example be reasonable because of the lexical meaning of the words in the sentence or it may be reasonable when the intention of the speaker is taken into account.

CHAPTER TWO

COULD MY PROBLEM BE
TRIVIALLY SOLVED?

1. Background

It has sometimes been maintained, by those engaged in the rare discussions of the problem of the relation of metaethical theories to ethics that (some) metaethical theories entail ethical statements. Furthermore there are quite a few metaethicists who seem to take this alleged entailment for granted. Clearly, if these theorists are right, if metaethical statements obviously entail ethical statements, then my problem dissolves into triviality. So let us see what can be said about this thesis.

It seems natural to start with an examination of some of the arguments advanced in support of the thesis that metaethical theories are non-neutral, i.e. entail ethical statements. The most thorough argumentation I know of in support of this view has been given by A. Gewirth in his article "Meta-ethics and Moral Neutrality". If I am correct, however, these arguments will be found to lack conclusiveness. Yet this will not settle the matter. For there are many metaethicists who think it obvious that metaethical statements *do* entail ethical statements.[1] Perhaps they know of independent reasons, which they have not even thought it necessary to state, in support of this view. But since they do not state them the only thing I can do is to present some arguments against their assertions. I think L. Bergström has given some good ones in his article "Meaning and Morals."

The problem will, however, turn out to be complicated, and no definite answer to the question whether there is some metaethical theory that entails some ethical statement can be reached. We will have to be content, at this stage of my investigation with the conclusion that *prima facie* good reasons speak against this view and that no explicitly stated reasons speak in its favor. I think this enough to show that we are not dealing with trivialities.

---

[1] L. Bergström has cited some prominent philosophers who seem to hold this view. C.f. "Meaning and Morals", the opening sections.

2. A. Gewirth on Ethical Non-neutrality

Some Central Concepts defined

The point of departure for Gewirth in his discussion is a distinction between what he calls two "senses" of moral neutrality. What complicates a rational assessment of Gewirth's argument is that he never clearly characterizes or defines his concept of metaethics and that he never clearly states what the relation is which he maintains holds between his two "senses" of moral neutrality and the concept of ethical neutrality (or, as Gewirth would rather say, I think, "moral neutrality"). Are Gewirth's two "senses" stipulative definitions of concepts of ethical neutrality, or does he conceive the question whether a theory which is non-neutral in one of his two senses is ethically or morally neutral, to be a synthetic one.

Since it appears to be easy to show that at least some metaethical statements satisfy the conditions of the *definientia* of the two senses of non-neutrality, and since it is far from clear that a theory which is non-neutral in Gewirth's senses is also non-neutral for example in the sense that it implies ethical statements, I shall interpret Gewirth in the latter way. Hence, the statement that a theory which is non-neutral in either of Gewirth's two senses is ethically non-neutral, i.e. implies ethical statements, will be interpreted to be synthetic. I am, however, not quite sure that this interpretation is correct (if it is, why talk of "senses"?). As a matter of fact, Gewirth seems to hold both views. But only in the interpretation I have chosen will his findings be of any interest in this connection. And this interpretation is in line with the idea that, if it is non-neutral, a metaethical theory *implies* ethical conclusions. This opinion Gewirth explicitly holds, and this is certainly not *obvious* when one considers the definition of, at least, *one* of the two "senses".

As regards the first mentioned complication, namely that Gewirth never explicitly defines his concept of metaethics, the following quotation may perhaps give at least a rough suggestion of his intention:

As is suggested by its affinity with 'metalanguage', metaethics is a certain kind of second-order moral discourse about first-order discourse. (p. 214)

But this, of course, is only an indication of some necessary, though not sufficient, criteria, and Gewirth is also faced with problems of "border-line cases", as he puts it. What about, Gewirth wonders, very *specific* assertions of the kind Bentham makes about a "utilitarian" meaning of ethical terms, and what about highly *general* assertions made by contemporary metaethicists about the meaning of ethical terms being "prescriptive", "descriptive", and so forth. Gewirth here chooses a loose and inclusive sense of "metaethics" where Bentham, as well as Hare, seem to be included. It is not clear, however, which *property* of statements about ethical language it is that makes them metaethical. For my purpose, however, it will be enough if my concept of metaethics is contained in Gewirth's. Then his thesis that metaethics is non-neutral will be relevant to my problem. And this, I think, is the case.

What, then, are Gewirth's two senses of "moral neutrality" (and "non-neutrality")?

Non-neutrality

Gewirth distinguishes between what he calls "referential neutrality" and "predicative neutrality". He never explicitly defines these terms, but let us see what we can do to interpret his characterizations, scattered about in the text. I think the following would be a descriptively reasonable interpretation of his words about "referential neutrality":

The metaethical assertion *t* is referentially neutral in relation to ethics, if, and only if, *t* is intended to fit all normative moral positions. Let us call this definition "(D1)".

At least Gewirth holds that the definiens of (D 1) accounts for *one* property of the concept of referential non-neutrality. He writes:

To say that a philosopher's metaethical assertion is morally neutral in the referential sense means that he does not intend to restrict the assertion's reference or application to that normative moral position which he himself regards as morally right; he intends it rather, to fit all normative moral positions, including those on which he holds no moral view at all. (p. 216)

But perhaps this is not meant as a defining characteristic but rather as an empirical statement *about* referentially neutral theories. There is another passage too, which has the appearance of a definition.

Gewirth writes:

In terms of its subject, the metaethical statement is morally neutral if its subject refers to the meaning or use of *any* term or judgement or the argument for any moral conclusion without restrictions to those moral judgements or uses which the metaethicist himself regards as morally right. If, on the other hand, the metaethicist does restrict in this way the reference of the subject of his metaethical statement, then his statement is not morally neutral. (The sense of 'morally neutral' here is, of course, the referential one.) (p. 217)

The following definition could be framed on the basis of this passage.

The metaethical assertion *t* is referentially neutral to ethics, if, and only if, its subject refers to the meaning or use of any term or judgment or the argument for any moral conclusion. Let us call this definition "(D1:1)".

(D1) and (D1:1) both give rise to questions about their reasonableness and about their correct interpretation. First of all, it is not at all clear to me how metaethical assertions can refer to *moral positions*. Is not metaethics a "second-order discourse", i.e. a discourse, not about moral positions, but about moral *language*, or *moral discourse*? But perhaps (D1) is to be interpreted so that references must not be exclusively made to assertions by *adherents* of certain positions? Then the difference between (D1) and (D1:1) apparently diminishes. Secondly, the expression "in this way" does indeed suggest that the condition in (D1:1) should be considered as sufficient though not necessary. An alternative way of being neutral would be to restrict the reference of *t* but to restrict it to statements of a position which the moral philosopher in question *is not in sympathy with*. This would make the concept of neutrality relative to a person, and probably also to a situation. I will, however, discount these interpretations (a parallel one could be given of (D1) as too queer to deserve any further attention.

I have taken (D1) to be different from (D1:1), and it is indeed expressed in different terms. But is the difference any deeper than that? Are two different concepts really involved here? It is hard to tell since the meaning of "fit" is so vague.

The concept of predicative neutrality is not central to the thesis that we are interested in. I mention it all the same, because it will be of some indirect importance. The following is, I believe, a fair interpretation:

The metaethical assertion *t* is predicatively neutral if, and only if, its predicate is descriptive, i.e. of the form "The use of moral terms *is* of the kind X", or, though normative, i.e. of the form "The use of moral terms *ought* to be of the kind X", non-moral in the sense that it uses a non-moral ought. Let us call this definition "(D2)".

In this distinction between referential and predicative neutrality Gewirth makes two assumptions, which reveal to some extent how he conceives metaethical statements. He assumes that metaethical statements can be analyzed into a subject and a predicate part, where the subject, to use his own words, "refers to the meaning or use of some moral term or judgment of the argument for some moral conclusion", and the predicate "assigns to this meaning or use some metaethical property, such as 'descriptive', 'empirical', or perhaps more particular terms specifically relevant to ethics". And he also assumes a "form" of metaethical statements, revealed by "The use of moral terms *is* of kind X" and "The use of moral terms *ought to be* of kind X".

Now, let us try to formulate Gewirth's theses and arguments.

Gewirth's Theses and His Arguments in Their Support

To Gewirth's distinction between referential and predicative neutrality two premises about the relation between metaethics and normative ethics correspond. I am, however, doubtful about their correct interpretation, especially that of the first one. All the same, what interests me here is but one out of three possible interpretations, all reasonable from a descriptive point of view. Two interpretations lack relevance to my problem in this study. Gewirth's premises could be cast into the following words:

P1.　　If a metaethical statement is not referentially neutral with reference to morality, then it is non-neutral with reference to morality in the sense that it implies ethical statements.

P2.　　If a metaethical statement is not predicatively neutral with reference to morality, then it is non-neutral with reference to morality in the sense that it explicitly contains some ethical statement.

Both P1 and P2 could be taken as points of departure for theories about the relation between metaethics and normative ethics, but only P1 is of interest at this stage of my investigation.

The reasons for doubt about the correct interpretation of Gewirth—P1 is obviously not the only possible way of understanding him—are, I think, clear from the following two passages, which could both be cited to support my interpretation:

For, in such a case (a metaethicist is putting forward a theory which is referentially non-neutral), his metaethical assertion implies or presupposes a specific normative moral position of his own. (p. 216)

In the former case (a referentially non-neutral assertion is made) the metaethical assertion implicitly makes a normative moral judgment . . . (p. 218)

The former quotation suggests indeed a kind of pragmatic interpretation. The metaethicist is, by his assent to, or acceptance of, a metaethical statement which is referentially non-neutral, letting us know, allowing us to infer, and so forth, *his* moral position. This, although far from clear, could be taken as independent support for the interpretation of the definition of 'referential neutrality' earlier discounted as too queer to deserve attention. The former quotation, furthermore, might, by its use of the word "presuppose", suggest some third kind of relation between metaethics and normative ethics, besides the logical one we have decided upon in our interpretation P1, and the pragmatical one. In chapter VI I shall discuss such interpretations. But for the moment let us leave these troublesome points. To make Gewirth relevant to *my* problem, I need the logical interpretation P1 and I am satisfied provided it is clear that this interpretation is reasonable even if it is not the only reasonable one, from a descriptive point of view.

Gewirth needs the premiss P1 for his argument for the following thesis:

(T)   '   There are metaethical theories which are interesting only because they imply ethical statements.

Clearly, if P1 is to give us (T), we shall also need the following premiss

P3.   There are metaethical theories which are interesting only because they are not referentially neutral.

This premiss is, of course, not quite non-controversial, and it is also far from clear what is the scope of the causal claims it makes. Yet *I* am very much in sympathy with it. In fact I think *this* is the best point that Gewirth makes in his article. In Chapter VI I shall end with, among other things, something which could be said to be an elaboration of this point. Besides that, I can, I think, accept it now just for the sake of argument. Then the crucial point will be P1, for I think there is no doubt that P1 and P3 together entail (T). And if (T) could be proved, it could also be proved that the problem of this study has a trivial solution.

Gewirth's Argumentation Examined

To refute P1 it is sufficient to show one instance of a metaethical theory which does not satisfy the conditions in the definiens of (D1)—or perhaps (D1:1)—and which does not imply any ethical statement. So let us look at some examples.

Example 1: Let us conceive of a metaethicist, *P*, who is a convinced ethical utilitarian. In one of his *metaethical* writings *P* makes the following assertion:

(t₁)   »Right means, to convinced utilitarians, *leads to a future state of the world which is as good (or which contains as great a balance of pleasure over pain) as that which any alternative would lead to.*

Now, it is clear, first of all that (t_1) is not referentially neutral in relation to (D1). For (t_1) is only intended to "fit" one particular moral position, viz. the utilitarian. The assertion is only meant to hold true of words used by utilitarians. Secondly, and in view of this, it is clear as well that (t_1) is not referentially neutral in relation to (D1:1) either, for the subject of (t_1) does not refer to the use of the term in question in statements of *any* moral position. Strangely enough, the conditions of the definiens of (D1:1) are not satisfied for another reason too, viz. because the referent of the subject of (t_1) is not just *any* ethical term but just the term "Right". I find this, however, too queer a consequence of Gewirth's characterization of the concept of referential neutrality to be anything but a slip of the pen.

The question now is: does (t_1) imply any ethical statements? Unfortunately Gewirth never gives any examples in his discussion. So what he would say about our example is left to our imagination. But *prima facie,* at least, it seems natural to conclude that (t_1) does not imply any ethical statements. For while (t_1) is a statement about a certain *word* (in the English language) ethical statements are usually about the rightness of actions, the value of characters etc. Thus it seems as though (t_1) and any ethical statement, are statements about different sorts of things.[2] And it is hard to see any good counterarguments. Why should the restricted field of application of (t_1) necessitate ethical implications?

A preliminary conclusion, then, is that we have found a metaethical statement which is non-neutral in the referential sense but which does not imply any ethical statements. But perhaps Gewirth would concede this, yet holding to his thesis, because *he* does not regard (t_1) as a (typical) metaethical statement.

Here Gewirth could refer to what he has said about the *form* of metaethical statements: 'The use of ethical terms is/ought to be of the kind X'. The statement (t_1) is perhaps too radical a deviation from this ideal form. What matters here is probably not that (t_1) is about the *meaning* while the form is about the *use* — Gewirth himself gives examples of both kinds — but that while (t_1) is about *one specified* ethical term the form deals with ethical terms *in general.*

Let us try to cope with this objection by changing our example accordingly.

Example 2: The same metaethicist, *P,* makes the following statement:

---

[2] Cf. Section 3 of this chapter where this point is developed.

(t₂)   The meanings of those ethical terms which are used by con-
         vinced utilitarians are definable in terms of the expression
         "Leads to a future state of the world which is as good (or
         which contains as great a balance of pleasure over pain) as
         that which any alternative leads to".

Even (t₂) is non-neutral in the referential sense, for here, again, a restriction is made in the scope of the statement to those statements which are made by *utilitarians* (though not to any particular terms). The prospects for deriving ethical conclusions from metaethics remain, however, poor. The metaethical statement is still about words, while statements about the rightness of actions, the value of characters or something of that kind, are *not* about words. The fact that (t₂) is non-neutral in the referential sense does *not* make it obvious that it implies ethical statements.

But perhaps Gewirth would concede this too, but disclaim the example as "irrelevant", since not even (t₂) is "metaethical", in *his* sense. The statement (t₂), Gewirth may hold, is still too much of a deviation from the ideal form of metaethical statements. While (t₂) is restricted (explicitly) to some uses of ethical terms, the form seems to require that no explicit restrictions of the field of application are made.

It is, however, important, though fairly obvious, to notice that if Gewirth choses *this* way out of the troubles he is faced with, when confronted with our examples, he would seriously weaken his premiss P1 while P3, and (T), would turn out to be very strong indeed. One would be tempted to ask whether there are any interesting metaethical theories at all, actual or possible, in Gewirth's sense of "metaethics". To see this, let us again try to cope with the objections.

Example 3: The same metaethicist, *P*, makes the following statement:

(t₃)   The meanings of ethical terms are definable in terms of the
         expression "Leads to a future state of the world which is as
         goos (or which contains as great a balance of pleasure over
         pain) as that which any alternative leads to".

We also suppose that *P*, while not stating it explicitly, is restricting the field of application of his assertion to uses made by utilitarians. But now, is it clear that (t₃) is not referentially neutral? In accordance with (D1) one may say that this is the case; (t₃) is not *intended* to fit every moral position. But this takes us away from our *logical* interpretation. If it is a proposition, then (t₃) contains no intentions and it is not dependent on any intentions whether (t_3) refers, or does not refer, to *any* ethical assertion.

Here two ways seem to be open. Either one chooses to try to base a pragmatic argument on the example, making use of the suggested interpretation of (D1) which stresses the word "intended", *or* the statement (t_3) will not be non-neutral in the referential sense, but false. The former way may have some plausibility. If the moral preferences of the metaethicist are well-known to his audience, or if the restrictions of the field of application are, for other reasons, obvious, one may perhaps infer (be entitled to infer) the moral position of the metaethicist, i.e. one may infer *that* he holds this view and that he wishes to have it generally accepted. This, however, is not enough to prove my problem trivial; it takes a logical argument to do this. The latter way out, in contradistinction to the former, has not much in its favour. It does not prove the thesis (T) and it does not prove that my problem is trivial either.

The Examination of Gewirth's Argumentation Concluded

In order definitely to answer the question whether there are metaethical theories that imply ethical statements one must probably proceed in one of the following two ways: either one gives an explicit definition of 'metaethics' or one makes one's answer relative to some examples of metaethical theories. Both approaches will be tried within this study. Right now, however, we must be satisfied with a preliminary conclusion.

As regards Gewirth the conclusion must be that he has not made it plausible, still less obvious, that there are metaethical theories which essentially imply ethical statements. As a matter of fact I have found, I think, *prima facie* good reasons for the view that there are no metaethical theories which in an essential way imply ethical statements, i.e. which owe their interest to their ethical implications.

An alternative way of arguing in support of Gewirth's point, which seems to have occurred to some of his adherents, would be to assert that non-neutral theories (in the referential sense) themselves imply a certain conception of morality. The metaethical theory is held to imply statements to the effect that these and only these statements are moral, these and only these opinions are ethical opinions, and so forth. Here a certain ambiguity should be noticed. This definition which is alleged to be implied may be of various sorts. It may be a naturalistic definition where the definiens takes either a "formal" ("ethical statements" are those and only those statements that are universalizable) or "material" ("ethical statements" are those and only those statements that are about

38

human welfare) character. Or it may be an evaluative definition where the definiens uses evaluative concepts ("ethical" are those and only those statements that *should* regulate human behavior). Now, it might perhaps be held that the *evaluative* definitions have a kind of moral import. So if they are implied by a metaethical theory this theory has ethical relevance. But I cannot see that this argument fares any better than the former ones.

First of all, it is not necessary to use evaluative definitions of 'ethical statement' in one's metaethic. This would simply create certain problems. The metaethical theory would become vague, since you would not know exactly what the theory is about. You would have to solve certain ethical problems before you could even try to test the metaethical theory.

Secondly, no matter whether the definiens is evaluative or not, I think it clear that the definition implied does not itself imply any ethical conclusion. For, again, the definition, if it is a statement at all, is a statement about the use of a certain term, a statement about a *word*—and ethical statements are *not* about language at all. It is true that all problems of definition (of a stipulative sort) involve a matter of decision. When you decide upon *one* conception of 'ethics' you decide upon which statements or sentences are to be examined. Hence, when you point out that these kinds of decisions are inevitable you say something which is perfectly true though neither sensational nor anything peculiarly metaethical. You indicate, simply, that there is a problem of evaluation within a discipline. One must be prepared to argue in support of one's choice of subject-matter. And this choice cannot be motivated only by theoretical reasons. Its fruitfulness is dependent on both theoretical and non-theoretical grounds. But this is one thesis; that the fruitfulness of your subject-matter is relative to some evaluative point of view. That non-neutrality obtains in the sense that ethical statements are implied, is quite another thing. Only the first thesis has been proved in the discussion about non-neutrality. And only the second thesis would be of interest for the purpose in hand.

I think the idea that evaluative definitions of 'ethics' are ethically relevant gains all its credibility from a failure to make a simple distinction, viz. the distinction between on the one hand *definitions* with an evaluative definiens and on the other hand *ethical principles* where the "definiendum" is evaluative and the "definiens" lays down certain criteria of the ethical concept in the "definiendum". An example of such a "definition", which is of course no definition at all, would be the statement that a use of language is "ethical"—where this *means* a use expressing a kind of statement that *should* regulate human behavior—if, and only if, it expresses a statement about human welfare. But of course no such *principles*, which are ordinary ethical principles, are implied by metaethical theories. On the other hand, *definitions* of 'ethical statement' and related concepts may very well *be* implied by metaethical statements. These definitions, however, in *their* turn, lack relevance to ethics.

Now, let us look a bit closer at the arguments I used against the view that (t_1), (t_2), and (t_3) imply ethical conclusions. These arguments have been put forward by L. Bergström in his article "Meaning and Morals".

3. L. Bergström on the Question Whether Metaethical Theories Imply Ethical Statements

Point of Departure

The point of departure for Bergström is, in my sense of the word, a "metaethical" definition of an ethical term. Similar cases may, according to Bergström, be treated in a similar way. The definition is this:

(1)   "Right" means the same as "Generally approved"

and the ethical conclusion Bergström tries to find out whether it follows logically from (1) is:

(2)   If an action is generally approved, then it is right.

Bergström tries to show by short quotations that many "influential" philosophers, for example Moore, Brandt and Ewing, have maintained that definitions of the same type as (1) do imply ethical conclusions of the same type as (2); this is the view Bergström wishes to question.

His argument covers two separate cases. First (1) and (2) are conceived as statements (propositional entities) and, secondly, they are conceived as sentences (linguistic entities).

Have Metaethical Statements Logical Consequences that are Ethical?

Bergström interprets the question whether metaethical statements contain ethical statements or entail ethical statements as the question whether ethical statements follow as *logical consequences* from metaethical ones.

But couldn't this be decided at once? For (2) is an ethical statement. Hence, someone may say, it lacks a truthvalue. And truthvalues are required if the concept of logical consequence is to apply.

This, however, would be to make the case too easy, Bergström retorts. And in order to avoid this he tries to generalize his concepts of 'logical consequence; giving to it application also in default of truthvalues. He does not wish to make his case rest on the "Hume-Poincaré" principle either, which would be another simple way out.

The concept of logical consequence Bergström defines in the following manner:

(D1) The statement p is a logical consequence of the statement q if and only if q is inconsistent with every statement which is inconsistent with p (p. 9).

To disprove the thesis that (2) is a logical consequence of (1) it is enough to find one statement inconsistent with (2) but not inconsistent with (1). The following statement is, according to Bergström, such an example:

(3)   Some actions which are generally approved are not right.

Clearly (3) is inconsistent with (2). But why not also with (1)? Bergström evokes three arguments in support of his thesis. Firstly, (1) is a statement about "right" and "generally approved", but (3) says nothing about these words. Secondly, (3) is a statement about actions, but (1) says nothing about actions. And, thirdly, (1) says nothing about the expressions which (3) contain, for (3) is a statement and does not contain any expressions.[3]

Do Ethical Sentences Follow as Logical Consequences of Metaethical Definitions of Ethical Terms?

Also when (1) and (2) are conceived as sentences Bergström interprets the question whether ethical conclusions are implied in terms of "logical consequence". Hence, he defines a concept that applies to pairs of sentences. This is done in the following manner:

(D2) The sentence P is a *logical consequence* of the sentence Q, if, and only if, i (P) is a logical consequence of i (Q) for every interpretation i (p. 10).

A special problem in connection with (D2) is how the domain of i, (which is a variable over functions, ordering statements to sentences,

---

[3] This argument may be even more simplified if we are willing to take the concept of logical consequence as primitive. Then we may right from the beginning conclude that (2) is not a logical consequence of (1) since (2) says nothing about words while (1) is about certain words and so forth.

thereby interpreting them) should be determined. Bergström's restrictions on the domain are rather rough. He requires that "an interpretation must not involve any deviation from "*the standard meaning of purely logical terms*" and that an interpretation "does not imply that one and the same expression has different meanings when it occurs in two different sentences". Furthermore he accepts, for the sake of argument, that no attention be paid to "unreasonable" interpretations.

Even in this case an example that shows that (2) does not follow from (1) is easily found. For (1) and (2) can reasonably be taken to express, respectively, that "right" means the same as "generally approved", and that if an action is generally approved, then it is right. And now the arguments above are relevant again, the *statement* (3) being inconsistent with the interpretation of (2) but not with the interpretation of (1).

The Examination of Bergström's Argumentation Concluded

After having discussed various possible objections to his argument, Bergström states his conclusion as follows:

In short, there seems to be no reason for rejecting my earlier conclusion that (2) does not follow from (1). Moreover, since my argument can easily be adapted to similar cases, we may also conclude that no definition of an ethical term entails or contains any moral principle. Some readers may find this trivial, but we have also seen that several moral philosophers appear to hold the opposite view. (p. 15).

Now, in what way is this conclusion relevant to my problem? Does it follow that my problem lacks the trivial solution I feared? Before we are entitled to draw this conclusion, at least four problematic points have to be clarified.

Firstly, it is essential to Bergström's argument that *we* know which statement *he* refers to when using the phrase ""Right" means the same as "generally approved"". But do we know this? What kind of statement is this? This knowledge seems to be required if a critical examination of the validity of Bergström's arguments is to be possible. How do we know that this statement *is* about certain words? For one possible interpretation this is obviously so. The statement can be taken to be to the effect that some actual group of people actually use the two phrases "right" and "generally approved" in the same way. Then Bergström's argument is obviously valid. But the statement could also be understood in other ways. It could, for example, be taken to be a statement of identity of certain meanings, or concepts, viz. the concepts expressed by the phrases "right" and "generally approved". It is here taken for granted

42

which concepts are expressed by these phrases. Now it is not so easy to tell what the statement is really about. Some would perhaps maintain that statements about statements are really statements about the world, cast in a special (meta-)form. And why not adopt this view of statements about concepts as well? I will go further into problems of this kind in Chapter VI, when I discuss the so-called "paradox of analysis". For the moment it must suffice to notice that there is at least one interpretation of Bergström for which his arguments seem to be valid—and Bergström himself does not claim to have proved more.

Secondly, and consequently, it is hard to tell what it amounts to when Bergström holds that "similar" cases may be treated in a "similar" way. Are all cases where a *word* is defined (no matter whether it is moral or not) "similar"? Or are the cases "similar" where an *ethical* term is defined (no matter whether it is a word or a concept) "similar"?

Thirdly, and as a consequence of my first and my second remarks, it is hard to know how to assess Bergström's assertion that many "influential" moral philosophers seem to have held a view opposite to the one Bergström himself holds about these matters. *Are* these philosophers really making the kind of statements that Bergström takes them to make?

Fourthly, I am in doubt whether Bergström has succeeded in avoiding letting his case rest on the "Hume-Poincaré" principle. For do not his arguments require, to be relevant, some sort of a "deductivistic" premiss as well? This, however, is perhaps not a very serious objection since Bergström himself has shown that the "Hume-Poincaré" principle, amended in a suitable way, is a reasonable principle.[4]

---

[4] Cf. his monograph *Imperatives and Ethics*.

CHAPTER THREE

THE RELEVANCE TO ETHICS OF
R. BRANDT'S NATURALISM

1. Background

In his book *Ethical Theory* R. Brandt pursues among other things, a general discussion about naturalism, conceived as a metaethical theory. The theory he himself advocates is furthermore naturally conceived as a "revised" form of naturalism, although the relation of his own theory to his own criterion of naturalism is far from clear.

Since R. Brandt in a way represents one very important "approach" in recent metaethical debate (where one could also point to such theorists as J. O. Urmson, in *The Emotive Theory of Ethics,* P. Ziff, in *Semantic Analysis,* and J. J. Katz, in "Semantic Theory and the Meaning of 'Good',just to mention a few) it seems fruitful and interesting to examine his theory from the point of view here adopted: has R. Brandt's kind of naturalism any relevance to ethics?

The recent approach here mentioned is chiefly distinguished by the fact that it deals with *linguistic* entities, i.e. parts of the English language; metaethics has elsewhere rather been interested in what people communicate with language, how they use language, and so forth.

The choice of what properties of linguistic entities, specified for example by quotation, one concentrates on, varies among the theorists of this linguistic approach. You could even say, I think, that it varies in a somewhat "rambling" manner. For usually no purpose is explicitly specified, in relation to which one may assess the adequacy of the conceptual framework in which the analysis is cast.

In Brandt's case there is a tendency towards *empirical* methods; and this too, is typical of this linguistic approach. At least in principle the results are thought to be empirically comfirmable. Brandt develops a definition of 'synonymy' which is almost "operational". And Ziff has similar aims since he intends to study "regularities" instead of "rules". On the other hand, empirical *investigations* are only seldom, if ever, pursued. The linguistic form of metaethics is only in its most primitive phase; the means by which it is pursued are highly speculative.

To be in a position to assess Brandt's kind of naturalism from the point of view I have chosen I shall try to give explicit definitions, both of the concept of naturalism and the concept of synonymy. As regards the concept of naturalism I shall give only a rough characterization of Brandt's view and try to define a concept which is at least as general as the one Brandt himself has in mind. In that way I hope to escape a debate over the question of what Brandt really meant where this is difficult to settle in any definite way.

2. R. Brandt's Concept of Naturalism

R. Brandt characterizes naturalism in various ways. Consider for example these two quotations from *Ethical Theory:*

The essential thesis of naturalism is the proposal that ethical statements can, after all, be confirmed, ethical questions answered by observation and inductive reasoning of the very sort that we use to confirm statements in the empirical sciences—and for a reason that the other theories overlook or do not take seriously: because of what ethical statements *mean.* In other words, it is held that on reflection we can see that the meaning of ethical statements is such that we can verify them just like the statements of psychology or chemistry. (p. 152)

Naturalism ... is a theory about the *meaning* of ethical statements. Naturalists hold that an ethical statement—that is, a statement with words like 'wrong' or 'undersirable'—is exactly identical in meaning with some other statement in which ethical words do not occur, and which everyone will recognize as a statement that can be confirmed or tested by the methods of science, by appeal to experience. Or, in other words, naturalists hold that any ethical statement can be translated, without any change of meaning, into a statement in the language of empirical science. (p. 155)

There are several passages that lack clarity in the quoted sections. Which are intended as statements *about* some form of naturalism, and which are intended as statements of defining criteria? What kind of a statement is an ethical statement? What is a statement in the language of empirical science? And incidentally, what is a statement? Brandt seems to refer *both* to logical entities, i.e. to what is expressed by language, and to linguistic entities, for example sentences, by his use of the term "statement". Statements can, at the same time, be verified and have meaning, contain words (that occur in them) and so forth.

Now, Brandt's discussion of the concept is only meant as a point of departure for me in this study so I shall side-step these difficulties simply by giving a definition of something I shall call "linguistic naturalism" without any serious demands for descriptive reasonableness. I shall be satisfied if there is some reasonable interpretation of my definition which is also a reasonable interpretation of Brandt's characterization. What he

45

has to say about naturalism may be seen as a specification, I think, of the concept I define. I leave some key concepts vague, or 'undefined'. My definition runs as follows:

(D1)   *t* is a linguistic naturalistic metaethical theory if, and only if, *t* implies the thesis that there are sentences *E* and *N* such that
    (i) *E* is an ethical sentence
    (ii) *N* is a naturalistic sentence and
    (iii) *E* and *N* are synonymous

The theses singled out by (D1) I shall call "linguistic metaethical statements". The phrase "is synonymous with" I will use synonymously with "have the same meaning as", just as Brandt seems to do.

Clearly (D1) singles out a group of rather heterogeneous metaethical statements, and the border-lines of this group are not sharp. The concepts 'naturalistic sentence' and 'ethical sentence' could be sharpened in various ways. The criteria used in the definition of these concepts could for example put a stress on the *function* of the sentences, on the *logical content* of them, and so forth. And the same is true of the concept 'naturalistic sentence'. *Some* ways, however, of sharpening the concepts are not mutually compatible. Incidentally Brandt's own characterizations seem to be of this kind! For Brandt characterizes ethical sentences as sentences containing certain words such as "good", "right", etc., or words synonymous with these. And naturalistic sentences (which is my term for "sentences in the language of empirical science") he characterizes as *not* containing these words. But now it seems impossible by definition, to fulfill the conditions of (D1), at least for a correct metaethical theory. For what is required by a linguistic naturalistic theory is that it implies that there are sentences which contain ethical words, or words synonymous with ethical words, which are synonymous with sentences containing only naturalistic terms. But whenever this seems to have occured, these naturalistic terms turn out *not* to be naturalistic but *ethical,* since terms synonymous with ethical terms are also ethical terms. At least this is so if we grant the principle that if two sentences are synonymous, the one containing an ethical term and the other a scientific term, in some crucial position, then also these *terms* are synonymous (in this context).[1]

Let us now leave these problems. Other less confusing interpretations of Brandt, are also possible, I think, though perhaps not so applicable to every context in Brandt. Let us now try to make only general state-

---

[1] Cf. page 2 of *Ethical Theory* about the definition of 'ethical term'!

ments about (D1) which are valid for all reasonable ways of making (D1) precise.

Confronted with the class of statements abstracted by (D1) there are several questions which one is tempted to ask. One kind of problem is, of course, whether there are any correct linguistic naturalistic statements; another is whether these statements are in any way relevant to ethics. Because of my narrow aim in this study I shall only deal with the latter kind of problem. These problems are, however, still too vaguely stated to allow for a rational solution. Any attempt to solve them must wait until we know more about the third condition of the definiens of (D1). Which concept of synonymy does Brandt use?

3. R. Brandt's Concept of Synonymy

Brandt's concept of synonymy is explicitly defined. Made only slightly more perspicuous his definition runs as follows:

(D2)   The two property-referring expressions X and Y are synonymous for the speech-habits of the person P if, and only if,
(i) for every actual thing or situation, P must, if called upon to judge, be willing either to apply both X and Y, to reject both, or must be in doubt about both, and
(ii) for every drawing of things, every description of things, or situations (not necessarily causally possible in nature), P must, if called upon to judge, be willing either to apply both X and Y, to reject both, or must be in doubt about both.

There are obvious, as well as more intricate problems, attached to this definition. One obvious problem is that while (D2) defines a relational concept the definition (D1), of naturalism, requires an absolute concept. Furthermore, while (D1) requires a concept that applies to sentences, (D2) applies to (property-referring) expressions. And in what sense is P "forced" to be willing; what does the obscure word "must" refer to in this context? It is probably thought that P is forced by his will to abide to his speech-habits, otherwise these have disappeared in the definiens. But, then, must not the concept be relativized to a *situation* as well? The speech-habits can, I suppose, change over a period of time. To avoid these *obvious* difficulties—leaving the intricate problems for further discussion—I propose the following modification of (D2), which, I think, catches at least some of Brandt's intensions (this definition is inspired by A. Naess in his *Empirisk semantik*):

(D2:1)   The two sentences U and V are synonymous if, and only if, for every not-too-special person P in every not-too-special situation S and for every possible world-description or "model" M, the propositions expressed by U and V for P in S are both true in M, or both false in M, and there is some M such that these propositions are true, and there is some M such that these propositions are false in it.

This formulation is not without its complications but we have at least got rid of the obscure talk of "speech-habits" and of P being "forced to accept" etc., and we have access to an absolute concept of synonymy, just like (D1) requires. Furthermore, (D2:1) defines a concept that applies to pairs of *sentences*. Yet two points are far from clear in my proposed definition. How do you know what proposition a sentence expresses to a person in a situation? Here some "operational test" should be supplied. And when is a person or situation "too-special"? All the same I think these areas of vagueness are harmless. Exactly how the definition should be made precise cannot be settled until one knows more about what kind of use Brandt is making of his concept, but when one knows that one probably also knows some manner of dispensing with the problems.

The last conditions of the definiens of (D2:1) are made necessary by the possibility of positively or negatively analytic sentences; unless we have these conditions, analytic sentences would all be synonymous with one another.

But even (D2:1) is problematic, in a less obvious manner. Which worlds are possible? Brandt writes that the class of possible worlds must not be restricted to those that are causally possible in nature (cf. (D2)!). But then, consider the following case. Suppose that we want to test the following pair of sentences for synonymy by the means that (D2:1) provides us with:

(1) All unmarried men are happy
(2) All bachelors are happy

If we disregard, for a moment, the problems posed by the fact that "bachelor" is ambiguous, these sentences do indeed seem to be synonymous. This conclusion could easily be rebutted, however, and so could any affirmative conclusion of this sort. One need only conceive a possible world where some unmarried men are *not* happy but where all bachelors *are*. In this world (1) is false and (2) is true. And there is no way of disposing with this apparent counter-instance as merely apparent because the world in question is not possible. For why is it not possible? In order to conclude this we require the very concept of synonymy which we are trying to define—or some related "intensional" concept like 'analyticity' or 'sameness of meaning'. This kind of problem is well-known to any reader of Quine or White on the concept of analyticity.

Even if the problems at this point seem overwhelming, let us nevertheless try to reach a preliminary solution which makes it possible to proceed. Perhaps there *is*, all the same, a way out of the troubles revealed by Quine's arguments. For when Quine denies[2] the availability of an adequate concept of analyticity (and hence of synonymy) his aims are epistemological, i.e. he wishes to destroy certain "dogmas of empiricism". But perhaps there is, all the same, some way for a metaethicist to define an adequate concept. This clearly, depends on his purposes, and these we are still partly ignorant of. But one way of proceeding here, which will work out "technically" at least, would be to be satisfied with a comparative concept of 'synonymy'. In that case, we relieve ourselves of the necessity of making a sharp distinction between synonymous and nonsynonymous sentences. Hence we will have to modify the definition of 'naturalism', (D1), too. Two sentences could now, for example, be more synonymous than an alternative pair if, and only if, roughly, the test works out well for *more* models in relation to these sentences than for the alternative pair. In the definiens of (D1) it could be reasonable to demand that E and N be synonymous *to a high degree*.

This, of course, is nothing but a rough "first aproximation". To be intelligible in terms of Brandt's "empirical" metaethics it must also be supplied with some "operational" device which makes it possible to "count models". Yet, for the time being these suggestions are good enough to allow us to proceed.

4. Further Problems with the Concept of 'Synonymy'

There is a complication in relation to (D2) which renders more difficult the solution of the problem of the relevance of linguistic naturalism. What is defined in (D2) is synonymy of *property-referring* expressions. In (D2:1) there seems to be required a corresponding restriction to some sort of "descriptive" sentences. But this restriction is not trivial. For it should not be taken for granted when one *defines* 'naturalism' that naturalism is true nor even that ethical terms refer to properties. This is denied by non-descriptivism of various sorts.

The reason why the test of synonymy presupposes that the sentences

[2] Cf. "Two Dogmas of Empiricism".

tested are descriptive, is not discussed by Brandt but it is obvious from the following distinction. It is one thing to apply a term on "linguistic" grounds and another to apply it on factual grounds. You could properly say of a cat that it is an "animal" *either* because the concept of animal is "included" in the concept of cat, i.e. because there is some linguistic rule or something like that, which combines the two terms, *or* you could properly say of a cat that it is an "animal" because there is some empirical law to the effect that all cats are animals. And the same goes for ethical terms. You could properly call an act of murder "immoral" either on linguistic grounds or on moral grounds, i.e. you may *by definition* refuse to talk of "murder" unless the act in question is immoral —or you may so speak of all acts of murder because you are of the *ethical conviction* that murder is always wrong.

Now, suppose we wish to examine whether the two sentences

(3) X is good

and

(4) X is an experience of pleasure

are synonymous. Let us suppose that we apply some test provided by the concept defined in (D2:1). And let us suppose that our test provides us with an affirmative conclusion. For every actual or hypothetical case all not-too-special people in not-too-special situations assent to the statements expressed by *both* sentences, dissent from the statements expressed by both sentences or are in doubt about both (this is a way of making the concept operational with which Brandt, I think, would be very much in sympathy). What kinds of conclusions could be drawn from this result? No definite conclusion at all, it appears. For we will not know whether this result is obtained because people have the axiological conviction that pleasure and nothing but pleasure is good, *or* because there is some linguistic rule which combines the two terms. And the restriction to descriptive sentences—or terms descriptive of properties—seems to be designed to dispose of these troubles. For if we in some way, grant that sentences in ethics are descriptive of natural facts, then the confrontation with models in conflict with the "laws of nature" would eliminate the possibility that what we have found is an ethical conviction. This way out, however, would be to put the cart before the horse, and we must find some other one. I suggest that we adopt the following method.

We try to design a "two-stage" method. First we proceed with the methods described in (D2:1) when faced with a pair of sentences for testing. This allows us to arrive at the hypothetical conclusion of the sort arrived at in relation to (3) and (4) above. Then we supply our test with the following procedure. We examine the speech habits of the persons in question, not only by confronting them with various actual and hypothetical situations (models), but also by making them imagine that they are accepting alternative moral positions to those they are actually in sympathy with. Now, two possibilities are open. Either the test will still yield the result that the two sentences are synonymous, or the new evidence will tell the other way. In the second case you can conclude that (3) and (4) are not synonymous but in the former case you can, with some confidence, conclude that they are.

Again, however, we are faced with the troubles revealed by Quine's argument. *Is* a moral position where experiences of happiness are not good *possible?*

There are still many problems in relation to linguistic naturalism but I think enough has been said to make us able to assess the relevance to ethics of this theory.

5. Is Linguistic Naturalism Relevant to Ethics?

The question whether linguistic naturalism is "relevant to ethics" can be interpreted in various different ways. This we saw in Chapter I. There is no given concept of relevance. Hence, let us start with Brandt's own views about this question, to see how he takes it and how he answers it. Let us then proceed, since his answers will turn out unsatisfactory, to weaken his concepts in reasonable ways. I shall have something to say about more "indirect" connections between metaethics and normative ethics.

Is Linguistic Naturalism Logically Relevant to Ethics?

R. Brandt himself seems to take it for granted that linguistic naturalism is logically relevant to ethics, i.e. he holds the view that we are in fact justified in deriving ethical conclusions from meataehical statements. This is obvious from the following passage of *Ethical Theory,* to mention only one example:

For instance, Perry's definitions enable us to say, 'Any act is right if and only if it will contribute more to harmonious happiness than anything else the agent could do instead'. (p. 178)

Now, how could this possibly be the case? How could one derive ethical conclusions from "reportive definitions", to use Brandt's term?[3]

---

[3] Perry's definition of 'right', according to Brandt, is that to "... say that an act is 'right' ... is to say that no other act can contribute more to the harmonious happiness of the group". (p. 170)

Brandt seems to have two separate ideas as to how this becomes possible.

On the one hand Brandt seems to be willing to weaken the concept of 'logical relevance' so that a metaethical theory *m* is logically relevant "in an empirical system", as I shall say, to an ethical statement *e* if, and only if, *m* together with some true empirical statements logically implies *e* and the empirical "extra" premisses do not themselves imply any ethical conclusions. This is, at least, how I interpret Brandt's implicit conceptualization. He writes:

It has been suggested that 'is desirable' means just 'is desired by somebody'. If this proposal is right, then, of course, observation can tell us what is desirable. (p. 152)

The idea now seems to be that the metaethical statement that "is desirable" means "is desired by somebody" implies that X is desirable if, and only if, X is desired by somebody, and that this principle, together with an empirical statement to the effect that for example pleasure is desired by a certain individual, implies that pleasure is desirable.

On the other hand Brandt seems to believe that metaethical theses imply that certain ethical principles are tautological and hence could be taken as basic premisses of systems of normative ethics. He writes:

The reason why all problems of ethics can be solved by the methods of science, if naturalism is true, is that the naturalist's definitions ... enable him to assert that some fundamental ethical statements are true by definition—statements he can use as the basic premisses of his normative ethics. (p. 178)

This second view obviously presupposes the view that if a statement implies that another statement is true by definition, then it also implies the latter statement itself.

Now, are Brandt's views of the logical relevance of linguistic naturalism valid? My thesis is that they are not.

Let us take the second line of argument first. I am not at all sure what it means, first of all, to say that some basic principles are "true by definition". Does this mean that they are tautological? But in that case they follow from *any* statement. And how could they then be taken as basic principles of any ethical system, given their emptiness?

Secondly, whatever "true by definition" means, can the property here referred to (this property of ethical statements) really be derived from metaethical generalizations about the use of words in a certain population, words like "desirable" and "is desired"?

The most that can be derived here seems to be that the *sentence*

"X is desirable, if, and only if, X is desired" is *analytic*. But what is the ethical relevance of *this* finding?

This question is naturally dealt with in connection with Brandt's former line of argument.

The idea underlying Brandt's former line of argument seems to be that the following argument is valid:

(1)   "desirable" means "is desired"
(2)   X is desirable if, and only if, X is desired
(3)   P desires A
(4)   A is desirable

where (2) is thought to follow from (1), (3) is a true empirical premiss, and (4) is thought to follow from (3) and (2).

The crucial point here, of course, is the step from (1) to (2). The question whether (2) follows from (1), furthermore, comes to much the same as the question whether the statement that "X is desirable if, and only if, X is desired" is analytic, implies the principle that X is desirable if, and only if, X is desired. And my answer to both these questions is, no. The reasons are the ones put forward by Lars Bergström in his essay "Meaning and Morals", which I discussed in Chapter II. The statements (1) and (2) are simply not statements about the same sort of things, the one being a statement about certain uses of certain words in some population, and the other being a statement about what is desirable. In Brandt's case it is *clear,* I think, that Bergström's argument applies, no matter what you may think of it in its *general* form.

The "deduction" from (1) to (4) is clearly dependent, as Brandt conceives it, not only on logic but on an empirical premiss as well. And I defined a concept which applies to such deductions. The acceptance of premiss (3) was of no help in this case. The "deduction" is still not valid because the step from (1) to (2) is not valid. But perhaps the weakened sense of "logical relevance in an empirical system" could suggest another way of deriving ethical conclusions. Perhaps it was only Brandt's *example* that was no good? Perhaps even the step from (1) to (2) could be taken if only we had access to some crucial empirical premisses? Here a field for examination opens up into which I shall not venture before Chapter VI.

Is Linguistic Naturalism of any Indirect Relevance to Ethics?

Explicitly Brandt himself only claims logical relevance for linguistic naturalism but he also makes some presuppositions which could be of some relevance to my question. In particular he presupposes that natu-

ralism is inconsistent with various philosophical views. And this indicates that he thinks naturalism implies that "there is knowledge in
ethics, knowledge like that of the empirical sciences", that "ethical
terms refer to properties", and that "ethical statements are either true
or false—in the sense of correctly or incorrectly representing some facts"
(203). He also holds that naturalism is a theory to the effect that ethical
beliefs are "generalizations, extrapolations, and so forth, of empirical
evidence" (p. 155). These are all theses, to be sure, of moral philosophy,
although not moral theses. Perhaps *these* are of some relevance to
ethics? Let us for the moment suppose that they are. Then the question
arises whether Brandt is right when he holds that "naturalism", in his
sense of the term, has these implications.

Now, this question is not very easy to answer. For what does it mean
to say that ethical statements "refer to properties", that ethical statements are "true" or "false" (in the sense of "correctly or incorrectly
representing some facts")? Does this imply that there *are* ethical facts
of some sort, or does it only imply that ethical statements make a claim
to truth, that they are made with the intention of describing facts? The
same also applies to the statements that "ethical knowledge" and ethical
beliefs are "generalizations, and so forth, of empirical evidence". Does
this mean that there *are* ethical facts which we can gain knowledge about
through generalizations of empirical evidence etc., or does it only mean
that this is what we think or intend our ethical convictions to be?

Obviously, only the "stronger" interpretations seem to be of any
immediate interest to the *moral* philosopher or the man who wants to
know what is right or wrong. But, as also seems obvious, Brandt's concept of naturalism is only to the latter effect. Moreover, I think it clear
that it does not *imply* conclusions of the former kind either. For these
stronger interpretations are statements about facts which are, again, of
quite a different kind from those which are ascertained by investigations
in accordance with Brandt's conception of naturalism. Again we must
remember that Brandt's conception of naturalism is a descriptive theory
of linguistic habits among some group of people. And even if you could
find means of ascertaining that all mankind uses some naturalistic term
synonymously with some ethical term this would not tell us anything
more than the fact that all mankind refuses to take an evaluative or
moral point of view *or* that ethical properties are of a natural kind.

The only way to escape this conclusion is, I think, to say that the
question whether there are ethical properties simply *is* a question
whether people actually and usually intend to refer to properties and so
forth when using some specified terms. Now, I can accept this if only

54

it is remembered and recognized that now the question whether there are ethical properties is in *its* turn of little philosophical significance and, hence, also of *prima facie* little ethical relevance. But I shall say more in Chapter VI about the significance for ontology and metaphysics of reports about actual word usage. For now I shall be content to conclude that such reports are of no obvious relevance to ontology, at least not if "ontology" is taken in a sense which seems ethically interesting.

6. Summary of the Chapter

The results of this chapter may be summarized in the following manner. I have found that for those interested in the relation between metaethics and ethics the important thing with R. Brandt's conception of naturalism, "linguistic naturalism", as I have called it, is not so much that it is naturalistic as that it is merely linguistic. This creates various problems and it affects in various ways the relation of the theory to ethics.

Firstly, I find it hard to understand exactly what kind of theory ethical naturalism is. The attempts I made to clarify and make comprehensive the concept of synonymy, used in the definition of 'linguistic naturalism' resulted in a concept which seems extremely difficult to apply and which is only *relative*. But at least I think I succeded in making a definition which is at the same time a fairly reasonable interpretation of Brandt and of a sort which could theoretically, at least, have application. The problem of making this concept absolute instead of comparative had to be solved, however, by quantification over some variables in a somewhat arbitrary way. And whether there is any good evidence to invoke in support of any linguistically naturalistic theory is open to serious doubt.

Secondly, it appeared to be far from clear what purpose linguistic naturalism was intended to serve. Hence it is hard to assess its fruitfulness. Assuming, however, that the theory is meant to have some *ethical* relevance or significance (as Brandt clearly holds that it has, whether this relevance is the sole purpose or not) I made some investigations which convinced me of the reasonableness of the tentative conclusion that *this* purpose is *not* fulfilled by the theory. And I am even more strongly convinced that Brandt's own arguments for this kind of relevance are deficient. The thesis that linguistic naturalism has logical relevance for ethics loses credit when one recognizes that metaethical, linguistically naturalistic statements, and ethical statements, are statements of quite different kinds, statements about radically different sorts of things.

The idea that linguistic naturalism is inconsistent with various views of metaphysics and ontology and, in particular, the thesis that the theory implies statements to the effect that there are ethical quialities of a peculiar sort, fared no better. This thesis appeared to be in conflict with the fact, again, that linguistically naturalistic statements are statements of a radically different kind from ontological or metaphysical statements, at least as long as the latter are conceived to be of some ethical importance.

The argument I pursued seems to go against Brandt's contentions about the relevance of metaethics to ethics. On two points, however, I had to leave the possibility open that further findings might partly upset my conclusion.

Firstly, I am not at all sure that Brandt has extracted from the term "logical relevance" all its interesting and fruitful meanings by his implicit use of concepts of relevance. More has to be said about various "weak" relations between ethics and metaethics.

Secondly, perhaps there is more to be said about the relation between "ontology" and "metaphysics" on one hand, and reports about speech, on the other. These two points will be left for the concluding chapter.

CHAPTER FOUR

THE RELEVANCE TO ETHICS OF
C. L. STEVENSON'S EMOTIVISM

1. Background

The question whether emotivism of the kind C. L. Stevenson develops, above all in *Ethics and Language* (from which all quotations in this chapter are taken unless otherwise stated) is relevant to ethics, is explicitly asked by Stevenson. The answer, however, is mainly implicit. In the first chapter of *Ethics and Language* Stevenson all the same makes some passing remarks about the problem. He there suggests that the study of metaethics may have what one could call a "therapeutic" relevance to ethics (more about this terminology of mine in Chapter VI, cf. also Chapter I), i.e. these kinds of studies would be of some help, in some way, to those trying to solve substantial moral problems. He writes:

> The purpose of an analytic or methodological study, whether of science or of ethics, is always indirect. It hopes to send others to their tasks with clearer heads and less wasteful habits of investigation. (p. 1)

Yet it is not quite clear, to me at least, exactly how Stevenson sees this aim realized by means of his theory. He does say, however, something about how it is *not* realized; emotivism is of no logical relevance (in my terms) to ethics. He writes the following about this:

> ... although normative questions constitute by far the most important branch of ethics, pervading all of common-sense life, and occupying most of professional attention of legislators, editorialists, didactic novelists, clergymen, and moral philosophers, these questions must here be left unanswered. The present volume has the limited tast of sharpening the tools which others employ. (p. 1)

I can see no reason to question the point made here by Stevenson as he denies that his theory has any ethical implication. His theory could be interpreted in different ways, but whatever reasonable interpretation we choose, the arguments put forward by L. Bergström, discussed in Chapter II and adapted to Brandt's naturalism in Chapter III, will apply. This, I think, will be obvious as we proceed to examine the different interpretations. On the other hand, this does not mean that Stevenson himself is quite free from ambiguities on this point; there *are* passages

indeed where he writes as though the above quoted passage did not exist
—cf. for example page 209 in *Ethics and Language* about this.

Now, how could the thesis that emotivism has some at least "therapeutic" relevance to ethics be rationally defended? Stevenson does
not say anything explicitly about this. But one answer seems to be
implicit in his way of arguing about certain implications of his theory.
Emotivism, Stevenson seems to hold, has some bearings of a "sceptical"
sort on the problem of finding methods for the rational justification of
ethical statements. It is far from clear what these would-be implications
are, but they seem significant enough, if they could be proved to follow
from the theory, to give to emotivism a kind of indirect relevance to
ethics. Stevenson's emotivism seems, if he is right about the implications
of it, to be of the utmost importance for all our moral "practice". Hence,
my first question to be dealt with in this chapter will be whether emotivism has ethically significant implications for the problem of the justification of ethical statements. This will take us far, but I think it worth-
while and even necessary to deal at some length with emotivism. The
emotive theory of ethics raises problems of a general character but the
theory is nevertheless often misrepresented and incorrectly interpreted.
The points about it that I shall make will turn out to be of a sort which
lend themselves naturally to generalizations. In Chapter VI when seeking
a general solution to my problem we shall see that the examination of
emotivism has prepared the way for a more definite answer to the question
whether there are any metaethical statements having relevance to ethics.

After having discussed Stevenson's own (implicit) views of the relation
between metaethics and ethics I shall deal with an argument put forward
by F. A. Olafson in defence of the thesis that emotivism is, in my terms,
"pragmatically relevant to ethics". His ideas could be considered as an
elaboration of the commonplace charge against Stevenson of "weakening
people's moral principles" and "letting caprice into people's moral
sense". These charges, which, if I am correctly informed, once almost
lost Stevenson his university post, are made by Olafson, in a less hostile,
though somewhat sharper manner than they used to be, in "Meta-ethics
and the Moral Life".

2. Emotivism and the Justification of Ethical Statements

Stevenson makes various assertions about what emotivism implies concerning the possibility of justifying one's ethical statements. He discusses the problem, roughly, from three different points of view, giving what
prima facie, at least, seem to be different arguments in support of what,

superficially, seems to be slightly different theses. I shall first try to give rough formulations of Stevenson's "sceptical" theses which he holds follow from emotivism. I then examine Stevenson's arguments in support of these theses under different interpretations (where it will turn out, as a matter of fact, that there is one reasonable interpretation common to all three of them). The rationale of all these arguments is Stevenson's metaethic (emotivism). Hence, this seems to give to emotivism an indirect kind of relevance to ethics.

Some Sceptical Theses

The "structure" of the relevant parts of *Ethics and Language* could be indicated in the following way. In Chapter I, Stevenson states some kind of a psychological theory about the nature of ethical disagreement. This theory is taken to support[1] his metaethical theory, i.e. his theory about the meaning of ethical terms. Stevenson tries to clarify the meaning of ethical terms, first in Chapter II where he gives his "working models", which are preliminary definitions of some key terms. He then develops a concept of meaning which is to enable him to be more precise in his statement of his metaethic. The theory is developed in Chapter IV into what he calls the "first pattern of analysis", and in Chapter IX into what he calls the "second pattern of analysis". Each time, after stating his metaethical views, Stevenson proceeds to draw some conclusions about the possibility of justifying ethical statements.

In Chapter II the thesis is that

(T1)   Ethical statements cannot be proved

which is supposed to be a consequence of the working models. In Chapter V the thesis is that

(T2)   The relation between the reasons in support of an ethical conclusion and the conclusion itself is psychological, not logical

where the argument is based *both* on the metaethical theory, now cast into the form of the "first pattern of analysis", and on characterizations

---

[1] Incidentally this "support" is of a somewhat peculiar sort. Stevenson seems to take his findings about ethical disagreement as positive evidence for his metaethical analysis of the meaning of ethical terms. But it is hard to see how this could be the case. How could a psychological theory about what is involved in a certain kind of interpersonal situation tell us anything about the meaning of certain utterances—and even less of certain words. A more natural way of taking the connection between the two theories would have been to take *consistency* with the theory of the psychological aspects of ethical disagreement to be a necessary condition of adequacy for any theory of the meaning of ethical terms. Then the theory of the psychology of morals would be a means of refuting metaethical theories but not a means of establishing them.

of some key concept such as 'reason', and in Chapter VII, *one* (out of several) thesis seems to be

(T3)   No ethical arguments are valid.

Here the argument is founded *both* on the first pattern of analysis and on characterizations of key concepts like 'validity' and 'truth'.

The problem of justification is discussed also in relation to the second pattern of analysis, in Chapter X, but here nothing important is added to the theses formulated above. So let us concentrate on these three formulations. How should they be interpreted and how does Stevenson try to support them?

3. Stevenson's Arguments in Support of his Sceptical Theses

The Working Model and the Possibility of Proof in Ethics

When first stating his problem of the possibility of rational justification in ethics granted the truth of emotivism (cf. Chapter II of *Ethics and Language* about this) Stevenson writes the following:

> The model for 'this is good' consists of the conjunction of (a) 'I approve of this' and (b) 'Do so as well'. If proof is possible for (a) and (b) taken separately, then and only then will it be possible for their conjunction. So let us see what can be done with the sentences separately. (p. 26)

Now, let us see what follows for the possibility of proofs in ethics, from the working models.

There seems to be something odd in this way of stating the problem. Stevenson seems to hold that *sentences* are being proved. But unless you were discussing a strictly formal calculus you would expect that proofs were given, not for the sentences themselves but for what is *expressed* by these sentences. What is referred to by "(a)" and "(b)" seem, however, to be sentences. Stevenson writes for example that "/s/entence (a) offers no trouble ..." and that "/s/entence (b) ... raises a question ..." And this raises the question how Stevenson conceives his metaethical deifnitions in this respect. In order to be able to deal with that question let us look at his original formulation of the working model for "This is good". Stevenson makes contextual "definitions" of the ethical terms. I shall call the definition of "good" "(WM1)":

(WM1)   "This is good" means *I approve of this; do so as well.*

In contradistinction to what is said in the quoted passage above the two "components" of the definiens are not within inverted commas in

(WM1). In (WM1) Stevenson seems to *use,* not to quote, the sentences in question. The opposite is the case in the passage quoted above. Hence, one could distinguish two directions of interpretation of (WM1) depending on whether one takes as his point of departure Stevenson's formulation of his analysis or his statements *about* it. These directions may be suggested in the following way:

(WM1.1) "This is good" expresses the statement 'I (the one using the sentence to make a statement) approve of this' and the imperative[2] 'Do so as well!'"

(WM1.2) "This is good" is synonymous with "I approve of this; do so as well!"

Hence, Stevenson's working models, exemplified by (WM1), can *either* be conceived of as a scheme for interpretations where "statements" (in my wide and inclusive sense) are correlated to sentences, *or* as an analytic scheme for statements of synonymy, statements asserting that specified sentences have the same meaning.

Both directions of interpretation of (VM1) raise difficulties for anyone who, like Stevenson, wishes to examine what the consequences of emotivism are for the possibility of ethical proofs. The line of interpretation suggested by (WM1:2) seems altogether irrelevant to this problem, for the piece of information that two specified sentences are synonymous is of no consequence for the problem of what sort of consideration (if any) is relevant to ethical conclusions. You can know *that* two sentences have the same meaning without knowing *which* meaning they have. Even if you did know their meaning, it is still far from clear to what effect this would be, but it is *quite* clear that if you *do not* know the meaning then, although you know that (WM1:2) is true, you are told nothing whatever about the prospects for a rational ethical justification.

A more specific problem in relation to this direction of interpretation is that it seems implausible that two sentence *types* (in contradistinction to sentence *tokens*) should ever express the same proposition in *every* context. Hence, this interpretation seems to presuppose that something is said also about the *contexts* in which the sentences appear, limiting the scope of the analysis to some specified contexts, for example where

---

[2] By "imperative" I denote, as is obvious from my use of simple quotation marks, a kind of proposition i.e. something *expressed* by the formulation in question. Perhaps someone would prefer to use the term "command" here but for the sake of simplicity I shall follow Stevenson in his use of "imperative".

the sentence in the definiendum is used "ethically"[3]—otherwise one shall have to choose a very weak concept of synonymy.

Stevenson's concept of meaning, which is presupposed in (WM1.2) —two sentences are anynonymous, according to Stevenson, if, and only if, they have the same meaning—raises various questions. I shall briefly indicate some of them here. They are all of consequence for the assessment of the relevance to ethics of emotivism in relation to the first and the second pattern of analysis as well as in relation to (WM1.2).

One naturally assumes that Stevenson's choice of his conceptual framework in general and his concept of meaning in particular is determined by his analytical aims, i.e. his wish to make well-founded statements about the possibility of justifying rationally one's ethical statements. Now Stevenson does take one step towards explicitly relating the adoption of his concept of meaning to his purposes. He imposes various conditions for the adequacy of his concept, i.e. conditions that must necessarily be fulfilled by any concept of meaning to be useful to Stevenson's purposes. Strangely enough, however, he does not argue in defence of these conditions. Why must they be fulfilled if Stevenson's aims are to be realized?

Stevenson requires that the concept of meaning be so defined that the meaning of a sign does not "vary in a bewildering way", that a sign could have meaning even if it is lacking "referent", that meanings are "conventional", that meanings are "psychological", that interjections could have meaning, and that "descriptive" and "emotive" meanings are "species" of the "genus" meaning.

Put in this compressed way questions of the correct interpretation of the conditions immediately arise. And, furthermore, since Stevenson does not argue in support of his conditions for the adequacy of his concept—save from the obviously false argument that some of these conditions must be fulfilled by *any* concept of meaning—one must seriously wonder whether they are reasonable. Let us, however, leave these problems and instead examine the very concept Stevenson defines and which he holds satisfies the conditions.[4]

Roughly, Stevenson defines a "causal" concept of meaning which could be suggested in the following way. The meaning of a sign *s* is a dispositional property of *s* where the response, varying with varying

---

[3] The most plausible interpretation would perhaps be to take (WM1.2) to be to the effect that the definiendum in ethical contexts means the same as does the definiens in the context of analysis, i.e. in the book *Ethics and Language*.

[4] This contention seems to be false in at least one respect. Stevenson's meanings are no more psychological than are the natural numbers. And his concept does not make meanings altogether free from variations either although they are perhaps not "bewildering".

attendant circumstances, consists of a psychological process in the hearer, and where the stimulus is hearing s.

This, although simplified, may seem a bit obscure, but perhaps it could be explained in the following way (where the simplification of only taking the *hearer* into account is dropped): Two signs, s_1, and s_2, have the same meaning (are synonymous) if, and only if, s_1, and s_2, if they were to be heard (read etc.) under similar attendant circumstances, would give rise to similar psychological processess in the hearer (reader etc), and if they were to be said (written etc.) under similar attendant circumstances, would stem from similar psychological processes in the speaker (writer etc.)

This definition is only vaguely suggested. Stevenson makes it sharper, for example by discussing more thoroughly the "psychological processes" in question. On these he places the following restriction:

A sign's disposition to affect a hearer is to be called a 'meaning ... only if it has been caused by, or would not have developed without, an elaborate process of conditioning which has attended the sign's use in communication. (p. 57)

This obviously, is intended to account for the fact that Stevenson's meanings are "conventional".

Stevenson indicates that perhaps the concept of meaning must be relativized in different ways (which is, it seems, inconsistent with what is said about "bewildering variations"). He writes the following about this:

In adopting the idiom, 'This sign has a meaning,' we must remember that the phrase is elliptical, and must often be expanded to the form 'This sign has a meaning for people of sort K.' This is parallel to saying that 'X is a stimulant' is elliptical, and must often be expanded to the form 'X is a stimulant for people of sort K'. Just as an X may be a stimulant for certain people and not for others, so a sign may have a meaning for certain people and not for others. (p. 56)

This restriction, of course, is needed unless all signs are trivially to lack meaning simply because people speak different languages, but it is doubtful whether Stevenson intends the restriction to say anything more than that.

With regard to the problem of the strength of the causal claims made in the definiens (expressed by the terms "give rise" and "stem from") we must remain uncertain since Stevenson says nothing on this point. This will be of some consequence for argument later.

Given this rough characterization of Stevenson's concept of meaning we encounter difficulties significant in relation to (WM1.2) and also, as we shall see later, in relation to the first and the second patterns of analysis.

Firstly, the concept of meaning is so defined that meanings are dispositional and, hence, the "traditional" difficulties attached to dispositional properties arise. The situations in which the same psychological responses are to appear include hypothetical ones as well as actual ones; but how can one confirm statements about hypothetical (counter-factual) situations? And how, exactly, is the subjunctive expression "if . . . would" to be interpreted?

Secondly, and partly as a consequence of what was said above, meanings will be extremely "complex" entities. They will, as a matter of fact, be "functions" (in a mathematical sense of the word) from a very large set of couples of utterances of words and situations into a set of psychological processes—if we, for short restrict our attention to the hearer's point of view. At the same time Stevenson, at least in some arguments, seems to presuppose that we can grasp these meanings simply by being presented with a phrase which is the bearer of them. But this I find implausible.

Thirdly, the talk of "similar situation" and "similar psychological response" is so imprecise that it seems practically impossible ever to decide, by the use of Stevenson's defining criteria, whether two signs or sentences are synonymous or not. Suppose, for example, that we are testing the words "ethics" and "morals" for synonymy. Let us assume that we have arrived at the preliminary conclusion that they *are* synonymous, after having gone through such a large number of different situations that our inductive hypothesis seems confirmed to a reasonable degree. But now, what conclusions can be drawn from this? Certainly not that the two words *are* synonymous. For our result might very well be a consequence of our, intentional or unintentional, "manipulation" of our variables. As soon as we seem to have run against a counter-instance to our hypothesis, the case could easily be dismissed because the difference in response is "explained", either by the assertion that the situations were not, after all, similar to an acceptable degree, or by the assertion that the psychological responses were, after all, similar to an acceptable degree. As long as no criterion by which relevant similarity could be recognized is stated, we could always in this way "manipulate" our variables—there are always *some* differences (at least temporally or spatially) which could be hypostatized as relevant. And Stevenson gives us no such criterion.

Fourthly, Stevenson's concept of meaning gives rise to problems similar to those discussed *à propos* of R. Brandt in Chapter III. Stevenson's concept of meaning is founded, it seems, on the idea of substitutions not *salva veritate* but with invariant psychological responses. Now, these "substitutions" cannot be allowed for in *all* contexts, granted that we are dealing (as we are) with a "non-extensional" language. For if you were to include all kinds of contexts, this would amount to the effect that no words were synonymous (not even two inscriptions of the same word) with each other. To see this, consider again the two words "ethics" and "morals". Even if the test has worked out very well for various kinds of contexts, you need only examine two contexts, similar in all respects you may think of, and both containing the occurrence of the linguistic component "the word ... contains the letter "r"" to get a counterinstance. Here, of course, the substitution of "ethics" for "morals" would lead to a change, in psychological response among literate people. Similar examples could be constructed for contexts where statements are made about beliefs and modalities, for example. Thus we need a criterion by which we can exclude problematic contexts, but can such a criterion be found without already having access to a concept of meaning?

I will say no more now about the difficulties pertaining to the interpretation (WM1.2) which are due to problems about the concept of meaning. These will all be of consequence to the first and second patterns of analysis, where they are impossible to avoid. Now we must proceed to the alternative interpretation of (WM1), i.e. (WM1.1), in order to examine whether it will prove less troublesome in connection with the question of whether there are proofs or rational arguments in ethics. Even if the concept of meaning were applicable and comprehensive, the conclusions about synonymy would still be irrelevant to the problem of justification for the reasons mentioned above; they would be especially irrelevant if it is implausible that we know *what* the meaning of a sign is, no matter what sign it is known to be synonymous with. Knowledge of the synonymy of a pair of sentences does not imply knowledge of the meaning of those sentences, and knowledge of a Stevenson meaning is furthermore a piece of highly complex *psychological* knowledge and, hence, *prima facie* devoid of all relevance to "logical" problems of proofs and so forth. So let us see whether (WM1.1) will turn out more promising.

The interpretation (WM1.1) is reasonable from a descriptive point of view, as is (WM1.2), and it seems *prima facie* relevant, too, to questions about justification in ethics. This interpretation *interprets* ethical sentences by assigning ethical statements to them. And what could be more natural than the view that if you wish to justify an ethical statement, you must know how to interpret the sentence by which it is communicated?

But even (WM1.1) is problematic. The fact that the definiendum is specified by *quotation* indicates that the sentence interpreted is a sentence-*type*. But how would one single out one and only one meaning of a sentence *type*? One would naturally think that the meaning (the statement expressed) varied from context to context. I can see but one way out of these problems. Though not explicitly saying so Stevenson analyses only a few uses of the sentence-types in question, i.e. only some *tokens* of the types are interpreted. I would suppose that these contexts that he examines are what could be called "the contexts that are most typical of normative ethics". As a matter of fact this is exactly what Stevenson calls some contexts singled out in *Ethics and Language,* on page 84, when he interrupts his clarification of the first pattern of analysis by a statement about what he calls the "function" of ethical terms— the function in the contexts just mentioned. This should perhaps not be taken to support my interpretation here, but at least it makes it somewhat more plausible. At least it is obvious that Stevenson is interested *both* in the meaning of sentence-types (when he uses the very concept of meaning he has defined) and in some semantic property possessed by sentence-tokens in certain typical contexts.

Now, let us examine possible implications of (WM1.1) for the possibility of proofs within ethics.

Stevenson's Arguments for the Impossibility of Proofs in Ethics

Stevenson states his answer to the question whether ethical statements can be proved in the following manner:

... ethical judgments are amenable only to a partial proof. So far as 'This is good' includes the meaning of (a) a proof is possible, but so far as it includes the meaning of (b) the very request for a proof is nonsensical. (p. 26)

As we remember, (a) and (b) are the parts of the definiens of (WM1). Since some metaethical definitions do consist in both (a) and (b)—or are incorrect, according to Stevenson—his thesis may be formulated as I formulated it above:

(T1)   Ethical statements cannot be proved.

Stevenson arrives at (T1) by the way of his view that statements of the kind (a) can easily be proved while statements of the kind (b) cannot possibly be proved. He writes:

Sentence (a) offers no trouble. It makes an assertion about the speaker's state of mind, and like any psychological statement, is open to empirical confirmation or disconfirmation, whether introspective or behavioristic. (p. 26)

and

Sentence (b), however, raises a question. Since it is an imperative it is not open to proof at all. (p. 26)

66

I have already dealt with the problems raised by Stevenson's talk of "sentences being confirmed" so let us proceed to an examination of Stevenson's argument in support of (T1) where we take "'This is good'" to denote a statement and where we take "the meaning of (a)" to denote the statement expressed by the sentence "I approve of this" and where we take "includes" to denote the relation of *being one link of a conjunction of statements* so that *p* is included in *q* whenever *q* is a conjunction of *p* and other statements (cf. the first of the three last quoted passages!).

Stevenson seems to base his thesis on three premisses:

(1)   A proof of a conjunction is only possible if a proof is possible of each of the links of the conjunction

(2)   Ethical sentences (in the contexts that are most typical of normative ethics) express a conjunction of a factual proposition and an imperative (ethical statements)

(3)   No proof is possible for imperatives

Premiss (1) is not likely to raise any problems; it seems to be true for all reasonable interpretations of "proof". Premiss (2) is a consequence of my interpretation of Stevenson's working model for "good", (WM1:1), and it is because this premiss occurs in the argument that the emotive theory of ethics seems to be of relevance for ethics in an indirect way. I shall not discuss the reasonableness of (2) since what interests me is what would happen if it *were* true. The crucial factor, then, is the premiss (3) since it admits of no doubt whatever that (1), (2) and (3) together are conclusive arguments for the thesis (T1).

In order to facilitate a rational assessment of the premiss (3), let us consider two examples of different kinds of "proofs" or "arguments":

(A)   (a) Communism in the interest of the people
       (b) If communism is in the interest of the people it will prevail

       (c) Communism will prevail

(B)   (a) Communism is in the interest of the people
       (b) If communism is in the interest of the people, make it prevail!

       (c) Make communism prevail!

Presented with these examples I think it clear that one can distinguish different interpretations of (T1) and of the premiss (3) by interpreting "proof" in different ways, and the resulting views will be of varying importance and reasonableness. One of these interpretations would be the following:

(T1:1)   No logically valid argument can have an ethical statement as the conclusion

as an interpretation of (T1) and (3) could be interpreted in the following, corresponding manner:

(3.1)   No logically valid argument can have an imperative as the conclusion.

Hence, "proof" is here interpreted as *logically valid argument*. In support of the interpretation (T1:1) from the descriptive point of view there is much to be said. On the other hand also a good deal against it. Let us examine the pro-arguments before we turn to the cons.

Firstly, Stevenson does seem to be of the opinion that no logical relations whatever can hold between the reasons for an ethical conslusion and the conclusion itself. This is for example obvious from his thesis (T2), which I shall soon discuss.

Secondly, this thesis (T2) could, according to Stevenson, be supported by the same arguments as those supporting (T1). And this suggests indeed an interpretation of (T1) which, like (T1:1), stresses that something is wanting from a logical point of view in ethical argumentation.

Thirdly, *persuasion* has, according to Stevenson, nothing to do with (logical) validity. As we shall see later, when discussing (T3), persuasion is at hand, under one reasonable interpretation, as soon as ethical (or normative) statements are being made.

Fourthly, Stevenson does explicitly write, *à propos* of his thesis (T1):

Clearly, the present account of methodology will fail to content a great number of theorists who are embarked on 'the quest for certainty'. The supporting reasons here mentioned have no sort of *logical* compulsion. (p. 30)

Fifthly, those arguments that can be adduced against the reasonableness of (T1:1), from a descriptive point of view, refer to facts that could perhaps be explained without dispensing with (T1:1). I shall consider this when I discuss these reasons presently.

Sixthly, one might perhaps add, Stevenson has often, in fact, been interpreted to hold the view expressed by (T1:1) and many "emotivists" have indeed held it. The view is a "radical" one which is *prima facie* of the very greatest consequence for ethics; hence it might be worth examining even for its own sake in relation to emotivism.

Against the reasonableness of (T1:1), from a descriptive point of view, we have the following.

Firstly, there are in *Ethics and Language* examples of arguments with an ethical conclusion which Stevenson seems to hold to be valid, for example on pp. 115–116 where he is implicitly assuming the validity of the following argument: Nothing which weakens people's sense of independence is good. A dole weakens people's sense of independence. Hence a dole is not good. This appears to speak against the reasonableness of the interpretation (T1:1). I shall discuss this example further later on, but it should be noticed here, that at least there are *some* comments, made by Stevenson, indicating that he takes this argument to be only "partly" valid. It's "validity" then, stems from the fact that the argument *would* be valid if we were to disregard the emotive (imperative) component of the statements. Stevenson's own comment on the example indicates that this is indeed his view:

In general, ethical statements, like all others that have at least *some* descriptive meaning, are amenable to the usual applications of formal logic. (p. 116)

and so does his note 6 on page 231:

It is assumed that logical relations are wholly unaffected by emotive meaning.

Secondly, (and perhaps this is an even stronger counter-argument), Stevenson explicitly asserts on pp. 134–35 that "... one may construct a valid syllogism with ethical premises and an ethical conclusion ...". But again, could one perhaps reasonably interpret "validity" as *partial* —due to the factual parts of the statements only. In support of this way of "dispensing" with the apparent counter-examples the passage could be cited where Stevenson asserts that what he calls "analytic" judgments "may be rejected for their emotive repercussions ..." (p. 134). Now, it is not quite clear what an analytic *judgment* is—one would have thought perhaps that analyticity is a property of sentences rather than of judgments—but all the same it could perhaps here simply be interpreted as *logical validity*? In that case logical validity may be possessed, obviously, even by statements whose "emotive" part *is not* "empty". Hence, emotive meaning seems to have been disregarded.

Enough now of the problems of the reasonableness of (T1:1) from a descriptive point of view. I cannot see that the arguments have been conclusive in any direction. The thesis (T1:1) is a "radical" and interesting thesis, however, and I think it should be discussed in connection with my main problem in this study regardless of whether Stevenson would be in sympathy of it or not. Even if interesting, however, the thesis (T1:1) appears, to my logical intuitions at least, to be false. To me the argument (B) seems as valid as the argument (A). This, however, I shall discuss in more detail later on.

The thesis (T1:1) is about a relation between the conclusions and premisses of certain arguments. One could, however, think of other interpretations as well. (T1) could be taken to be a thesis not about the relation between premisses and conclusions, but about the premisses themselves. Let us try to formulate such interpretations.

Stevenson seems to hold several views about the premisses of ethical arguments besides what has been said about their relation to the conclusions. As compared to factual premisses ethical premisses are, according to Stevenson, less "certain" or "objective". Among other things Stevenson writes the following about this:

... even if the propounding of inductive canons reflects only a *resolution* to accept them, it reflects one that is likely ... to be shared by all others who trouble to understand them. In ethics a parallel situation cannot be hoped for. (p. 173)

One descriptively reasonable interpretation of this might be the following thesis:

(T1:2)   The premisses of logically valid arguments with an ethical conclusion are never generally agreed upon

Here a difference between factual arguments and ethical arguments would obtain, according to Stevenson, since (T1:2) is intended to hold also for ultimate[5] premisses and since, as is obvious from the quoted passage, ultimate factual premisses *are* agreed upon, according to Stevenson.

The corresponding interpretation of the premiss (3) will now be the following:

(3.2)   The premisses of logically valid arguments with an imperative conclusion are never generally agreed upon

I shall deal with the question of the reasonableness of the various theses I attribute to Stevenson later. But the superficial validity of (T1:2) is low. The thesis will be denied by those who take ethical statements of an ultimate sort to be rather certain as well as by those who question the claim to certainty as regards factual statements. I shall return to this.

[5] By "ultimate premisses" I mean, roughly, those premisses that one will retort to in the very last instance when trying to defend one's position to a strenuous inquisitor, who doubts whatever statement one makes.

Perhaps the formulation (T1:2) expresses too strong a thesis to be a reasonable interpretation of Stevenson. Perhaps the difference, in the respect discussed between factual and ethical premisses should rather be conceived as gradual than as absolute, according to Stevenson. This would call for an interpretation of the following sort:

(T1:3)   The premisses of any logically valid argument with an ethical conclusion are less generally agreed upon than are the premisses of some logically valid argument with a factual conclusion

(3.3)   The premisses of any logically valid argument with an imperative conclusion are less generally agreed upon than are the premisses of some logically valid argument with a factual conclusion

All the same it could, reasonably, be retorted that these interpretations—(T1:2) and (T1:3)—are much too "superficial". And a way of delving deeper into the problem is indicated by Stevenson's conception of ethical statements as in some way "subjective". He asserts for example that "... temperamental differences in people's aspirations might lead to insoluble controversies". (p. 173). Perhaps Stevenson here also perceives a difference, in this respect, between factual and ethical statements? His thesis could, then, be interpreted in the following manner:

(T1:4)   Some premisses (viz. the ethical ones—cf. what is said in relation to (T1:5) about this) of logically valid arguments with an ethical conclusion are "subjective" in the sense that different premisses are only "reflections" of "temperamental differences in people's aspirations"

and the premiss (3) correspondingly:

(3.4)   Some premisses (viz. the imperative ones) of logically valid arguments with an imperative conclusion are "subjective" in the sense that different premisses are only "reflections" of "temperamental differences in people's aspirations"

These interpretations are, indeed, somewhat metaphorically expressed here, but should they later turn out to be fruitful for my purposes, there are various interesting ways of making them more precise.

All of the interpretations (T1:2)—(T1:4), as a matter of fact, are rather *lines* of interpretation than clear cut examples of unambiguously expressed theses. This must be kept in mind as we proceed.

All of the interpretations made hitherto, seem to accord well with the following passage, if interpreted in a suitable manner:

Those who seek an absolutely definitive method for normative ethics, and who want to rule out the possibility of rival moral codes, each equally well supported by reasons, will find that the present account gives them less than they want. (p. 31)

All of the theses (T1:1)—(T1:4) seem to be such that, if true, they will each prevent there being "absolutely definitive methods for normative ethics". But the above quoted passage could be read in another way as well. It could be taken to contain only the view that none of Stevenson's metaethical views *grant* that there are definitive methods while the question whether there are such methods is left open. This would make possible the following, "weaker" interpretation of (T1):

(T1:5)   No logically valid argument with an ethical conclusion can have only factual premisses

and the corresponding interpretation of (3) would now be:

(3.5)   No logically valid argument with an imperative conclusion can have only factual premisses.

This interpretation is interesting because it gives an "explanation" of the former theses. It is because of what is here asserted that the premisses of a valid ethical argument must contain ethical statements, and it is because they contain ethical statements that the alleged differences between factual and ethical arguments obtain, i.e. because of differences between ethical and factual statements.

What makes this interpretation descriptively reasonable, (besides the just quoted passage interpreted in the suggested way), is the fact that Stevenson seems, sometimes at least, to conceive reasons as purely *factual* statements. This is suggested in the following passage:

The way in which the reasons support the imperative is simply this: The imperative is used to alter the hearer's attitudes or actions ... The supporting reasons then describe the situation which the imperative seeks to bring about ... (p. 27)

Also the fact that Stevenson, characterizing the concept of a reason (I shall discuss this presently), holds that (only?) statements about matters of fact could be adduced as reasons, speaks *prima facie* in support of this interpretation.

The interpretation (T1:5) is, obviously, a rough formulation of the so-called Hume-Poincaré-principle.

I shall now try to make sharp Stevenson's theses (T2) and (T3). I shall at the same time try to give an account of some natural interpertations of the reasons adduced in support of these theses by Stevenson. I hope, after that, to be in a position rationally to assess the relevance to ethics of emotivism. This will be attempted in Section 4.

The Relation between the Premisses and the Conclusions of Ethical Arguments

When I tried to formulate Stevenson's view of ethical argumentation, in a preliminary manner, I formulated three different theses, (T1) discussed above, (T2) to be discussed now and (T3), to be discussed in the next section. Let us now turn to (T2).

Stevenson himself formulates his thesis in the following way:

> The reasons which support or attack an ethical judgment have previously been mentioned. Subject to some exceptions that will be noted as we proceed, they are related to the judgment psychologically rather than logically. (p. 113)

> Many modern writers accept the maxim. 'To understand what a sentence means, ask how you would verify it' ... For the first pattern, so long as sentences describing the 'verification' of an ethical judgment are identified ... with the reasons that support it, the maxim will be of no service at all. The ethical judgment and its supporting reasons become logically independent by this pattern, apart from exceptions that will be mentioned. (p. 114)

Apparently, Stevenson here makes at least two different assertions, so perhaps I had better 'split' my thesis (T2) into two independent theses:

(T2:1)   The reasons which support or attack an ethical judgment are not related logically to the judgment

(T2:2)   The reasons which support or attack an ethical judgment are related psychologically to the judgment

The thesis (T2:1) seems to imply (T1:1), discussed above, or are they perhaps even identical?

The exceptions to (T2) are exceptions to (T2:1), according to Stevenson, if I have understood him correctly, but probably not to (T2:2). They are exemplified in the following argument:

> *A*: It would be a good thing to have a dole for the unemployed. *B*: But you have just said that a dole would weaken people's sense of independence, and you have admitted that *nothing* which has that consequence is good. (pp. 115–6)

Stevenson's own comment on this example is as follows:

> Here B attacks A's position by pointing out a formal inconsistency. In general, ethical statements, like all others that have at least *some* descriptive meaning, are amenable to the usual applications of formal logic. (p. 116)

73

It seems, then, as if Stevenson would hold that moral positions of the kind: 'X is good' and 'Nothing that has Y is good' are inconsistent if X as a matter of fact has Y. And this is due to the "descriptive meaning" of the two statements. I suppose that Stevenson would argue in the following manner to prove his point. If two statements entail statements that are inconsistent, then they are themselves inconsistent. But what "X is good" said by a person, A, expresses, entails the statement that A approves of X. And this statement is inconsistent with a statement entailed by what is expressed by "Nothing which has Y is good" said by A, together with the statement that X has Y viz. the statement that A does not approve of X. The crucial argument, then, is the following:

(1) A approves of nothing which has Y
(2) X has Y

---

(3) Hence, A does not approve of X

If this argument is valid, then there appears to be some logical relations between the premises and the conclusions of some ethical arguments. Or at least it is possible to contradict oneself in ethics. But are arguments of this kind valid?

First of all it must be noted that the relevance of this argument, even if it is valid, is rather slight. The only thing here noted is that it is possible to contradict oneself in ethics. The example is not to the effect that there are relations of entailment in ethics. Even if (3) follows from (1) and (2) it is not thereby shown that it follows from the statement that nothing which has Y is good and that X has Y that X is not good. Whether the latter argument is valid or not, depends on the effect of the emotive meaning of the premises and the conclusion. Stevenson himself has argued that since there is an imperative component in ethical statement, these cannot be entailed by any statements—this was at least my interpretation (T1:1) of him.

Secondly, it seems as though the validity of the argument presupposes a very special sense of "approve", in Stevenson's formulation of his metaethical theory. For could it not reasonably be held that (3) might be false although (2) and (1) are true? If A *did not know* that (2) were true, he might perfectly well approve of nothing which has Y *and* yet approve of X, it might be held. In order to avoid this consequence Stevenson must take a person who approves of some generic thing like a kind of action or a trait of character to approve of every *instance* of that generic thing. Unless he approves of every instance he does not approve of the generic thing, in Stevenson's sense of "approve", no matter what the man himself says. And it is not only *actual* instances, but also *possible* ones he must approve of. As far as I can see this interpretation will grant that all general positive ethical statements are false! This, I think, will also be the case if the ethical statement is taken to be a hypothesis about how a person would react to an instance if he were confronted with it. One single instance which runs counter to the hypothesis is enough to falsify it.

I think that the interpretation of "approve" which saves the validity of the argument from (1) and (2) to (3) is the one which results in the least plausible metaethical theory. But it is hard to think of precise and plausible alternatives. This I think is a genuine difficulty of subjectivism of Stevenson's kind. One way of avoiding the difficulty is to refuse to recognize general ethical assertions as meaningful at all. But this is not a very plausible view. For we do make such assertions and we seem to understand them perfectly well. Another way is to take approvals of general things to be approvals of typical examples of general things. Or you may chose a "platonic" solution where the generic "things" themself are thought to be the objects of your attitudes. But is this psychologically or ontologically sound? I have really no idea about how this problem is most reasonably solved. Perhaps it has no solution? This is perhaps a good reason why we should reject subjectivism. However that may be I feel certain that a reasonable solution must admit that you may disapprove of murder in general although there is some case of murder which you do not disapprove of, either because you are ignorant of the character of the act in question or because you are in this very case irrational.

In Stevenson's formulation of (T2) the words "a reason" appear, and the concept of reason is, of course, central to the understanding of the thesis. Now, which concept of a reason is Stevenson using? The nearest he comes to an explicit definition is the following:

Any statement about *any* matter of fact which *any* speaker considers likely to alter attitudes may be adduced as a reason for or against an ethical judgment. (p. 114)

The quoted passage raises at least three questions. Firstly, is Stevenson here intending to give a definition, with both necessary and sufficient conditions, or are the conditions only intended to be sufficient? And, *if* a definition, could it be considered a definition of 'a reason', or only of 'what could be adduced *as* a reason', i.e. are there "reasons", in Stevenson's sense, that cannot be adduced? Secondly, what does Stevenson mean by "matter of fact", and "likely to alter attitudes"? These phrases are rather vague. Thirdly, what is a *statement*? Let us deal with these questions one by one.

Several facts indicate that Stevenson is not intending the lines quoted to express a definition. His way of expression does indeed suggest that it should only be considered an expression of sufficient conditions. Even the reference to the "likelihood" of "altering attitudes" would turn out to be problematic if it were considered a necessary characteristic. Apparently there are reasons, even good ones, which nobody (we *know* that, I think) is prepared to commit themselves to, and, hence, which we do not consider likely to "alter any attitudes".

The reference to "matter of fact" is not only vague but it is also, I think, ambiguous. Is it intended to preclude ethical statements from being reasons, granted the truth of some version of non-cognitivism? Or is it only used to express the view that it is of no importance what a statement is about for it to be a reason? The following example of a reason indicates that the latter is the case:

A: The proposed tax bill is on the whole very bad.
B: I know little about it, but have been inclined to favor it on the ground that higher taxes are preferable to further borrowing. (p. 118)

But what is a *statement,* according to Stevenson? What *sort* of entity is a statement? What answer is natural and reasonable to give to this question depends on what use one is going to make of the concept of reason, obviously. Three candidates announce themselves. First arguments or reasons may be sentences, i.e. linguistic entities, secondly, they may be conceived of as propositions, i.e. what I have called "statements", and, thirdly, they may be conceived of as states of affairs. And, in the last case, states of affairs may either be of the kind: the aggressive US war against Vietnam, which is a reason for taking up actions against the US governement; or of the kind: acceptances of statements, in the way that my realizing the effects of the US agression may be a reason for me to take up some sort of action.

I leave the various possibilities open here, since Stevenson's formulations are not at all precise. The various possibilities will be discussed in the sequel as I proceed to examine Stevenson's argumentation.

Stevenson's Arguments in Favor in the View that the Relation
between the Premises and the Conclusions of Ethical
Arguments are Psychological Rather than Logical

Stevenson's thesis (T2) could, as we saw, be split into two theses, (T2:1) and (T2:2), the one to the effect that there are no logical relations between the premisses and the conclusions of ethical arguments, and the other to the effect that these relations are psychological. This way of "splitting" the thesis will, however, turn out to be problematic. In relation to one concept of reason the thesis will seem altogether inconceivable.

The problematic character of (T2), when both statements which it expresses are taken into account, will be apparent as one realizes that if (T2:2), which asserts a psychological relation, is correct, then (T2:1), which denies any logical relation, is quite *trivial,* and true. If reasons are entities which are psychologically, pragmatically, related to the ethical conclusion, then they cannot be *logical* entities. They must, then be pragmatical entities, like acceptances of statements. But now, of course, (T2:1) is completely trivial. For there cannot be logical relations between pragmatic entities. I cannot see, either, that (T2:2) would be very sensational in this interpretation. Of course there are *some* correspondences between which ethical convictions you hold and other convictions of yours.

The absurd character of the thesis (T2) when both statements expressed by it are taken into account will be obvious as soon as one tries to solve the problem raised above by giving to (T2:1) a more interesting content. If "a reason" is interpreted to refer to logical entities, the thesis (T2:1) will imply the "nihilistic" thesis (T1:1), discussed earlier. It is now asserted that no logical relations hold between what is concluded in an ethical argument and the premisses that "lead" to this conclusion. And this, of course, is a powerful and interesting consequence of emotivism. Now, however, (T2:2) will turn out to be altogether inconceivable. For this thesis will now assert that logical entities, "statements" in my vocabulary, have *causal* relations. But statements do not "exist" in time and space.

Here the only way out of the problem seems to be to abandon any interpretation of Stevenson that is too literal. And the most reasonable way of doing this, I think, is by interpreting him as using different concepts of reason in his two theses (T2:1) and (T2:2)—in spite of the fact that he only uses the word "reason" once in his statement of the dual thesis. While (T2:1) is about reasons in the logical sense, (T2:2) is about pragmatic entities.

Now, (T2:2), though not very sensational, can be conceived as a sort of an explanation of the sense of paradox we are faced with when confronted with (T2:1). When we grasp the idea that the statement that the grass is green is, from the logical point of view, as good a reason for the ethical statement that one ought not to harm people as is the statement that to harm people is evil, we are, very naturally, astonished. According to (T2:2), then, this astonishment is only due to our psychological constitution: it is *hard* for us to accept that it is evil to harm people but not that one ought not to harm them while it is *easy* to accept that the grass is green and that one may harm people. This psychological finding we mistake for a logical one.

Now, in what way does all this confer ethical relevance on the emotive theory of ethics? Well, the thesis (T2) interpreted as (T2:1) and (T2:2), with attention paid to my comments on the concept 'a reason', is *prima facie* of great significance for ethics, even if it is hard to tell in detail what are the relations between it and normative problems. So let us see how Stevenson tries to support his thesis about argumentation. If the emotive theory here plays a crucial role, it will to some extent share the ethical relevance of (T2), whatever that may be.

In his argument in support of (T2), in Chapter V of Ethics and Language, Stevenson both makes a reference back to his discussion in Chapter II of what I have called (T1) and in addition evokes some independent reasons for (T2). The former fact is perhaps a bit astonishing since (T2)—especially the part (T2:1)—seems to be stronger than (T1)—interpreted as (T1:1). While (T2:1) denies that there are any logical relations whatever between premisses and conclusions, save for the exceptions which I think I have found reasons to discount, (T1:1) seems only to deny that there are relations of entailment but not, for example, that the premisses and the conclusion may be inconsistent. Let us, however, not go into these difficulties. Perhaps Stevenson is willing to strengthen his view about imperatives so that they cannot, in his conception, contradict each other either.[6] What is most interesting, then, is to see whether Stevenson finds any good *independent* reasons in support of (T2:1).

The point of departure for Stevenson is, again, his metaethical analysis. But his analysis can, as we have seen earlier, be conceived in different ways. The common core of these various conceptions is the statement that ethical language has an emotive component. But here you may, I think, choose between at least three lines of making the analysis more precise, all of equal reasonableness. Firstly, you may interpret Stevenson as making the assertion that some typical "ethical terms", i.e. some specified class of word-*types,* have emotive meaning. As we recall, statements about "meaning", in Stevenson's sense, are state-

---

[6] This would be a very natural thing to do, for if it is taken for granted that imperatives may be inconsistent with one another it follows that they may entail each others as well—if entailment is defined in the manner described on p. 41 i.e. in terms of inconsistency.

78

ments about tendencies of words to produce, in specific circumstances, certain specific psychological responses among the hearers, and to be the result of specific psychological processes, in specific circumstances, in those who use them. This, of course, supports this first line of interpretation.

Secondly, you may interpret Stevenson as making the assertion that some typical "ethical terms", in some "typical contexts", i.e. typical of normative ethics, have a sort of emotive function. This function would perhaps be understood as the tendency of these words, in these types of circumstances, to produce emotive psychological processes in the hearer and to be, in these types of circumstances, the results of emotive psychological processes in those who use them. This line of interpretation gains credibility from the passage where Stevenson writes about the "function" and from the fact that Stevenson has to admit that emotive *meaning* is nothing peculiar to ethical or normative language. *Any* word has emotive effects in *some* context and, hence, emotive meaning.

Thirdly, you may interpret Stevenson as making the assertion that the *way* of using language, typical of ethical communication (a peculiar kind of speech-act), involves emotions. He could, for example, be interpreted as holding that no one is using language in the ethical way unless he has certain emotions, on the whole or in this very situation, and that no one has accepted or understood what is asserted when language is used in the ethical way unless he (the hearer) has certain emotions, on the whole or in this very situation. This interpretation gains credibility from the fact that it is hard to see why Stevenson should pay any attention to *which* words are used, when he does not ascribe the emotive properties to the words but to words in situations. Why not, then, take the natural further step and ascribe the properties to *ways* of using language (to kinds of speech-acts).

Stevenson may, then, be interpreted as holding a view, either of the properties possessed by some word-*types,* or of the properties possessed by *these words as used in certain contexts,* or of certain *ways* of using language, no matter which words are used. All these interpretations, or lines of interpretation, seem reasonable from a descriptive point of view.

A version of the two latter lines of interpretation will be a natural point of departure for an argument of Stevenson's which I have already discussed. If emotions are taken to be *semantic* (logical) entities, and if they are correlated, by the first pattern of analysis, to certain ways of using language, or to certain tokens of certain words, then the first pattern of analysis will turn out to be equal to the so called "working models", in the interpretation (WM1:1) of mine, save for the fact that *emotions* have been substituted for *imperatives*. Hence, the argument in defence of (T1) may be adapted to (T2:1) as well, granted only that emotions (and imperatives) lack, not only relations of logical consequence, but all logical relations whatever. But since I am now searching for *independent* reasons in support of (T2) this line of interpretation of emotivism will not be developed any further.

The aspect of ethical language and communication Stevenson seems to concentrate on in his argument in defence of (T2), and which he in many places in *Ethics and Language* explicitly declares to be his main interest, is the causal, or pragmatic one. But is it because ethical language is *effective* in a certain way that (T2:1), according to Stevenson, holds? Stevenson writes things like the following:

... beliefs here, I think, conceived as pragmatic entities alter attitudes in virtue of being intermediaries, as it were, between a given attitude and certain others. A belief reinforces an attitude, or diminishes its strength, by disclosing new objects of favor or disfavor, in such a way that several attitudes act concurrently, with a mutual modification of them all. (p. 115)

This seems very reasonable, but what is astonishing is that Stevenson does not supply observations like these with any further arguments for his thesis about the (lack of) logical properties of ethical *statements*. Both (T2:1) and (T2:3) seems all the same to be considered by Stevenson to be consequences of his psychological findings about ethical communication. And this seems to be due to an implicit view of logical properties and psychological properties as in some way being *alternatives*. This is true, of course, in the sense that it is not the same entities that possess the two kinds of properties—it is "reasons" in the pragmatic sense that have pragmatic properties, and it is "reasons" in the logical sense that have logical properties, yet this does not mean that ethical language cannot have both a pragmatic and a logical "dimension". But this seems to be what Stevenson implicitly holds. Stevenson writes, for example, the following:

Reasons ... become 'practical' or 'ethical' depending upon their psychological milieu; when they direct attitudes they are 'practical'. This relational characteristic does not change their nature nor does it free *them* from the ordinary canons of inductive logic. (p. 133)

where the stress on "*them*" indicates that, in contradistinction, the "step" from reasons to conclusion in this way *is* freed from "the ordinary canons of inductive logic".

But this conclusion is unwarranted. For even the most "scientific" one among statements probably has emotive effects, and it would be rash to conclude, only because of this, that it has no logical relations to other statements.

I now leave the thesis (T2) and proceed to the thesis (T3), which is the third, and the last, thesis about ethical argumentation which I will examine in relation to emotivism. After having discussed this thesis I hope to be in a better position rationally to assess the relevance to ethics of the emotive theory of ethics. The relation between emotivism and ethics has hitherto been only dimly seen.

Stevenson's Argument in Favor of the View that No Ethical Arguments are Valid

In Chapter VII of *Ethics and Language* Stevenson argues in support of a thesis, which I have called "(T3)", to the effect that no ethical arguments are valid. His arguments in Chapter VII are independent[7] of his arguments in support of the theses that I have called "(T1)" and "(T2)".

The thesis (T3) is rather precisely stated here I think, if only one disregards the fact that the world "valid" is ambiguous and allows for different interpretations. The most natural interpretation of that word, in this context, would be to take it to express the concept of logical validity. So let us start with the following interpretation, which makes (T3) equal to (T1:1):

(T3:1)   No ethical arguments are logically valid.

The reasonableness of the interpretation (T3:1) is, however, far from certain, from the descriptive point of view; so at the end of the next section I shall propose alternative interpretations.

What makes (T3:1) interesting is *both* that this thesis is shared by many adherents of emotivism, who take it to be a consequence of their metaethic, *and* that it is a thesis which is, *prima facie,* of consequence for normative ethics. And even if it is far from clear whether Stevenson really explicitly gives his assent to it, it is clear that Stevenson hints at some arguments, in Chapter VII of *Ethics and Language,* which, if true, *do* establish it. If one wishes, it is also possible to construct a sort of a defense of the view that Stevenson really assents to (T3:1). I shall suggest briefly how this defence would run.

---

[7] Though independent I have hinted at these arguments when discussing Stevenson's view that the thesis (T2:1) has certain "exceptions". The arguments evoked in defence of the assertion about exceptions turned out to be arguments, rather, in support of the thesis itself.

The first formulation in Chapter VII with relevance for the present thesis is the following:

... validity has nothing to do with persuasive methods. It is cognitively non-sensical to speak either of 'valid' or of 'invalid' persuasion. (p. 152)

If interpreted weakly this indicates at least that Stevenson holds that persuasive methods are never valid. We need not worry in this weak interpretation of what he means by "cognitively nonsensical" above this. The import of this assertion will not be clear, however, until we have more clearly grasped the sense of the terms "method" and "persuasion". It is also necessary to know something about Stevenson's view of rational methods in ethics and of validity.

Stevenson makes a distinction between rational and nonrational methods, in Chapter VI of *Ethics and Language*. The crucial question in this distinction is whether or not attitudes are changed by a change of beliefs. A method which establishes a conviction by changing beliefs is rational while a method which does the same by some *other* way is non-rational. The persuasive methods are included among the non-rational ones. The common core of these persuasive methods is their dependence on "the sheer, direct emotional impact of words—emotive meaning, rhetorical cadence, apt metaphor, stentorian, stimulating, or pleading tones of voice, dramatic gestures, care in establishing *rapport* with the hearer or audience, and so on". Thus, the specific characteristic of persuasive methods (as a *species* of non-rational methods), seems to be the use of *language*.

Now it is important to notice that the word "method" is equivocal. Either it refers to an argument in a logical sense viz. a set of premises and a conclusion or to some sort of activity. And here a first interpretation of Stevenson's assertion that "validity has nothing to do with persuasive methods" can be attempted. This assertion must be taken to be about methods of a logical sort unless it be quite trivial. For, of course, no *activities* whatever are valid. But how does Stevenson conceive, in more detail, of persuasive methods?

It is important to notice that Stevenson makes the following stipulation about the term "belief": "... the term 'belief' must not, at least for the moment, include reference to ethical convictions ..." (cf. p. 2). Now, if rational methods are to proceed *via* changes in beliefs, i.e. in a "logical" formulation, if rational methods are those arguments where all the premises are purely *factual,* or at least not *ethical,* then Stevenson's assertion that validity has nothing to do with persuasive methods seems to be an assertion to the effect that no arguments containing ethical premisses can be valid. This, I think, is a reasonable (from the descriptive point of view) interpretation of Stevenson. But how does one get the thesis (T3:1) from this?

As we just saw, rational methods correspond to arguments containing *no* ethical premisses. But this kind of argument in support of ethical conclusions cannot, according to Stevenson, be valid either. Just like persuasive arguments they are never valid since such an argument "... does not exemplify any inductive or deductive procedure ..." (p. 153). Now, these two views taken together, the view that ethical arguments containing at least one ethical premiss, and hence persuasion, are never valid, and the view that ethical arguments containing no ethical premisses are never valid either, yield the view that no arguments with an ethical conclusion may be valid. And this is the thesis (T3:1). Then, how does Stevenson go about proving (T3:1), besides adapting to it the arguments evoked in support of (T1:1) and (T2:1)?

Some Premisses with Relevance to the Thesis that No Valid Arguments are Possible in Ethics

Although I am far from certain whether Stevenson assents to the thesis (T3:1) or not, I think it clear that he assents to some premisses which together entail this thesis. So let us consider these premisses.

What Stevenson *is* arguing, no doubt, is that in ethical arguments the (factual) reasons are not there to ensure the truth of the ethical conclusion (cf. Chapter VII of *Ethics and Language*). This premiss, together with two other premisses, is the rationale of (T3:1). One of the other premisses is about the concept of truth and the other one is about the concept of validity. Stevenson explicitly states his premiss about 'validity' and he presupposes a premiss about 'truth'.

The premiss about the concept of validity is stated thus:

No matter how else we may define 'valid', we shall very likely want to retain a sense which is intimately related to 'true'. The precise way in which the terms are to be related, and the precise meaning of them both, may occasion no little perplexity; but we shall in any case want to say that a 'valid' method is more conducive to establishing truths, or probable truths, than any 'invalid' one. (p. 154)

Clearly, Stevenson uses a concept of validity which applies to arguments (methods). This concept seems to be defined in terms of 'truth'. But what exactly the relation between these two concepts is he does not say. And what does Stevenson mean by "is more conducive to establishing truths?" Do you get true conclusions from them, more "often" than you get when you use an invalid method? But does not this depend also on whether the premises are true or not?

Perhaps Stevenson's view is consistent with the possibility that you get only true conclusions from an invalid method and false premises: but it is hard to tell since the phrase "conducive ... to" is so vague. A way of sharpening Stevenson's concept of validity, however, would be exemplified by the following definition:

Def. (valid inference): 'p, so q' is a valid inference=df.

it is necessarily the case that if 'p' is true, then 'q' is true

I think this is *one* fairly reasonable interpretation of Stevenson's views and it is certainly a reasonable account of the view of quite a few emotivist.[8] It is, however, rather vague as long as we have not yet decided what to express by "truth". So let us see what can be said about Stevenson's second premiss.

Apparently, Stevenson's second premiss consists of a statement to the effect that truth is a question of correspondence with facts, i.e. Stevenson is using a kind of "Aristotelian" concept of truth. 'I approve of this' is true, if, and only if, I really approve of this. But Stevenson is never particularly precise about his choice of concept.

What, then, do Stevenson's two premisses, about validity and truth, show?

Here I wish to recall that there is at least one reasonable interpretation of Stevenson which makes his metaethic a scheme for interpretations of ethical sentences in contexts that are typical of normative ethics. This interpretation of mine is not quite consistent with what Stevenson says about the concept of meaning, which should be so defined, he holds, that meanings are psychological entities, but on the other hand it is the only one consistent with his assertion that (descriptive) meanings could be true or false. Furthermore, the sentence "This is good", is interpreted by Stevenson, in his working models, and his first pattern of analysis, to express the statement 'I approve of this' in the contexts considered. (It is *also* interpreted to express the statement 'Do so as well!', but this "statement" will, Stevenson seems to hold, be totally irrelevant from the point of view of truth granted you are dealing with an Aristotelian concept).[9]

---

[8] Cf. I. Hedenius, who in *Om Rätt och Moral* (p. 120) draws heavily on this kind of conception of valid inference when arguing in defence of a "nihilistic" thesis similar to (T3:1).
[9] Here it is somewhat hard to follow Stevenson. Why cannot the emotive part of the ethical statements, roughly represented by 'Do so as well!', be true or false in an "Ari-

84

If now we examine a typical ethical argument we will find that the thesis (T3:1) is indeed implied by Stevenson's two premises. Consider for example an argument expressed in the following way:

(4) All kinds of socialism are good
(5) Communism is a kind of socialism

(6) Communism is good

When interpreting these sentences, disregarding emotive meaning, Stevenson would come up with the following argument:

(7) I approve of all kinds of socialism
(8) Communism is a kind of socialism

(9) I approve of communism

Now it is obvious that Stevenson's two premises do entail his thesis (T3:1). For, whatever Stevenson himself would say to this, I think it obvious that (9) does not follow from (7) and (8). As a matter of fact I think there are people, some anarchists for example, who can truthfully utter (4) which seems to be a sentence, thereby expressing (7), which seems to be a statement, and yet refuse to utter (6) since (9) is not true of them *in spite* of the fact that (8), I think, is true, something which they seem to be unable to realize. Therefore, the truth of (7) and (8) does not guarantee the truth of the conclusion (9). The argument is not *valid,* in Stevenson's terms. And if, in this manner, not even the descriptive parts of the argument are valid, how could then the argument itself be valid?

Enough now of the interpretation (T3:1) of Stevenson's views in Chapter VII of *Ethics and Language.* Before I proceed to discuss Stevenson's arguments in support of his "nihilistic" thesis, I shall indicate some alternative interpretations of (T3).

One thesis which I think it clear that Stevenson assents to in Chapter VII, is the following one:

---

stotelian" sense? Granted for example the concept of truth that Tarski has explicated, in "The Semantic Concept of Truth", this kind of statement may very well be true or false. In his conception it would seem natural to take an imperative to be true or valid when, and only when, what is commanded really ought to be done. Granted, on the other hand, some stronger conception of truth, with stronger ontological commitments, imperatives would probably come to lack truth-values. As a matter of fact it seems as though Stevenson would be ambivalent on this very point. For in *Ethics and Language* he mentions a concept without ontological commitments, of Tarski's sort, and dismisses it. This very concept he adopts in *Facts and Values.* This means that *this* argument in support of (T3) is not derivable from the emotive theory of *Facts and Values.*

(T3:2)   When people argue in defence of ethical conclusions the
           problem of the truth of these is never under debate

This thesis is supported by a premiss to the effect that people, when
arguing in support of ethical conclusions, are only trying to support the
"emotive" component of the conclusion, not the "descriptive" one, as
long as we stick to the first pattern of analysis or the working models.
This premiss (which I think is a good reason against the reasonableness
of the autobiographical component of Stevenson's emotive analysis!),
together with the premiss stating the "Aristotelian" nature of truth (*with*
ontic commitments), gives to Stevenson his thesis (T3:2).

A third way of interpreting Stevenson in Chapter VI is to take him
to hold the following view:

(T3:3)   No factual reasons are conclusive for an ethical statement

The problem is set forth in the following passage:

... if "R" and "E" stand respectively for a set of reasons and an ethical conclusion, related neither deductively nor inductively, then is it of interest to ask
whether an inference from R to E is valid?
    Clearly, the inference will be neither demonstratively nor inductively valid, by
hypothesis ...
    The only interesting issue is of another sort ... is there not some other kind
of validity, peculiar to normative arguments, that deserves equal emphasis?

Stevenson's answer to the question he himself has formulated is, that
"unless "valid" is to have a misleadingly extended sense, the question,
"Does R permit a valid inference to E?" is devoid of interest" (p. 155)

Stevenson's own argument in support of (T3:3) is the thesis (T3:2)
and his conception of validity in terms of truth. But I think that this
argument is not sufficient to prove its point. For even if the truth of
the descriptive part of ethical statements is never under debate in ethical
arguments, why not say that 'R, hence E' is an ethically valid argument
or that R is a conclusive reason for E provided that there is some valid
ethical principle, consistent with R, which together with R implies E but
does not do this itself?[1] This you may reasonably, I think, call a case of
"ethical validity". In order to dismiss this view as implausible Stevenson
would have either to resort to his theses (T1:1), (T2:1) or (T3:1) i.e.
to some view of ethical arguments as defective from a logical point of
view, or to his theses (T1:2) or (T2:1) i.e. to some view to the effect
that ethical principles are always "subjective" or "uncertain", in some
way.

---

[1] This definition of 'conclusive factual reason for an ethical statement' or 'ethically valid
reason' is clearly analogous to my definition of moral relevance to ethics, cf. pp. 172–173.

A fourth way of interpreting Stevenson in Chapter VII would be to take him as there expressing only the "Hume-Poincaré"-principle, viz. the following thesis:

(T3:4)   No valid argument with an ethical conclusion has only factual premisses.

The descriptive reasonableness of this interpretation could be defended with the same reasons as those I invoked in defense of the interpretation (T1:5) of (T1). (T1:5) and (T3:4) are obviously identical.

I have now concluded my examination of Stevenson's various views of the connection between emotivism and the possibility of rational justification in ethics. I have explicated his arguments for the "sceptical" views of justification he seems to hold. I must now turn to the task of giving a rational assessment of his views from the point of view I have chosen. Do the connections Stevenson asserts to hold, really hold? And, in that case: in which way do these connections confer upon meatethics any relevance to ethics?

4. Do the Alleged Consequences of Emotivism
for the Possibilities of Rational Justification in Ethics
Prove Emotivism Relevant to Ethics?

A rational assessment of the relevance to ethics of emotivism, based on a consideration of Stevenson's views of ethical argumentation, must proceed in two stages. What I am searching for is, namely, a sort of indirect relevance. Emotivism is alleged to be relevant to problems of argumentation and solutions to these are assumed to be of some ethical significance in their turn. Hence, my two questions to be dealt with must be, firstly, whether Stevenson really establishes his views of ethical argumentation, his statement of the emotive theory being at least one premiss and, secondly, whether Stevenson's views of argumentation really are of any ethical significance themselves.

Some Critical Remarks on the Way Stevenson Tries to
Establish His Views of Ethical Argumentation

Departing from my formulations (T1), (T2), and (T3), of three of Stevenson's views of the solution to the problem of justification in ethics, I made various interpretations, more or less reasonable from a descriptive point of view, viz. (T1:1), (T1:2), (T1:3), (T1:4), (T1:5), (T2:1), (T2:2), (T3:1), (T3:2), (T3:3) and (T3:4). Some of these were theses to the effect that some sort of uncertainty, relative to factual premisses or absolutely, was attached to ethical premisses of ethical arguments, viz. (T1:2), (T1:3), (T1:4) and (T3:3), while others were theses to the effect that the *relation* between premisses and conclusions of ethical argumentations was in some way deficient from a "logical" point of view, viz. (T1:1), (T2:1), and (T3:1). Two interpretations, (T1:5) and (T3:4) were simply rough formulations of the "Hume-Poincaré"-principle. The remaining two interpretations, (T2:2) and (T3:2), were statements of empirical findings about ethical argumentation, the one to the effect that the acceptance of arguments are sometimes "effective" and the other to the effect that people, when arguing about ethical matters, are not questioning the truth of the ethical conclusion.

Out of these interpretations the theses (T1:1), (T2:1), and (T3:1) are of special interest for my purposes. As we saw, (T2:1) seemed to imply (T1:1). And (T3:1) could be considered only a slightly different formulation of the same statement that (T1:1) expresses. So it seems as though one could find a common core here, viz. the statement that no logically valid argument can have an ethical conclusion. Let us call this thesis, which will be of the outmost importance in the next section, the "nihilistic" thesis.[2] Now, has Stevenson really shown the truth of the nihilistic thesis? I can see various grounds for doubt on this point.

One way of arguing in support of the nihilistic thesis proceeded, as we may recall, via the premiss that imperatives can never be the conclusions of valid arguments; but, firstly, this premiss is itself far from obvious, indeed quite the contrary, and, secondly, it is hard rationally to assess it since the concept 'imperative' is not clearly defined by Stevenson. Thus we do not know whether anything is gained by pointing out that since imperatives lack logical properties then norms must also do so, for perhaps imperatives *are* norms. Thirdly, the thesis presupposes, to be vindicated through reference to emotivism, that emotivism is given an interpretation which makes it a theory about *logical* properties of ethical *statements*, and this is but one out of many reasonable interpretations of Stevenson, perhaps not even the most reasonable one.

Another way of arguing in defence of the nihilistic thesis would be to proceed *via* statements about the nature of truth and validity, together with a statement of emotivism. But this line of argument seems even weaker than the former. For here, as J. O. Urmson has pointed out in

---

[2] The nihilistic thesis was held by the members of the so-called "Uppsala School". The members of this school were also called "value nihilists", hence my adoption of the term. A comprehensive defense of the views of the Uppsala school is found in *Om Rätt och Moral* by I. Hedenius.

The Emotive Theory of Ethics, a counter-intuitive conclusion is derived from premisses that themselves, depend, ultimately, on—very weak—intuitions.

This seems to be the rationale of Urmson's criticism, although I am not sure that I have been able to follow him on all points. First of all, as Urmson points out, it is, from an intuitive point of view, clear that ethical arguments *can* be valid or invalid, while it is far from clear that there is a connection between 'validity' and 'truth'. Secondly, it is not difficult to think of concepts of truth which allow for the truth or falsity of (the emotive component of) ethical statements as well as of factual ones,[3] and these concepts are, at least, no less intuitive than the thesis Stevenson is trying to defend. Stevenson's argument on this point, implicit in Chapter VII of *Ethics and Language,* presupposes, again, a "logical" interpretation of the emotive theory.

A third way of defending the nihilistic thesis was implicit in what Stevenson said about "exceptions" to (T2:1) contrary to what he himself believed. For, as we saw, the descriptive part of the premisses and of the conclusions of ethical arguments became logically independent by the first pattern of analysis, and by the working models. This, however, is not a good argument in defence of the nihilistic thesis. Rather, I think, it should be considered an argument against Stevenson's analysis concerning the "autobiographical" statements he asserts are expressed by ethical sentences. Moreover, this "deficiency" of ethical arguments could easily be repaired by always adding to one's arguments a premiss stating something which makes the descriptive part of one's statement more reasonable.

A fourth way of defending the nihilist thesis seems to be based on the idea that *either* ethical language has, roughly, an "emotive" function viz. some sort of psychological effect, *or* it functions in a "logical" way, by expressing what I have called "statements". This argument, presupposed by Stevenson mainly in relation to (T2:1) is not very con-

---

[3] Actually, Tarski's concept of truth will do here, as I noticed before (cf. note 2 on p. 84), adapted to statements instead of sentences. Tarski writes about his concept in "The Semantic Concept of Truth": "In fact, the semantic definition of truth implies nothing regarding the conditions under which a sentence like (1):
(1) Snow is white
can be asserted. It implies only that, whenever we assert or reject this sentence, we must be ready to assert or reject the correlated sentence
(2) The sentence 'Snow is white' is true
Thus we may accept the semantic conception of truth without giving up any epistemological attitudes we may have had; we may remain naive realists, critical realists or idealists, empiricists or metaphysicians—whatever we were before. The semantic conception is completely neutral toward all these issues".

vincing either. The premiss on which it is based has been ably criticized, for example, by H. Ofstad in *Objectivity of Norms*. Again a "logical" interpretation of emotivism is presupposed.

Some theses are not at all *argued* for by Stevenson, but only indicated by his formulations. Among these are the various theses, such as (T1:2)—(T1:4), about the uncertainty of ethical premisses of ethical arguments. (Also the thesis (T3:3) seems to be based on a view of ethical principles as "subjective", in some way.) But perhaps they are more or less obvious when you consider emotivism according to a logical interpretation. One thesis is rather trivial, viz. (T2:2), to the effect that acceptances of ethical reasons sometimes are *effective*. If it is not made more specific hardly anyone can doubt that it is true. Another thesis too is rather unproblematic, viz. (T3:3) to the effect that one is not arguing for or against the truth of ethical conclusions, granted the empirical fact that one is never arguing about the "descriptive" part of ethical statements, granted the truth of the emotive theory in a logical version and granted the reasonableness of Stevenson's statements about the nature of truth to the effect that truth is a matter of correspondence with (natural) facts.

There is not much to be added about those interpretations which are statements of the "Hume-Poincaré"-principle. Perhaps this principle is enhanced by Stevenson's metaethical theory, but it is hard to say something more definite since the thesis is so vaguely expressed by Stevenson.

I leave the question of the reasonableness of Stevenson's views about justification in ethics with these, mostly critical, remarks. I leave it because I am willing, for the sake of argument, to concede to the statement that, at least, emotivism makes *some* of Stevenson's views of justification *somewhat* more reasonable. If this is so, will emotivism turn out to be relevant to ethics? Clearly, this depends on the ethical significance of Stevenson's views on justification, themselves.

Are Stevenson's Conclusions about the Problem of Justification in Ethics of any Ethical Significance?

I left the problem of the reasonableness of the various theses put forward by Stevenson about justification in ethics with some hesitation. But for the sake of argument I assumed that some of these theses, at least, could be proved with a statement of emotivism as one essential premiss. Would this confer ethical relevance on emotivism? Are Stevenson's derived theses about argumentation, of any ethical significance?

The question whether for example the nihilistic thesis is relevant to ethics seems to make necessary the following distinction. There are, roughly, on the one hand, kinds of problems which I will call "ethical" problems, problems where one is seeking answers to questions about what to do, what one ought to do, what is right to do, what is good, fair etc., and, on the other hand, there are problems of a kind which I will call "descriptively ethical" ones, problems where one seeks answers to questions about what people accept as good reasons for or against statements communicated by sentences like "X is right", "X is a duty", "X is morally good", etc. in certain typical contexts, and, more generally, problems where one seeks answers to questions about the nature of the language people use (in ethical contexts) or the nature of the ways of using language that are typical of normative contexts. This distinction is only a preliminary one but I think it will do as a point of departure; moreover distinctions similar or equal to it are often drawn by people writing introductions to moral philosophy, cf., for example, *Ethics* by W. Frankena.

A reasonable, preliminary, way of conceiving of the question whether metaethics is relevant to ethics is, I think, to hold that this question has not been answered affirmatively in a rational way until one has been able to point out how some metaethical theory gives us knowledge relevant to the solution of an *ethical* problem. If light is shed, by all metaethical theories, only on the latter kind of problems, the descriptively ethical ones, they are *not* relevant to ethics; though of course, this does not prevent them from being interesting for some other purpose. Even if some descriptively ethical problem were to be *solved* with reference to a metaethical theory this would not make the theory relevant to *ethics*.

But Stevenson's views of ethical language, his emotive theory of ethics, is at most relevant to problems within descriptive ethics. Not even the strong "nihilistic" thesis will be of much interest to those worried by ethical problems. I shall try to explain this in some detail.

A problem that becomes acute when one considers Stevenson's nihilistic thesis, or his other theses about ethical argumentation, is that one does not know exactly what these theses are *about*. But *if* these theses are to follow from his emotivist analysis of ethical language, they must have the same field of application as the metaethical analysis itself. So all restrictions imposed on the field to which the emotive analysis apply are also restrictions on the field to which the theory of argumentation applies. The nihilist thesis is about ethical statements. But the word "ethical statement", here, must refer to statements that we get some knowledge about from the emotivist analysis, the working models or the first or the second pattern of analysis. What are these statements?

The uncertainty about how the emotive theory is to be correctly interpreted appears in different respects. One interpretation takes the theory to assert something about certain word-tokens, another about word-types, and a third about certain ways of using language. These are the variations in one respect. But, furthermore, there are two principally different ways of interpreting Stevenson as regards what he asserts *about* those words, tokens of words, or ways of using language. Either he is taken to hold a causal view about what he has identified as the object of his analysis, as he clearly himself says that he does, or he is taken to hold a view of a logical sort about it, which is the only interpretation consistent with his idea that meanings are true or false. This is another type of variation we have to consider when searching for the most interesting and reasonable account of Stevenson's views.

For methodological reasons I will have to choose an interpretation of Stevenson which makes him hold a logical theory of ethical communication *as well* as a causal theory. Otherwise it would seem altogether mysterious how Stevenson can attempt to derive conclusions about argumentation from his analysis. On the former point, regarding the object of the analysis, I will presently have more to say. Before that a *third* kind of variation in the interpretation of Stevenson must be noted, a kind which I have not yet discussed.

The third kind of variation in the interpretation of Stevenson is due to his vagueness about the *causal* claims he makes with his theory. The relevant part of the theory here is the one to the effect that, roughly, attitudes and feelings, *emotions* of the logical sort, are involved in ethical argumentation, and in communication. But this "pairing" of linguistic elements with statements could be conceived as making stronger or weaker causal claims. A "minimal" interpretation takes the theory to be a statement of a (positive) statistical correlation with some significance. In a large percentage of the contexts observed, emotions are communicated. A strong interpretation takes the theory to be a statement of some "law-like" connection. The theory is about counterfactual, hypothetical situations as well as actual ones.

Now, let us consider for example a case where a person is trying to solve an ethical problem to see how what has been said about the field of application of Stevenson's emotivism makes his views of justification of no help to this person. I think Stevenson would have somewhat the following to say to a person who tells him that he, is trying to decide whether to join the Communist Party or not, which is clearly a moral (ethical) problem.

– You, my friend, are worried by a moral problem. Either you ought to join the Party or you ought not. Of course there are lots of problems here, that must be solved before you can reach a conclusion. You must seek empirical information of various kinds as well as a reasoned normative system. I cannot help you in any direct way on these points *qua* moral philosopher, at least not as a metaethicist. But I can do something else. For I have found out that when you and other people are trying to solve your problems you are proceeding with *wasteful habits of investigation.* You are, as a matter of fact, trying to do what cannot be done! If you try to formulate your problem in the form of the question 'Ought I to join the Communist Party?' you will find that the answer to this question—that you ought to, that you ought not to, or that you may do as you please—is an ethical statement which cannot be supported with a logically binding argument (or with an argument based on absolutely certain premisses, and so forth). So you had better, at least, not try to find *such* reasons any more. At most you can try various arguments to see what *effects* they have on your choice. *Which* reasons you are allowed to try is a moral problem, and here I can, again, do nothing to advice you. But at least it is clear that whatever reasons you try they are not logically binding on your conclusion.

This argument is only indicated. There are gaps to be filled in, and points to be made more precise. But what is worse, the argument is, I think, based on false premisses. As far as I can see, there are various ways out of the "dilemma" set by Stevenson for "objectivism".

First of all, his theory could be taken to be a pragmatic theory of the causal aspects of ethical communication. Then his theory will be of no relevance whatever for questions of rational justification. This problem, however, I have decided to avoid by interpreting Stevenson as holding a logical theory.

Secondly, his theory i.e. the emotive theory and also the "derived" theory of argumentation, could, in one interpretation, be taken to be only statistical. But then, how can I ever be sure that Stevenson's findings apply to *my* statements? This argument, Stevenson will have to meet by strengthening his theory so that it will make assertions with claims to lawlike validity.

Thirdly, however, even as a statement of a finding of an empirical law, emotivism seems to lack ethical relevance in the respect here discussed. Stevenson's theories may either be taken to be theories about certain *words* (types or tokens), or about certain *ways of using language.* In the former case Stevenson's alleged effects are simply avoided by a *linguistic reform,* if we like to make such a reform. We choose to talk another language, to use other words, and so forth. If there is a peculiar property possessed by "good" which makes statements expressed by sentences containing "good" devoid of normal logical relations, then, let us not use this term any more! At least Stevenson has said nothing to support the assertion that one shouldn't do this, or that this would be impossible. But what about the latter case? Suppose Stevenson would reply to this that his theory is not about words, but about ways of using language, or about some kind of "speech-acts".

Now, it is not so easy consistently to hold that we do not know whether Stevenson's emotivist theses, in this interpretation, apply to *our* ethical statements. In relation to the linguistic interpretation of emotivism it could be said that the theory of argumentation is a theory about logical properties of *statements* while the emotivist theses are about *language;* and we have said nothing about how we would prefer to express the ethical statement in question. This argument applies, somewhat modified, to *some* versions of Stevenson's emotive theory, when interpreted as a theory about certain *ways* of using language. How does Stevenson know that his findings are not dependent on properties possessed by ways of using language in ethical contexts that are not "essential", in the sense that one can use language in *another* way and yet express the *same* statements? But this objection does not work for *all* versions of emotivism taken as a theory about ways of using language. Stevenson could reply that to him two ways of using language are relevantly "the same", if, and only if, the same statement is expressed by them.

If interpreted in this way it seems clear that the emotive theory *does* apply to my statement that I ought, ought not, may or may not, join the Communist Party. If Stevenson could show that this statement of mine cannot be supported by logically binding reasons, has he not then, given me a reason for not looking, in vain, for such a ground for my judgment? I think there is, all the same, a place for doubts on this point. For wouldn't another way of responding to this observation of Stevenson's be to reply that earlier I was not quite clear about the nature of my statements which I expressed when using language in the way typical of ethical contexts. Now that I see that they are of a "nihilist" sort I therefore prefer to *reform* my conceptual framework. This, I may hold, I do for good reasons, for "Nihilistic" statements are not solutions to *my* problems nor even are they ever solutions to *moral* problems. Thus Stevenson may have told me what sort of statements a person so-and-so, or even any person in the world, has made when stating his moral views, but this descriptively ethical piece of knowledge is of no immediate help to trying to find out, not how people *usually* deliberate about moral problems but *how to act,* what *is* right, wrong, and so forth.

The conclusion here must be that one crucial premiss in Stevenson's argument is missing. He has not, as he should have, shown that a linguistic or conceptual reform is not *possible.* He should have produced some reasons to the effect that no statement that is not nihilistic *can* be a solution to my problem, or to moral problems in general. This, however, cannot be done with reference only to descriptive findings about language, speech, or conceptual habits. Perhaps there is a non-nihilistic counterpart to any ethical statement ever used in ethical communication, counterparts that apply to exactly the same acts or characters, and so forth, as do the original statements!

I leave Stevenson's discussion on this point, with these comments. It should be noticed, however, that what has here been discussed is a rather "strong" sort of indirect relation between metaethics and ethics. The question what can be learnt from observations about language, speech, and conceptual habits, must be taken up again. This will be done in Chapter VI.

A Brief Summary of the Section

To sum up this section I conclude that the apparent relevance of Stevenson's views of ethical argumentation has turned out to be merely apparent. The conclusion that they are relevant is based on a failure to make clear the distinction between ethical problems and descriptively ethical ones. Only knowledge about the latter kind of problems can be gained from the emotive theory of ethics Stevenson puts forward. This puts Stevenson in a "dilemma". Either he has to give up the idea that his theory of argumentation may be derived from his metaethical analysis or he has to face the conclusion that his theory of argumentation falls within descriptive ethics.

Besides this I found, at the beginning of this section, grounds for doubting that the theory of ethical argumentation follows from the meta-ethical analysis.

On one point I had to make a reservation, however, as regards my negative conclusion. For even if they are not "immediatly" relevant, in any strong sense, to ethics, yet findings of an empirical sort about speech, linguistic, and conceptual habits, are perhaps of *some* interest to ethics. This problem, I will return to.

5. F. A. Olafson in Defense of the View that Emotivism has a Sort of Pragmatic Relevance to Ethics

Background

When I indicated, in Chapter I, various concepts of ethical relevance I distinguished between logical, pragmatical, and therapeutic concepts. I have a feeling that particularly the latter two kinds of concept are fruitful in relation to my problem, while the former kind of concept in most cases seems to be altogether too strong. The relations involved here, however, are rarely discussed. What I have called "therapeutic" relations are often presupposed to hold but I know of no thorough discussion about them. I will not discuss this kind of relation until Chapter VI. As for the "pragmatic" relations between metaethics and normative ethics I know of only one more thorough discussion, viz. the one pursued by F. A. Olafson in "Meta-ethics and the Moral Life", where the pragmatic effects of the acceptance of emotivism are discussed.

Since Olafson has achieved quite a reputation in the debate about metaethics and ethics (his conclusions are often taken for granted) I think it worth while to dwell on Olafson's thesis and arguments for a while. At the same time it should be noticed that Olafson's conclusion is put forward in an extremely vague manner, that his conception of emotivism seems to be mischievously confused, being based on an incorrect interpretation of Stevenson—and that his arguments in favour of his thesis are only scantily indicated. Moreover, I am not sure that his concept of pragmatic relevance is the most fruitful one, at least not for my purpose.

Olafson's Thesis Formulated

The point of departure for Olafson is an observed "discrepancy" between what common sense believes and what the emotive theory asserts about ethical statements. According to our common sense beliefs "an admission that a conflicting moral judgment is true would amount to a subversion of one's moral position", while, according to emotivism "it is at least not clear that the standard or typical use of such statements as 'X is good' requires that they be logically incompatible with the truth of the statement 'X is bad'" (To be interesting this last quoted passage must be understood in such a way that the statements will have reference to, at least, the same *time* and *situation* and *respect*. I think, however, that this is what Olafson means.)

Now Olafson claims roughly, that when people accept emotivism their way of "taking morality" is changed. This is a matter of fact and partly it is due to the fact that their earlier, common sense beliefs, are changed.

Instead of this talk about changes the interesting relation could here be explained, more simply, as a relation between the acceptance of emotivism and a certain *way of* accepting ethical statements. The former "necessitates" (causally, I believe) the latter. This is clearly a kind of relation which I have earlier called "pragmatic". Let us study it in more detail. How does Olafson, for example, conceive the change in question, i.e. how does a person proceed when accepting ethical statements after having accepted emotivism? The question is not easy to answer.

Although Olafson uses many words to explain the nature of the "change" it remains, to me at least, obscure. Olafson writes, among other things, the following about it:

There is still no reason to suppose that any specific modification in the content of our moral views will be entailed by a shift from one meta-ethic to another ... But this is not the only possible form of first-level moral change. The acceptance of such a theory may affect the way we hold our moral views. Although a meta-ethical characterization of moral judgments does not answer the substantive question, 'What shall I do?' it may still have an effect upon the *person* who asks and answers this question. The answer, whatever it may be, will now stand in a different relation to the person who gives it, and the relation will be different because one of its terms—the moral judgment—has been drastically reinterpreted as a result of a metaethical argument. If a logician were to show that all declarative sentences are really questions, we might go on making the same statements, but it would be implausible to suggest that nothing had been changed, since we would now be making then *as* questions, even if we retained the declarative form. And just as asking questions is very different from making statements, so issuing a command is very different from uttering a quasi-descriptive proposition, even though the 'content' may be the same. The logical characterization of what is said determines the nature of the act of utterance; and the latter, in turn, sets its stamp upon the whole moral life. (p. 172)

This characterization raises two questions which may, perhaps, at first seem trifling but which are, we shall see, of the very greatest consequence.

First af all, what does Olafson mean by two acts of utterance being *different*—a question in one case and a quasi-description in the other— while the content is *the same*? Is he here referring to cases of inadequate intentions exemplified by an Englishman who may say, in Italy, "acqua calda", intending to refer to cold water, though actually referring to hot water? Or does he mean that the logical content of two statements may be the same although one statement is a question and the other a description?

Secondly, if the passage about the effects on the person involved in a "moral practice" is essential, which it seems to be, what do these effects more precisely consist in?

Since I can see no way of definitly answering these questions I shall simply, for the sake of argument, *assume* that the "change" in question is ethically significant in some way, perhaps "setting its stamp on one's moral life". Then the important thing will be to examine Olafson's arguments in favour of the view that emotivism brings about such a change, if accepted. Perhaps this examination will shed some light on Olafson's thesis too. As I proceed I will try to clarify the nature of the "change" here talked about.

Olafson's Conception of Emotivism

Olafson seems to hold that the acceptance of emotivism has certain "effects" of importance. The acceptance of emotivism "necessitates" a certain *way* of accepting ethical statements. So how does Olafson conceive of emotivism?

There are two ways of explicating Olafson's concept of emotivism. Either you stress what he explicitly says about the concept, or you stress the concept which seems to be implicit in his argumentation. These two methods will lead, I think, to mutually inconsistent results. Here I shall try the first one, leaving the second one until I examine Olafson's argumentation.

Strangely enough Olafson takes as his point of departure the discussion in "The Philosophy of G. E. Moore" by Stevenson about the *naturalistic* analysis which "translates" for example "This is good" into "I approve of this". Olafson claims that this analysis has been accepted by Stevenson! But that assertion of his presupposes, to be true, a very weak concept of translation indeed.

Anyway, according to Olafson, emotivism holds (1) that "X is good" may be translated into "I approve of X" and that "X is bad" may be translated into "I disapprove of X", at least in "standard" or "typical" usage. The thesis (1) is supplied, by Olafson in his characterization of emotivism, with a thesis, (2), about ethical disagreement and to the effect that two persons who disagree in ethical matters, making statements expressed by "X is good" and "X is bad" respectively, both might make true statements although they might have a tendency to perform actions that "collide".

The thesis (1) and (2), where the first part of (2) seems to be implied by (1), exhaust what Olafson says explicitly in defining 'emotivism'. Now, one must seriously doubt whether Stevenson would accept *this* as an account of his theory. Furthermore, Olafson seems to be confused himself about the nature of (1), and hence of (2). In fact, he does not distinguish (1), it seems, from the view (3) that *according to common sense* (1) is true. Thus he seems to think it possible to refute (1) by confirming the denial of (3). He writes for example:

> If these translations are accepted, then the 'Is' appearing in them would normally refer to different persons, and so the statements might both be true ... This is the claim I wish to challenge. I hope to show that in typical cases of ethical disagreement the contestants are not prepared to concede that a moral view conflicting with their own can be 'true' and that they regard the two judgments as mutually incompatible. (p. 161)

Since all this is obscure, to say the least, and since nothing is said, in the explicit characterization of emotivism, about emotive meaning (!), let us leave the problem and return to it when we have seen which concept of emotivism Olafson actually *uses* in his argumentation.

Olafson's Argument in Defense of the View that
Emotivism has Pragmatic Effects

As we have seen, what Olafson sets about to show is that the acceptance of emotivism has, as a matter of fact, effects on those who accept it— in the way that it makes necessary a certain *way* of accepting ethical statements. Now, this is an empirical hypothesis which can hardly be confirmed without empirical investigations. And Olafson does not try to confirm it either. What he does is something more preliminary. He sets out to show that a change of the sort described, in one's moral practice, would be *the rational thing to do* for anyone who had accepted emotivism. This, however, far from diminishes my interest in his conclusions. On the contrary! For, of course, from *my* point of view, rational effects of the acceptance of a metaethical theory are of *special* interest.[4] Effects stemming from, for example, confusion about the real import of a theory, are *prima facie* of less interest than effects which result from a deliberate, rational acceptance of it.

---

[4] The distinction between rational and non-rational effects must not be confused with the distinction beteeen specific and non-specific effects, discussed in chapter I in connection with the account of conditions of adequacy for the concept of relevance to ethics. A specific consequence of the acceptance of a metaethical theory is, roughly, a consequence which could not have been obtained as well by the acceptance of some other kind of theory, say some theory of formal logic, physics or chemistry. A specific consequence is not necessarily a rational consequence. Consequences stemming for example from confusion may be specific of a metaethical theory. Of course, these connections between metaethics and ethics are not the most interesting ones, but all the same they might be well worth an examination. And there is no one but the metametaethicist to make them.

Olafson supports the view that the change in question would be rational, granted the truth of emotivism, by asserting three premisses about the implications of emotivism.

P1.   Ethical statements are not objective if emotivism is true

P2.   No rational justification of (the acceptance of) ethical statements is possible if emotivism is true

P3.   Ethical statements are actions if emotivism is true

Olafson seems to take P3 to be a pro-argument for P1, and P1 to be a pro-argument for P2. Pl–P3 are together thought, by Olafson, to be good reasons for a change in one's moral life.

One problem now is how P1–P3 are to be interpreted. I shall put forward interpretations based on Olafson's vague expressions. At the same time I shall discuss the reasonableness of P1–P3. When this has been done, I hope to be in a position rationally to assess Olafson's thesis that emotivism has a sort of pragmatic relevance to ethics.

A crucial point will be the examination of the nature of the change that according to Olafson *follows* from the acceptance of emotivism.

Let us start by examining P3 which seems to underlie the other two premisses. That Olafson really holds a view that could be expressed by P3 is obvious from the following passages:

One who accepts emotivism is forced to see that his favored moral judgments and their opposites are profoundly alike in being non-logical acts of preference ... (p. 173)

Under the non-cognitivist dispensation, a moral assertion is no longer primarily a description of something distinct from the assertion itself; it is itself an act ... (p. 174)

A non-cognitivist meta-ethic goes far toward obliterating this distinction between moral discourse and action by assimilating the former to the latter, and in doing so, it changes the complexion of the moral life as a whole. (p. 174)

Olafson tries to show the relevance of this premiss by asserting that "... a performatory analysis of moral statements/where P3 is an example/generates a performatory moral life". But as far as I can see, P3 rests wholly on the confusion of two different interpretations of expressions like "statement" and "judgment". On the one hand, ethical statements can be *conceived* as logical entities, which is the way I use the word "statement" in this study, and on the other hand they can be *conceived* as (speech-)*acts* of stating so or so. This, however, is nothing specific to *ethical* statement, it is true of descriptions, commands, and questions as well. And emotivism by no means makes this distinction collapse.

Olafson's overlooking of this distinction is very serious for his argument, since he bases a great deal of it on the premiss P3. But perhaps something of it could be saved by the following "reinterpretations" of P3:

P3:1.   When people use ethical language in contexts that are typical of normative ethics, they express something *more* than empirical, factual statements, if emotivism is true.

P3:2   When people use ethical language in contexts that are typical of normative ethics, they express *nothing at all*—in an ordinary "semantic" sense of "express", if emotivism is true.

P3:2 in particular could be considered an interpretation of the claim that ethical judgments are, nothing but, actions. According to P3:2 the semantic "dimension" is, in a relevant sense, empty. Perhaps P3:1 could, too, be considered at least a "step in this direction".

Of course P3, in both interpretations, is false if "emotivism" is taken in Olafson's explicitly defined sense. And at least P3:2 is false relative to Stevenson's theory. I think the only way out of these problems is to take P3, interpreted as P3:1, as a *definition,* not as the statement of a consequence, of emotivism. Then the question whether the acceptance of emotivism does necessitate a particular way of accepting ethical statements so far remains open.

The premiss P1 seems to be a statement to the effect that there are no ethical facts, according to emotivism. Olafson writes:

There is ... a similarity between the views taken of moral action by emotivists and existentialists ... both are concerned to deny the possibility of any legitimizing reality with which moral views must coincide if they are to be valid. (p. 176–77)

It /the emotive theory/ rules out any use of the factual model for interpeting moral validity and provides no new means by which we can express an order of values that is not merely individual. (p. 173)

But does emotivism have this consequence? As far as I can see: no. Neither P3:1 nor Olafson's explicit conception of emotivism does imply that there are no ethical facts of a nonnatural sort, in accordance with the view of, say, the "intuitionists". The most you can reasonably derive from P3:1 is that ethical statements are not, exclusively, descriptive of *natural* facts. Of course P3:2, on the other hand, *does* imply that ethical statements are not descriptive of anything, simply because there are no ethical statements expressed by ethical language. But this view is probably not Stevenson's, it is probably false, and it is inconsistent with Olafson's own interpretations of ethical language when trying to give an account of "emotivism".

Finally, let us consider the premiss P2. It is formulated by Olafson in the following way, among others:

> To the extent that he /a person confronted with emotivism/ does not merely identify with his own preferences, but tries to accept a moral principle only when the grounds for its acceptance are such as to be equally compelling for everyone, he searches for a standard that is not itself internal to one of the two conflicting views. At this final level of the moral life, however, there is none to be found. (p. 173)

There is much that is obscure in this passage, but at least it seems to be clear to the extent that it expresses a statement about the *acceptance* of ethical statements. I think it fair to interpret Olafson here to be asserting that the acceptance of ethical statements, if emotivism is true, cannot be given a rational justification. There is also something said about this concept of rational justification, viz. that rational grounds for the acceptance of a statement are to be such that they are equally compelling for everyone.

Now, P2 seems quite counter-intuitive. Being an *act,* why cannot the act of accepting an ethical statement be rationally justified simply with reference to an ethical system, like *any* act will be justified? Here, I think, Olafson is keeping a special sort of justification in mind which precludes this possibility. What Olafson would accept as an affirmative answer to the question whether a rational justification in ethics is possible, would be a specification of a method of determining how a person would assess an ethical statement if his motives were purley rational.

There is obviously an analogous problem of what it is that constitutes a rational acceptance of empirical statements, or are these problems even the same?

We are here touching difficult problems of epistemology. Any answer claiming to be definite should contain a definition of the concept of rationality. This Olafson never attempts to do. He seems to presuppose, however, that if an acceptance of a certain statement q by a certain person P is to be made rational, P's grounds for his acceptance of q must be equally compelling for everyone. But I am not at all happy with this as a conception of rationality. Is it not both much too narrow and too inclusive? Do we not often accept statements (ethical or empirical) rationally without having any *reasons* for them? Is not this the case with all "ultimate" knowledge? And may it not sometimes be rash to accept statements although we have rather good reasons in their support, for example categorical statements about the future? But let us all the same stick to Olafson's own conception. Is it then true that emotivism puts any obstacles to the rational acceptance of ethical statements?

Again Olafson's own conception of emotivism seems altogether irrelevant. According to Olafson ethical statements in the emotivist's conception are statements to the effect that the speaker approves or disapproves of something. And of course such statements may be founded on sound empirical evidence. But what about emotivism conceived in accordance with P3:1 or P3:2?

As far as I can see *some* ethical statements cannot be accepted rationally now; but for the same reasons that may be adapted to the acceptance also of empirical statements. We cannot support *every* statement with a reason. All arguments must come to a stop somewhere.

But may not *some* acceptances of ethical statements be rational? As far as I can see, yes. At least according to P3:1. For this premiss is consistent with the fact that ethical statements besides being empirical autobiographical assertions about the speaker also be *imperatives*, as Stevenson holds in his Working Models. And imperatives may probably be supported with logically good reasons as we have seen à *propos* of Stevenson's theory.

Emotivism conceived of in accordance with P3:2, on the other hand, is probably inconsistent with rational acceptance of ethical statements in Olafson's conception of rationality. If nothing at all is "expressed", in a semantical sense, by ethical language, it is hard to see that ethical argumentation is possible. When a person says "This is good" certain psychological processes are taking place in him and certain words are coming out of his mouth but he does not *say* anything; he does not *refer* to anything nor does he *predicate* anything about anything at all. The psychological processes and the words are all there is to it. There is nothing there to be logically implied or contradicted by any other statements. In that case there *is* a collision between Olafson's conception of rationality and his conception of emotivism.

The following passage could perhaps with some reason be cited in support of the interpretation P3:2 i.e. in support of the interpretation of Olafson where he is taken to hold that ethical language, according to emotivism, is semantically speaking empty:

Since no inference from factual premises to moral conclusions can be shown to be logically necessary and since there is no absurdity in substituting, for any particular moral conclusion, its contradictory, the uniqueness of a given moral

103

principle reduces to a kind of psychological *trompe l'oeil*. The special authority attaching to 'valid' moral principles is shown to be conditional upon an emotive push, since it does not even have propositional form, there can be nothing like any general rational sanction. (p. 172–73)

Here ethical "statements" are perhaps not taken to have any semantical content at all. This is at least one possible interpretation of the thesis that they lack "propositional" form. But two other arguments seem to be given as well in the quoted passage in support of the thesis that ethical statements cannot be given a rational sanction. *Prima facie* these two arguments seem not to require such a strong interpretation of "emotivism" that ethical language be semantically empty. Olafson asserts that since no inference from factual premises to moral conclusions can be shown to be logically necessary "the uniqueness of a given moral principle reduces to a kind of psychological *trompe l'oeil*". Here it is obviously not presupposed that ethical statements are not properly statements at all, only that they are non-factual. But is this argument sound? I think not. Why could not the "uniqueness" consist in the fact that a certain ethical conclusion is based on very good reasons, ethical as well as factual ones? I think it can, but Olafson seems to think that it cannot. This view of his is expressed by the words that "there is no absurdity in substitution, for any particular moral conclusion, its contradictory. This seems to be a view of ethical argumentation *in general*. I have already indicated my reasons why I think this second argument of Olafson's unwarranted, unless ethical statements be taken as altogether empty. Even if taken as imperatives, ethical statements *can* be supported by logically binding reasons, "equally compelling for everyone".

I conclude, then, that contrary to what appears in some of Olafson's arguments, a conception of emotivism is required which takes ethical sentences to be without semantic content. Otherwise Olafson's thesis P2 about rationality, according to his conception of it, does not hold.

But is this conception of emotivism, which is inconsistent with Olafson's own explicit definition of 'emotivism', really consistent with Stevenson's intentions? And is this conception of rationality really fruitful?

Has Olafson Shown that Emotivism is Pragmatically Relevant to Ethics?

The results of my examination of Olafson's views have been meagre. Firstly, the formulation of his thesis is unclear. Secondly, the conception of emotivism that he uses proved to be so vague that one must seriously wonder what the thesis is about. Thirdly, the arguments in support of the thesis, to the effect that there are good reasons to revise one's way of accepting ethical statements, if emotivism is true, are either false, under the most natural interpretation, or presuppose a conception of emotivism which is far from Stevenson's (and which makes emotivism most probably a false theory). Fourthly, since we do not know the exact nature of the way of accepting ethical statements, which Olafson says is necessitated by the acceptance of emotivism, we do not know whether this effect is of any ethical significance.

On the other hand it could hardly be denied that Olafson is touching upon an interesting and important problem. Pragmatic effects seem to constitute a promising field of examination for those who take an interest in the problem of the relation between metaethics and ethics. So let us briefly see what Olafson has shown, if we take as our point of departure our most sympathetic interpretations of him. I shall also return to the problem of pragmatic effects, in Chapter VI, where it will be discussed in a more general manner.

The only line of argument that did not obviously prove delusive was based on a conception of emotivism where the emotive theory was taken to imply that ethical language (in contexts typical of normative ethics) does not express anything at all, at least not in a semantic sense of "express". There is no logical content in ethical statements. In that case, it seems rational to follow Olafson in his contention that the acceptance of ethical statements cannot be made "rational", in Olafson's sense where rationality implies that good reasons are given in support of the acceptance. It seems also, then, reasonable to conclude that ethical statements are not descriptive of any "ethical facts" or of any "legitimizing reality", as Olafson puts it. This non-rationality and lack of objectivity, in their turn, are by Olafson taken to be good reasons for my not accepting ethical statements in the "usual" manner. Can a certain "flippancy" perhaps now be permitted?

I seriously doubt, however, the rationality of this change in one's ethical practice. Not because emotivism does not really have this implication, which it probably has, for some sense of "rational", but because a linguistic or conceptual *reform* would now be a possible, and reasonable, response. I have a reform in mind of the sort discussed in relation to Stevenson's views of ethical argumentation. A rational person would simply reply, I think, to the emotivist's alleged findings, that *he* would not accept that sentences that express nothing at all can express the answers to his formulations of his problems, or, even, that such sentences can express answers to any moral questions at all. If the emotivist holds that this is *impossible,* I must ask him to prove this.

For emotivism itself does not make it reasonable to conclude that there is no truth in ethics, that statements claiming to ethical truth cannot be supported by logically binding reasons and so forth.

If I am right on this point, discussed at some length in the preceding section, this will make Olafson's results even less interesting from my point of view, besides the fact that his queer concept of emotivism makes his discussion non-representative. Yet, there is a possibility that there is more to Olafson's ideas than I have been able to find here. For suppose there are certain non-rational, though specific, effects of the acceptance of emotivism. I will return to this problem in Chapter VI.

6. The Chapter Concluded

The results of this chapter are mainly negative. I have studied emotivism in C. L. Stevenson's version of it, with an eye to its logical relevance to ethics, both in immediate, and in more indirect, respects. I have found that it is far from clear how Stevenson should, from a descriptive point of view, be interpreted, but I have also found that for all descriptively reasonable interpretations that I have been able to make, the theory does not have any ethical relevance of a logical sort. The theory does not itself imply any ethical conclusions. This is Stevenson's view too. But while *he* seems to hold that his theory of argumentation, at least, has some relevance to ethics, and that thereby his emotive theory of ethics gains relevance too, *I* have found reasons to believe that also that part of his theory lacks relevance to ethics, in a logical sense. At least this is the case, unless you give to his theory of argumentation such a strong interpretation that it does not *follow* from the emotive theory of ethics.

But logical relevance is not the only possible form of relevance to ethics. Perhaps emotivism has some pragmatic relevance to ethics? Here the more definite conclusions will have to wait. Stevenson does not himself discuss this possibility, and most of the conclusions of F. A. Olafson, who does, turned out to be unwarranted. The rest were based on a very strange conception of emotivism and of the nature of the alleged relevance. Also in relation to Olafson, in the most reasonable interpretation of him, the dilemma occurred that either an interpretation is made of the alleged consequences of emotivism that makes them relevant to ethics but not really consequences of emotivism. Or an interpretation is made of the alleged consequences that does make them consequences of emotivism, but then they are irrelevant to ethics.

None the less, pragmatic relations between metaethics and ethics seemed to be a promising object of investigation. I will return to a discussion of it in Chapter VI, where I study all possible kinds of metaethical theories. Before that, however, I shall conclude my examination of representative, actual, metaethical theories, by an investigation of the relevance to ethics of R. M. Hare's universal prescriptivism.

CHAPTER FIVE

THE RELEVANCE TO ETHICS OF R. M. HARE'S
UNIVERSAL PRESCRIPTIVISM

1. Background

The third theory which I have decided to examine closer with regard to its relevance to ethics, is R. M. Hare's *universal prescriptivism*. This theory he has put forward mainly in *The Language of Morals* and *Freedom and Reason*.

Universal prescriptivism is of interest in at least three respects for an investigation of the relation between metaethics and ethics. The theory consists, if one restricts one's attention to those parts which are "meta-ethical" in my sense, of two parts. There is one thesis to the effect that ethical language is *prescriptive,* which Hare calls "(p)" and in this I will follow him, and there is another thesis to the effect that ethical language is "universal", or "universalizable", which Hare calls "(u)" and this terminology I will use as well. The exact import and meaning of (p) and (u) will be discussed when it becomes necessary for the sake of clarity of my argument.

Now Hare himself seems to hold, roughly, the views that (p) is relevant to the problem whether "ought" implies "can", that (u) is relevant to the problem whether there is any difference between act- and rule-utilitarianism, and that (p) and (u) together "entail", in some sense, some sort of an answer to the question how ethical deliberation and argumentation are or should be pursued. And since all these three "derived" conclusions, or sorts of conclusions, seem to be of no little *prima facie* ethical consequence I had better examine the arguments leading up to these conclusions, one by one.

2. Does "Ought" Imply "Can?"

In Chapter 4 of *Freedom and Reason* (from which book all quotations in this section are taken unless otherwise stated) R. M. Hare espouses the thesis that "ought" implies "can". Since Hare's metaethical principle (p) plays a crucial role in the argument in defense of this thesis, (p) seems here to achieve relevance to ethics. For the question whether "ought" implies "can" seems to be of some ethical significance. This is obvious if you consider the "contraposition" i.e. the thesis that "cannot" implies "oughtn't", or "must not". It seems, in fact, as though Hare, by the use of his metaethic, were able to restrict the scope of normative ethics.

One's curiosity is raised even more when one looks closer at the word "can". Hare does not define its meaning, but it is clear at least that he has in mind some concept stronger than that of sheer logical possibility. Then "can" applies only if one has a physical ability to do the thing in question and perhaps one must also have a psychological ability; here Hare is himself in doubt. On the other hand, nothing is *by definition* said about some alternative not being determined.

Now, let us start with a rough formulation of Hare's thesis, viz.

(T1)   "Ought" implies "can"

and let us see, first of all, how it should be interpreted, and, secondly, how it could be (and is) defended (by Hare).

What Does Hare Mean by "ought" and "can?"

The formulation of (T1) is clearly "metaphorical". Of course, Hare does not mean that the *word* "ought" implies the *word* "can". But, then, what *does* he mean?

Here three directions of interpretation seem at first to be open.

First of all, Hare could mean that all sentences containing the word "ought" imply some sentence containing the word "can".

Secondly, Hare could mean that some sentence-tokens containing the word "ought" imply some sentence-tokens containing the word "can".

Thirdly, Hare could mean that some ways of using language to form sentences and to make statements, where some typical ways of using "ought" are representative, imply some ways of using language to form sentences and to make statements, where some specified ways of using "can" are representative.

The first of these directions we need not enter into at all, since Hare writes:

... it is not universally true that 'ought' ... implies 'can'; that is to say, there are many uses of 'ought' in which it by no means is inconsistent with 'cannot'. (p. 51–2)

This leaves us with the other two possibilities, or with some combination of them. But which?

As for the word "ought" Hare requires, at least, that the word in question be *prescriptive*. And a word is "prescriptive" if, and only if, "it is intended to serve as a guide to anybody's actions". But here, what is it exactly that possesses the property of prescriptivity? Is it the word "ought" in the actual contexts, or is it what is expressed by that word, or is it a certain way of using language, a speech-act of a certain type? It is hard to say, since Hare does not use the word "prescriptive" consistently. Sometimes it applies to judgments, sometimes to the meanings of words, and sometimes to uses of words. But when he discusses the thesis (T1) he seems to hold that not only the word "ought" implies "can" but also other ethical words, if only they are used prescriptively. This indicates, I think, that (T1) is really to the effect that prescriptive statements, which are perhaps statements expressed by sentences containing some term which is used prescriptively, imply statements about the physical and logical and perhaps psychological ability of some agent. A slightly different interpretation would be to take (T1) to be to the effect that statements made by people using language in a prescriptive manner, imply statements about the physical and logical and perhaps psychological ability of the agent. Let us call the statements so specified "ought"-statements and "can"-statements respectively.

There is, however, a further possibility. And it has some descriptive reasonableness as well. For Hare is actually speaking of uses implying one another. And this makes reasonable an interpretation where certain sentence-tokens containing the word "ought" (used with the intention to guide actions) imply statements (here we must choose an interpretation where the stress is not upon certain words, since Hare sometimes talks about "can" and sometimes about "ability") about physical, logical, and perhaps psychological ability. Let us call these sentence-tokens and statements "ought"-sentences and "can"-statements respectively. Now the two interpretations can be stated thus:

(T1:1)   "Ought"-statements imply "can"-statements
(T1:2)   "Ought"-sentences imply "can"-statements.

These interpretations raise two questions. What kind of relation is the relation of "implication"? The relation in (T1:2) especially seems somewhat "unusual". And how could (T1:1) and (T1:2) be supported by reasons? Let us deal with these two questions simultaneously.

The Concept of Implication and Hare's Arguments in Defense of (T1)
Hare himself frankly says that

... it is because they are prescriptive that moral words possess that property which is summed up ... in the slogan '"ought" implies "can"' (p. 51)

110

One way of basing an argument on this quoted passage would be to use the argument which for example Stevenson touches upon in *Ethics and Language* when he discusses what he calls "avoidability". Since ethical language is used to reform people, he seems to hold, it will only operate if people are free to choose. But this, of course, is not enough to guarantee that just *that* agent be free to whom you address your ethical statements. It will be enough if there is some agent who is free some time in the future. At the first glance at Hare's argument, it seems to differ from Stevenson's. I think that the following would be a good first approximation to it, and a short one too (it is in fact rather complicated): Prescriptive use, Hare seems to maintain, implies *by definition* an imperative. And imperatives *do* imply "can"-statements. So prescriptive language implies "can"-statements.

In support of this interpretation one may point to the fact that Hare seems to identify prescriptive and universal usage with evaluative usage, and the latter is by definition, in *The Language of Morals* (p. 168–9), made to imply imperatives. Also his discussion of "prescriptive", "ought"- and "practical" questions points in this direction. This discussion is not quite easy to follow unless you know what it is for a question to "arise", since Hare writes that unless "the practical question (the "Shall I?"-question) arises, the "ought"-question cannot arise, if "ought" has its full force . . ." (p. 56). If one transforms this talk of relations between questions into a talk about relations between statements, (I shall discuss presently in more detail what it is for a question to arise,) my hypothesis is that what we will come up with is the statement that "ought"-statements imply imperatives. For Hare seems to hold that imperatives are *the* answers to practical questions, and the concept of implication seems to be definable in terms of questions arising. But what is Hare's concept of implication?

The Concept of Implication

My preliminary, rough account of the argument invoked by Hare in support of the thesis (T1) will not be intelligible before one knows what he means by "imply". When Hare tries to explain this he turns to Strawson and writes:

The sense of 'imply' in which 'ought' implies 'can' is not that of logical entailment. It is a weaker relation, analogous to that which Mr. Strawson has claimed to exist between the statement that the King of France is wise, and the statement that there is a King of France. If there is no King of France, then the question whether the King of France is wise does not arise. And so, by saying that the King of France is wise, we give our hearers to understand that we think, at least, that the question arises to which this is one possible answer, and that, accordingly, there is a King of France. (p. 54)

From the last lines of this quoted passage one may conclude that if a person, *P*, by his explicit assent to a statement, *p*, weakly implies another statement, *q*, then *P* is giving his hearers (if there are any) to understand that he thinks that the question arises to which *p* is a possible answer and, accordingly, *P* is giving his hearers to understand that he believes *q*.

If you take Hare to hold a view of 'ought'-sentences, not statements, you would have to modify this conclusion somewhat. You would have, then, to conclude that if a person, *P*, by his use of the sentence *S*, weakly implies the statement *q*, then *P*, by his use of the sentence *S*, is giving his hearers (if there are any) to understand that he thinks that the question, to which *S* expresses a possible answer, arises and, accordingly, *P* gives his hearers to understand that he believes *q*. Let us for the moment be satisfied with the former version.

There is one problem in Hare's formulation that has been dealt with in my reformulation of his views. The "hearers" that appear in Hare's quoted lines have by me been taken to be of a "hypothetical" sort. To be exact I should have used, perhaps, rather a *subjunctive* formulation. The point is, if I have understood him correctly, that *if there were* any hearers they *would* be given to understand, and so forth. This modification of Hare I take to be quite unproblematic. To avoid contradictions my explication should also have been made relative to a certain situation or time. Also this, I think, Hare would accept. But there are two more serious problems concerning which one may wonder what Hare really means. First of all, what does he mean by the word "accordingly" and, secondly, what does he mean by "*the* question ... to which .. is an answer"?

The word "accordingly" indicates that, should the defined relation hold between *p* and *q*, the values of these variables must be chosen so that it be impossible to give one's hearers to understand that one believes that the question to which *p* is a possible answer arises without also to give one's hearers to understand that one believes *q*.

Now, this seems to be the case whenever the question, to which *p* is a possible answer, cannot arise unless *q* is true. When will this happen? This is hard to tell before you have answered the other question I raised above, about the phrase " *the* question ... to which ... is an answer"? And it is also hard to tell before one knows more about what it is for a question to "arise".

Are there *unique* questions corresponding to each statement? Hare writes as if there were. But take the statement that the King of France is wise. Does not this statement correspond to the question whether there are any wise men in France and whether the King of France is stupid as well as to the question whether the King of France is wise? How does one cope with this?

One idea would be to amend Hare's characterization of the concept of weak implication so that *all* questions, to which *p* is a possible answer, are such that they cannot arise unless *q* is true. But this will lead to very strange results. For why should not the question whether there are any wise men in France arise unless there is a King of France? But then, the only way to make conceivable what Hare writes seems to be to take "corresponding question" in a very special sense. And I think this reasonable from a descriptive point of view. I think Hare conceives of every statement as having a corresponding question which is only an interrogative "reformulation" of the statement itself. But since this relation is a relation between logical entities, not between formulations, it is not easy to understand what this view really amounts to. It must suffice to notice what the problems are which here become acute. And the main problem is that it is presupposed that one has a method of analyzing every statement into a "referential" and a "predicative" part. This presupposition is very controversial indeed.

Next, what is the meaning of the term "arise"? This concept Hare characterizes in the following manner:

> The point is that, for a question to be said to arise in the required sense, it must be the case that, if asked, we should be able to understand it in the sense, not merely of knowing what the words mean in their normal acceptation, but of not being driven to ask, with an air of bafflement, 'What on earth is being asked'? If a question is, in a certain situation, incomprehensible in this sense, then it does not (in the sense required) arise in that situation (p. 59)

Notice that this concept is relative to a situation. This is another reason for making the concept of weak implication relative too, to a situation or a time (compare what was said above on this.) What besides that, can one learn from the quoted passage?

The concept here defined seems to be of a "pragmatic" or "psychological" sort. Whether a question arises or not depends on what one can *think of* as comprehensible *in a certain situation*. A troublesome point here is that Hare does not clearly distinguish between sentences and what is expressed by sentences. Is a question a type of sentence or do questions constitute a logical category? In this context they seem to be sentences. But, on the other hand, Hare's interpretation here in the context of ought-statements seems to require that they be logical entities. And also the interpretation that takes him to hold a view of ought-sentences requires, in order to be cogent, that a restriction is made to certain *tokens* of a certain class of sentences. So perhaps the most natural way to interpret what Hare says about "questions arising" is to take him to hold the view that what is expressed by these sentences is quite unproblematic. "Is the King of France wise"? is taken to express the question whether the King of France is wise, and we are supposed to know very well which question this is. Should this, however, turn out to be problematic, Hare would have to accept, I think, that his view is rather about logical entities than about formulations. The concept 'arise' would then apply when, and only when, a relation between *questions* (of a logical sort), *situations,* and *persons* holds. A question is said to arise for a person in a situation if, and only if, the person can grasp the question in that situation without being perplexed by its occurrence. This is not very clear but at least it is a rough indication of Hare's conception of what it means for a question to arise.

Hare's Discussion

Let us now turn to Hare's discussion about "ought" and "can". His general idea seems to be that whenever a person (explicitly) assents to the statement that P ought to do X he is giving his hearers (if there are any) to understand that he thinks that the question whether P ought to do X arises. This is in accordance with some general pragmatic "law". But this question, according to Hare, is related to another question, viz. the question whether P should do X. He holds that

The two questions are ... related, in the following way: unless the practical question (i.e. the 'should'-question) arises, the 'ought'-question cannot arise ... (p. 56)

This is one premiss in Hare's argument. Another premiss is that the practical, should-question, cannot arise unless P *can* do X. Hence, when a person assents to the statement that P ought to do X he weakly implies that P can do X. What, then, about the reasonableness of Hare's two premisses?

The first premiss, that the 'ought'-question cannot arise unless the 'should'-question arises, is simply a statement to the effect that 'ought'-statements in the required, "weak", sense imply imperatives, since imperatives are *the* answers to practical questions (by definition, I believe), while 'ought'-statements are *the* answers to 'ought'-questions.

114

And this premiss I shall not question since it is simply a version of Hare's metaethical theory.

The second premiss, however, that imperatives weakly imply 'can'-statements, must be questioned. Why is it that you cannot comprehend the question whether P should do X in a situation where P cannot do X? Or, rather, where you *think* P cannot do X?

I think there are two possible lines of argument open here. Hare, however, is only developing his reasoning along one of them, and not very explicitly either. The other one seems to be implicit in another of his views, however, viz. his view of what it is to assent to an ethical statement.

Hare claims, I think, that imperatives have no "function" unless P *can* do X. He writes that "... the fact that a man cannot but do what he is going to do stops any practical questions arising for him; and therefore there is no place for a decision or an imperative" (p. 55), and "If I tell or ask someone to do something ... I give him to understand that I think that the question to which I have given him an answer arises —i.e. that a decision is open to him. It would not do to tell a soldier to pick up his rifle if it were fixed to the ground". (p. 54)

The general idea seems to be that ought-statements imply imperatives and that imperatives have the function of guiding choices; the latter property is transferred to 'ought'-statements too, since these imply the imperatives.

What, then, about this second premiss? Is it a good reason in support of Hare's thesis? I doubt this. For even if a person cannot but do what he is going to do, or could not have acted otherwise in a certain situation, this does not prevent my practical remark from having a guiding function for that very person. He may be guided in some *other* situation by my remark about *this* situation. Furthermore, there may be other persons that are guided and there may be other functions of the command, besides the guiding one. Consider the following example. A man who refuses to do his military service is commanded to pick up a rifle and shoot although it is quite clear that it is psychologically impossible for him to obey. This command may indeed have a "function". It makes it possible to send the man to prison because of his refusal to carry arms. Or, consider a leader of a militant strike who is arrested and commanded to stop the strike. Even if it is altogether impossible for him to stop the strike, the command may have a function. It makes it "politically possible" to imprison or even kill the leader of the strike. This is one ground for doubt. Another one is that even if practical discourse, and *a fortiori*, moral discourse, *has* a practical or guiding func-

115

tion, this does not preclude this discourse from having a more "theoretical" function as well. One may perhaps give one's assent to the imperative that P should do X or the 'ought'-statement that P ought to do X merely because one finds this to be a *correct* view. At least Hare has not proved these two possibilities, the theoretical and the guiding one, to be mutually exclusive. Moreover, even if *imperatives* presuppose the ability of the agent to do the prescribed act this does not mean that *other* sorts of statements as well are not implied by 'ought'-statements, so that the theoretical question may arise equally well.

It is a problem here that Hare does not explicitly define his concepts of imperative and norm. Because of this vagueness it is hard definitely to assess his claim that *because* norms imply imperatives they also imply 'can'-statements.

On the other hand Hare could have chosen another line of argument. When he writes that "... the fact that a man cannot but do what he is going to do stops any practical questions arising *for him*" (p. 55) he puts a stress on the *agent*. Why is this so? Hithereto it was the man passing the judgment who entered into the relation with the question arising in the situation. This may be simply a slip of the pen. But it may also be the consequence of a certain view of what it is to "assent" to an imperative. Hare seems to take this to be to have some sort of disposition to do what is commanded. And this is something that only the agent can do. Under these circumstances, does it also imply an ability to do the act considered? This, however, would imply that only the agent can "accept", in Hare's sense, an imperative or a normative statement. Perhaps this idea should be generalized a bit so that for me to accept an imperative or normative statement that P ought to do X, is for me to have some disposition or tendency to make true the statement that P does X, if I have the opportunity. And perhaps this implies that P *can* do X, for how else could I be in a position to make him do X?

Now I am not at all sure that this is a reasonable account of a view which seems implicit in Hare's discussion of assent to moral principles, but perhaps it is. I *am* sure, however, that this in no way constitutes a good reason for the view that "ought" implies "can". For of course *I* can have a disposition to make P do X if I have the opportunity even if P cannot do X. The first phrase has to be read subjunctively, of course, and then it does not imply that P can do X. It is only said that if the situation *were to* come about where I could make P do X I *would* not hesitate to make him do so.

116

What Does Hare's Argument Prove?

There are various grounds for disappointment when one considers the arguments Hare invokes in support of the thesis that "ought" implies "can", especially from the point of view of an interest in the relevance of metaethics to normative ethics.

First of all the sense of "imply" turned out to be so weak that it could very well be that a person actually ought to do a certain act in spite of his inability to do so. What the thesis asserts is only something about some psychological effects on a (hypothetical) person confronted with the explicit assertion by someone, in a certain situation, that a certain obligation holds—where the agent is unable to do as he is commanded. From this, it is hard to see that we can learn anything of ethical import. 'Implication' has here become a pragmatic concept. So no ethical conclusions are logically implied by Hare's thesis (T1). The only kind of conclusions that are implied are that if a person asserts that someone ought to do a certain action this person believes that this action is performable. That Hare's concept of implication is pragmatic does not mean that the thesis (p) is pragmatically relevant to ethics either. It is not. The belief in (T1) is no reason for the acceptance, or rejection, of any ethical statement. At least Hare has said nothing to make plausible that it is.

Secondly, a crucial premiss in the argument seems to be wanting. Hare is trying to prove his thesis with reference to the premiss that 'ought'-statements imply (weakly) imperatives, and that imperatives imply 'can'-statements. Hare fails to prove the latter contention, however. The former I have not discussed since it is simply an aspect of Hare's metaethic. As far as I can see neither the fact that imperatives guide choices nor the fact that acceptance of imperatives perhaps must be conceived to include a willingness to make true what is commanded, if possible, is sufficient to guarantee that the agent must have the ability to do what is commanded if the command is to have any function. On the one hand you may very well tell someone to do something simply because he *should* really do it, disregarding the fact altogether whether anyone finds any guidance in your command. Whether this is inconsistent with Hare's prescriptivism or not, depends on whether he holds that ethical language *always,* in every particular situation, guides choices *in that situation,* or whether he holds some less universal view. This I have not been able to discover. What is certain, however, is that it is possible that ethical language has *both* a "theoretical" and a "practical" function. Hare has mentioned nothing that makes this combination of functions impossible. On the other hand, even if Hare were to hold the view that every ethical statement in every situation has a guiding function (in that situation—

a view which I find most certainly false), this would not require that the agent in that very situation can do what is ordered. It is enough if there is *some* situation *sometimes* where he is free to act in the relevant way. How else would we understand prescriptions or norms in past tense, according to Hare?

There is no way out of the dilemma set by my first remark, I think. Hare has weakened his concept of implication so that it is of no practical importance to know that 'ought'-statements imply 'can'-statements. I think it is possible to conclude this, although it is far from clear *exactly* what Hare means by "imply". There is, however, one move Hare could try in relation to my second remark that he has not proved that a practical function is inconsistent with the agent's inability to do what is prescribed by ethical language. He could take "guiding", or "practical" function to include reference to the ability of the agent to do what is commanded in the sense that the thesis that "ought" implies (weakly) "can" is implied (logically) by Hare's prescriptivism. This move, however, would make the prescriptive theory most certainly false, yet the gain would be small, since the pragmatic character of the implication-relation remains.

3. Does Hare's Universalism Make the Distinction between Act- and Rule-Utilitarianism Collapse?

While the prescriptivist thesis, (p), is supposed to account for our moral freedom, the thesis of universalism, (u), is supposed to account for our rationality in ethics. These functions of Hare's metaethic I shall study in the next section. First, however, I shall deal briefly with another kind of *prima facie* relevance to ethics, besides the one just discussed and also of a more special kind. For Hare seems to hold that his thesis (u) makes the conflict between act- and rule-utilitarianism dissolve. And if this is true it would be, at least, of *some* consequence to ethics. Perhaps one could here find a case for the judgment that metaethics, of the kind that (u) exemplifies, is relevant to ethics. I shall first of all formulate more precisely the thesis that there is no conflict between rule- and act-utilitarianism, secondly I shall make more precise the concepts of act-utilitarianism and rule-utilitarianism, thirdly, I shall examine more closely Hare's arguments in defense of his thesis, and, fourthly, I shall try to assess the relevance to ethics of Hare's findings.

The Thesis that there is No Conflict between Act- and Rule-Utilitarianism

Hare states his thesis in the following words:

I shall argue that if 'ought'-judgments are universalizable, there is less difference between these two theories than might appear. (p. 130)

Once the universalizability of moral judgments about individual acts is granted, the two theories collapse into each other ... in nearly all cases. (p. 135)

Roughly, Hare's thesis seems to be that rule-utilitarianism and act-utilitarianism are extensionally equivalent, i.e. the application of the two principles, to any particular action, will yield the same result as to its normative status. This is clear from the fact that Hare argues that there is no particular act which ought to be done according to act-utilitarianism but not according to rule-utilitarianism, that there is no act which ought to be done according to rule-utilitarianism but not according to act-utilitarianism, and that act-utilitarianism is "really" a sort of rule-utilitarianism. These are his three basic premisses. Thus the qualifications suggested by "less" and "nearly" in the quoted passages above seem to be superfluous. If Hare is right about his arguments then his thesis is valid in its most general version.

What are Act-Utilitarianism and Rule-Utilitarianism?

The principles Hare refers to by "act-utilitarianism" and "rule-utilitarianism" are characterized in the following manner:

Act-utilitarianism is the view that we have to apply the so-called 'principle of utility' directly to individual acts; what we have to do is to assess the effect on total satisfactions of the individual act in question and its individual alternatives, and judge accordingly. Rule-utilitarianism, on the other hand, is the view that this test is not to be applied to individual actions but *kinds* of actions. The assessment of the morality of an action then becomes a two-stage process. Actions are to be assessed by asking whether they are forbidden or enjoined by certain moral rules or principles; and it is only when we start to ask which moral rules or principles we are to adopt for assessing actions that we apply the utilitarian test. (p. 130)

To depart from this quoted passage is perhaps a bit rash when one searches for clear-cut definitions of the concepts. But Hare does not say much more about the two kinds of utilitarianism. When one considers Hare's arguments I think all the same that the following two principles give a fairly reasonable account of Hare's intentions and at least they do not make Hare's argument less convincing.

(AU) A particular act, *h*, ought to be done if, and only if, *h* but none of the alternatives to *h*, brings about a maximum of satisfaction.

(RU) A particular act, *h*, ought to be done, if, and only if, *h*, but none of the alternatives to *h*, is prescribed by some rule, the general observance of which brings about a maximum of satisfaction

Let us now turn to the problem how the thesis of extensional equivalence of (AU) and (RU) is defended by Hare.

Hare's Argument in Defense of the Thesis that (AU)
and (RU) are Extensionally Equivalent

As I mentioned above, Hare's argument is founded on three premisses. He holds that there is no act "consistent" with (AU) which is not "consistent" with (RU), that there is no act "consistent" with (RU) which is not "consistent" with (AU), and that, on closer inspection, (AU) turns out to be to the same effect as (RU). Let us examine these premisses one by one.

With regard to his first premiss Hare concludes that the only case where (AU) but not (RU) would make an act obligatory would be where "it were possible to apply the principle of utility directly to actions without the intermediacy of any subordinate principle". But this is, according to Hare, impossible. And he seems to have a "logical" impossibility in mind. This premiss is based on a statement to the effect that each consequence of an act is dependent on some *property* possessed by the act itself; "dependent" is here taken in a strong sense so that two acts which are "similar" cannot have "different" consequences. As far as I can see, this statement is not obviously true,[1] and I am not even quite sure exactly what it means since "similar" and "different" are not defined. Furthermore, I do not think that Hare's argument in defense of it makes it any more probable. For his argument is of an "epistemological" sort which seems irrelevant to his conclusion. He writes:

For how could it be the case that an action could be *known* to be such as to maximize satisfactions, without it being *known* that it did so *because* of the sort of action that it was? (p. 131, italicized by me)

The main weakness with Hare's position here, besides the fact that he tries to establish an "ontological" point on epistemic grounds, is

[1] Cf. J. Harrison, "Utilitarianism, Universalization and Our Duty to be Just" for an account of the opposite view; according to Harrison relevantly similar acts may have consequences of very different kinds and value. (pp. 114–118)

120

that *prima facie* you may easily imagine situations where two "similar" (in a natural sense) acts have consequences of different value as well as of "different" sort (in a natural sense of "different"). Take for example the act of going to the country instead of participating in a general election. Depending on other persons' voting in the elections this act may result in different states of affairs. The act may be crucial if the election of the one and only progressive candidate depends on it or if not it may be without any consequence for his success. If we wish to avoid this we will have to describe the act in such a manner that the "situation", including a description of other peoples' activities and so forth, is built into it. But then one is in fact abandoning (RU) for (AU). For the whole point in (RU), in situations like this, I think, is to make voting obligatory *regardless* of other peoples' actions. This is at least one reasonable interpretation of (RU), where it is taken to be a way of solving the pradox inherent in the fact that in situations like this no one's vote seems to be crucial to the outcome of the election. Here the results of conformity to (AU) by all parties involved would seem to be disastrous—everyone goes to the country since *his* vote is unimportant. I cannot see how any epistemic considerations could prove that the interpretation of (RU) which forbids this is normatively or descriptively unreasonable, even less can I see that it it "impossible".

When trying to establish his second premiss Hare concludes that a case where (RU) makes an act obligatory but (AU) does not would be a case of for example ", . . an individual act of promise-keeping which could not be justified directly by appeal to the demand for a universal prescription for cases *precisely* like this, but could be justified by appeal to some more *general* rule . . . which in turn was justified by asking 'Are we prepared to prescribe universal obedience to this more general rule'"?. But even this case Hare finds implausible. And the reason is that the acceptance of rules, according to Hare, is performed in a certain way. As a matter of fact, when we try to find out whether a rule is acceptable we go through all particular implications (and applications) of the rule and assess *them*. Hare writes:

. . . to accept any rule is, given the way the world is, to accept, by implication, a multitude of particular prescriptions about individual concrete cases. (p. 135)

Let us call this principle of Hare's "(q)".

What does Hare mean exactly by this quoted passage? Does he contend that universal rules are only a sort of "rule of thumb"? A sort of inductive generalization from particular cases? But this will give rise to various questions. For now one will most certainly find that, given a set of moral "intuitions", or "observations", there are several principles all consistent with the "evidence", which are mutually inconsistent. And how shall one be able to decide between them? Furthermore, this implies that one may never definitely accept, or assent to, a principle. For this acceptance or assent would imply complete knowledge about the world. Most of all, however, one must wonder what Hare has to say to those who, all the same, accept ethical principles, like the Rule-utilitarians or Rule-deontologists clearly do, after having made an assessment of the principle itself, without regard to what happens when it is applied, only concerning themselves with what *would* happen if everyone *would* obey it. Hare seems to try to denounce this position by using the argument that *actually* people reject a principle, no matter how reasonable it is, if only it has a counter-intuitive application. This I take to be the meaning of "... to accept any rule *is, given the way the world is ...*" But this argument does not prove Hare's conclusion that (AU and (RU) are extensionally equivalent. It is only a statement to the effect that there are, actually, no Rule-utilitarians!

Perhaps Hare's premiss (q) is rather to be interpreted as a kind of "meta-norm" to the effect that only those ethical principles that lack counter-intuitive applications are valid? But this argument fares no better. For now it is proved that (RU), in most versions, is invalid. But it is not proved that (RU) and (AU) are equivalent.

The third premiss on which Hare has based his argument in defense of his view that (RU) and (AU) are extensionally equivalent is to the effect that (AU) in a sense may be "reduced" to (RU). This may seem a bit odd when one considers the second premiss, which seemed to be to the opposite effect. The third premiss is indicated in the following passage:

... unless the argument of this book is totally mistaken even in deciding on the morality of an individual act by reference to its consequences, as the act-utilitarians bid us, we are at the same time deciding whether to accept or reject a rule applicable to all acts of a certain kind, as the rule-utilitarians bid us. (p. 131)

In the next section of this chapter I shall discuss various ways of interpreting (u). Here I shall only use one implication of (u), which Hare obviously takes to follow from it:

(r)   If some action ought to be done then all actions relevantly similar to it ought to be done as well.

Now, Hare's point seems to be that if (AU) is applied to a particular act, it is, because of (r), at the same time applied to the corresponding generic act; and to justify the generic act is, according to Hare, to justify a *rule* of the kind required by (RU).

But this conclusion is, I think, mistaken. It seems to me to be founded on a misconception of relevant similarity. For, according to Hare, (u), and thus also (r), are purely *logical* theses and thus not *ethical* principles. Hence, (r) cannot tell us *which* similarities *are* the relevant ones (to some particular moral view). Hare seems not to have noticed, astonishing as this may seem, that criteria of *relevant similarity* vary from one ethical system to another. Consider, for example, the following proposals:

(a) h_1 and h_2 are relevantly similar if, and only if, h_1 and h_2 possess the same causal properties in virtue of which the universal performance of acts of that kind would produce some utility or disutility[2]

(b) h_1 and h_2 are relevantly similar if, and only if, h_1 and h_2 are, from an intuitive point of view, the same kind of actions, i.e. they are both instances of murder, or of stealing, or of lying, and so forth

(c) h_1 and h_2 are relevantly similar if, and only if, h_1 and h_2 are both unique in their "spectrum" of alternatives in that they both maximize satisfaction or neither of them does maximize satisfaction.

When Hare concludes that, granted the truth of (r), the application of (AU) involves the normative assessment of a "rule" in the sense required by (RU) he seems to presuppose that the "relevant similarity" referred to in (r) is *not* of the kind (b), for example. But on what grounds can Hare make that claim? Here some *normative* premiss is wanting. For one descriptively reasonable interpretation of (RU) would operate with a criterion of relevant similarity of the kind (b). Perhaps this is not reasonable from a *normative* point of view, but that cannot be shown by meta-ethical considerations.

To conclude, the problem whether (AU) and (RU) are extensionally equivalent, depends for its solution on what criteria of relevant similarity are built into the theories. If (RU), for example, operates with (a)-kind criteria then, perhaps as D. Lyons has maintained in *Forms and Limits of Utilitarianism,* equivalence will obtain. But if (RU), on the other hand operates with (b)-kind criteria, it seems, to me at least, obvious that the theories will *not* be equivalent. If (RU) is taken to operate with (c)-kind

---

[2] This criterion is accepted on normative grounds by D. Lyons in his book *Forms and Limits of Utilitarianism,* p. 57.

criteria it is *obvious* that (AU) and (RU) are equivalent. And so forth. All these choices must be justified by ethical considerations. Here the thesis (r) will be of no help at all.

Conclusion

My conclusions have again been negative. The thesis that the conflict between act- and rule-utilitarianism dissolves, granted the truth of universal prescriptivism, turned out to be false.

Hare's argument in defense of his thesis was developed along three different lines. Strangely enough these three lines of his argument seem to be inconsistent. Hence, the relevance of his argument taken as a whole is beyond doubt (any statement is implied by an inconsistency) but its validity must be doubted. It seems as though Hare hesitates about the choice of which moral system to employ in order to resolve the conflict between (AU) and (RU), before finally deciding to resolve it *both* ways! It is not to be wondered at, then, that the arguments turn out to be defective.

The first line of argument presupposes a false premiss to the effect that similar acts have consequences of a similar sort and of equal value. This view is wrongly held by Hare to follow from the epistemological view that an action can only be *known* to maximize satisfactions if it is *known* to do so because of the *sort* of action that it is. Furthermore I am not clear as to how Hare conceives of the relation between this, probably false, epistemological principle, and his metaethical principles (p) and (u). But he gives no reason why it should be a logical consequence of these principles.

The second line of argument was based on either the premiss that no one accepts, as a matter of fact, (RU) or on the premiss that (RU) is invalid. The former premiss may very well be a logical consequence of Hare's metaethic but hardly the second premiss, being a normatively ethical view cast only in a "meta"-form. However this may be both premisses are clearly irrelevant to Hare's thesis of extensional equivalence between (RU) and (AU). This *logical* relation between the two principles is independent of whether they are respectively valid or generally accepted.

The third line of argument presupposed *certain* interpretations of (RU) and (AU) which cannot be justified unless one adopts a *moral* point of view.

4. Ethical Argumentation and Deliberation in the Light of Universal Prescriptivism

Background

The purpose behind Hare's choice of metaethical methodology seems to be a desire to be able to draw significant and well-founded conclusions about ethical argumentation and deliberation. Hare seems to be in agreement with Stevenson when the latter holds that metaethics has some relevance to ethics of an indirect sort. Hare would also say, in agreement with the the spirit of Stevenson, that this relevance is, at least partly, a matter of the implications for the theory of ethical argumentation and deliberation. Hare writes, for example:

Ethical theory, which determines the meanings and functions of the moral words, and thus the 'rules' of the moral 'game', provides only a clarification of the conceptual framework within which moral reasoning takes place; it is therefore, in the required sense, neutral as between different moral opinions. But it is highly relevant to moral reasoning because, as with the rules of a game, there could be no such thing as moral reasoning without this framework, and the framework dictates the form of the reasoning. (p. 89)

Here "ethical theory" seems, roughly, to denote what I have called "metaethics".

The idea expressed here seems to be that, although metaethical statements do not imply any ethical conclusions they have implications for the theory of ethical argumentation. Metaethical statements "dictate the form of" moral reasoning.

I shall try to discover in more detail what this means, i.e. *what* restrictions on how to pursue moral reasoning and deliberation Hare takes to follow from his metaethical views, and I shall try to assess the reasonableness of his view about this connection between metaethics and the theory of ethical argumentation. For the sake of simplicity I shall not distinguish between Hare's views about argumentation and deliberation since his views about the two kinds of activity or discourse seem to be to the same effect. For the most part he does not distinguish between them himself.

As I discuss whether Hare's view about the relation between metaethics and the theory of argumentation are sound, I shall also try to assess the relevance to ethics of those views of the relation between metaethics and ethical argumentation which I consider to be founded on good reasons. Hare's views about the *relation* between metaethics and ethical argumentation, in contradistinction to his metaethical views, I will *not* take for granted. While I examine only the *relevance* of metaethical statements, I have to examine also the *validity* of statements to the effect that a relation holds between metaethics and theories about ethical argumentation.

The Structure of Ethical Arguments

When trying generally to characterize his views of the structure of ethical arguments Hare has, among other things, the following to say:

When we are trying, in a concrete case, to decide what we ought to do, what we are looking for . . . is an action to which we can commit ourselves (prescriptivity) but which we are at the same time prepared to accept as exemplifying a principle of action to be prescribed for others in like circumstances (universalizability) (pp. 89–90)

More particularily, the view held by Hare of the structure of ethical argumentation may be exemplified by Hare's use of the parable of Matthew (xviii. 23). This is the parable of the man, A, who owes money to another man, B, who in his turn owes money to a third man, C. Neither B nor A can pay their debtors.

Now, B is confronted with a problem which could be stated in the following question:

(1)   Ought I, B, to put A into prison?

In order to answer rationally this question B, according to Hare's theory of argumentation, makes the hypothetical assumption that

(2)   B ought to put A into prison.

This hypothetical assumption, according to Hare, may be taken as the point of departure for a kind of "deduction". From (2)—and I think together with the universalistic metaethical thesis (u)—B deduces that

(3)   for all persons x and y, if x is relevantly similar to B and y is relevantly similar to A then x ought to put y into prison.

But what does this mean? What is a "relevant" similarity? I think the idea is that from the point of view of the theory of argumentation this must be left open. Any similarity *may* be relevant—with some exceptions.

What is important to my purpose here are the exceptions, for if there were no exceptions nothing would prevent that the property that made the pair a and b, say, relevantly similar to B and A, would be that a ought to put b into prison. This, however, is explicitly denied by Hare. And I think the reason for this is that he holds that (2) implies—I think together with his metaethical thesis (u)—that

(4)   for all persons x and y, if x is similar to B, and y is similar to A, in all respects except, possibly, for *numerical, nominal,* and *non-natural* properties, then x ought to put y into prison.

The statement (4) is not quite unambiguously stated here. I will not be able to make it altogether sharp since Hare's suggestions do not allow for this, but I shall say something to indicate what I mean by "numerical", "nominal", and "non-natural" properties.

When it is allowed that x and y are different from B and A in a "nominal" respect this only means that x and y do not have to bear the same *names* as B and A. When a universalization is made, no reference must be made to proper names or singular terms. Hare writes about this:

There are two stages in the process of universalization. The first is passed when we have found a universal principle, not containing proper names or other singular terms ... (p. 217)

The idea about "numerical" properties is that the fact that a *particular* person is involved, and not another person, must not be taken to be of ethical importance. If something is right for me, then it is also right for anyone exactly like me in all respects except that he is "numerically" different from me, i.e. except that he is not me but another person. Hare writes:

If a man is prepared to make positive moral judgments about his own ... but not about others ... he must either produce ... some principle which makes him hold different moral opinions about apparently similar cases, or else admit that the judgments he is making are not moral ones. (p. 102)

The exception for non-natural properties excludes cases where two persons are exactly similar in all *natural* respects but where one ought to do something which the other ought not to do. It is only because Hare denies the existence of such properties, I think, that he allows for this kind of exception.

Does the fact that (2), if Hare is right, implies, perhaps together with (u), (4), have any ethical importance? It seems so. This is because of the exceptions Hare takes it to be possible to make. There is something about the "form" of ethical argumentation that precludes certain ethical positions. These positions are perhaps not very reasonable, but all the same conceivable. Perhaps someone has even been willing to assent to some of them; in order to see this, let us consider an example.

Suppose there are two people, faced with a serious moral problem.

127

Ought they to join the liberation movement of their country which is fighting US imperialism? Now the following three arguments presented to them by friends who have studied at European universities may be refuted after the two people have consulted Hare. First of all the view that although the two persons are exactly similar in all natural respects the one simply ought to join the liberation movement but the other ought not since there are no ethical "principles" and every case has to be considered on its own merits (this argument is presented by a comrade who has been to Paris). Secondly, although the two persons are exactly similar in all natural respects, one ought to join the liberation movement and the other ought not to do so since one of the two persons is *me* (this argument is put forth by one of the two persons themselves, who has studied in Oxford) and it is true of me that heavier duties rest on me than on anyone else. Thirdly, one ought to join the liberation movement and the other ought not in spite of their being similar in all natural respects save for the name, because the name of one of them is *Trung* (and being a Trung she has special obligations).

These three moral positions, or kinds of moral positions, are perhaps not too clearly set out here, and there is perhaps some good reason against accepting any one of them, but I think they are all the same clearly *conceivable*. And this is all that is needed to prove that there are *ethical* implications in Hare's theory of argumentation, at least if it can be granted that the fact that a moral position is "precluded" by the theory of argumentation makes it impossible for this position to be valid.

In the original example it will now turn out that since B is similar to A and C is similar to B in all except, possibly, nominal, numerical, and nonnatural respects (and according to Hare, *actually* except numerical and nominal respects), i.e. B owes C money just as A owes B money, C ought to put B into prison. This conclusion B has to draw from his original hypothetical assumption.

There is another aspect of Hare's theory of argumentation as well, corresponding to his idea of prescriptivity. He also holds that from norms, perhaps together with the principle of prescriptivity (p), one can, in some sense, "deduce" imperatives. This means that B has not only to admit that if C is similar to B and B is similar to A, in all respects except possibly for numerical, nominal, and nonnatural ones, then C ought to put B into prison, but also that if C is similar to B, and so on, then, C, put B into prison! I shall restrict my examination to the universalist part of Hare's theory since I think it extremely hard to tell what Hare means by this latter idea and since I think the more reasonable part of Hare's theory is the one about universality. It is this part of the theory that Hare himself elaborates most and it is also this part of the theory which *prima facie* seems to be most relevant to ethics.

One could now recast the whole argument in the following way (for the sake of completeness I also mention the steps in the argument that are demanded by the principle of prescriptivity even if I do not discuss these steps):

(1)   Ought I, B, to put A into prison?

(2)   B ought to put A into prison (hypothetical assumption)

(4)   For all x and y, if x is similar to B, and y is similar to A, in all respects except possibly for *nominal, numerical,* and *nonnatural* ones, then x ought to put y into prison ((2) & (u))

(5)   If C is similar to B and B is similar to A in all respects except possibly for *nominal, numerical,* and *nonnatural* ones, then C ought to put B into prison ((4) by universal specification)

(6)   C is similar to B and B is similar to A in all respects except possibly for *nominal, numerical,* and *nonnatural* ones (factual premiss)

(7)   C ought to put B into prison ((5) & (6))

(8)   C, put B into prison! ((7) & (p))

(9)   Not-(2) or (8) (elmination of the hypothesis (2))

On the right I have indicated how the steps of the argument seem to be justified by Hare.

The *actual* character of this argument is not essential, according to Hare. It remains in force if (6) is dropped. Then (7) and (8) must be given hypothetical, subjunctive, formulations. The point, then, is that *if there were* a C, he *would* be obliged to put B into prison provided B ought to put A into prison. And this is considered no easier for B to accept than that C *actually* ought to put him into prison.

This is only a rough sketch of Hare's view of ethical argumentation. But I think it a good point of departure at least for an examination of the question of whether Hare's metaethical views are relevant to ethics on account of their implications for the theory of ethical argumentation. There are, however, some questions that must be satisfactorily answered before a conclusion about this can be reached. I am thinking of the question of what role is played by the thesis (u) in the step from (2) to (4) and of what kind of relation holds between (4) and (2). (Similar questions could be asked in relation to the prescriptive aspect of the theory.)

Several of the steps of the "deduction" above are taken by means of the application of ordinary rules of predicate logic. Perhaps *all* of them are so to be taken. Hare often asserts most emphatically that his thesis (u) is a logical principle, and so it also sometimes seems to be. He illustrates, for example, how he conceives of his principle by pointing out that when someone asserts that this is red he has to admit that there is a property such that this has it and such that everything that has it is red, i.e. he seems to take the principle (u) to be to the same effect as the principle of second-order predicate logic:

$$g(a) \rightarrow \exists f[f(a) \mathbin{\&} \forall x(f(x) \rightarrow g(x))]$$

Here "g" and "a" are predicate- and individual constants respectively and "*f*" and "*x*" are pedicate- and individual variables respectively.

Now, since (u) is a logical thesis it has no essential role to play in the argument. If (4) follows from (2) & (u) it follows from (2) alone. But *does* it follow from (2)? I think the answer is, no. The (invalid) argument to the effect that (4) *does* follow from (2) would probably take the following form. When it is asserted in (2) that B ought to put A into prison it is asserted that a certain particular act, B's putting A into prison, ought to be done. But then there is some property of this act such that if any other act shares it it ought to be done as well. Then, if another act is similar in *all* respects to this act it must also be similar in the *relevant* respect, and, hence, it ought to be done as well (it possesses also the relevant property). But what have been forgotten in this argument are the *exceptions* allowed for in (4) for numerical, nominal, and nonnatural properties. The *relevant* property may be among these. Of course the idea of the exceptions may be dropped. But at a very high price. For then (4) will not tell us anything more than does (2) itself.

I think this shows the inadequacy of this line of interpretation for my purposes. Here the principle (u) has not been shown relevant to ethics at all; it does not at all affect the theory of argumentation.

Suppose, then, that (u) is not really a "logical" principle in the sense that it is a truth of logic but rather a thesis about words and the meaning of words (this is a sense of "logical" which Hare explicitly defines or indicates). Is there, in that case, any way of making the argument cogent (provided the argument is still taken to have a logical form)? As far as I can see, no. If (4), with the exceptions indicated, is to be taken to follow from (2) and (u) logically then (u) has to be taken to have a normative content. Only ethical considerations can prove that certain properties such as nominal, numerical, and nonnatural ones, are not relevant to ethics. No thesis about the meaning of certain words will do in this kind of deduction; at least this was the tentative conclusion I arrived at in Chapter II, and Hare has said nothing that would do as the rationale of a rebuttal of this conclusion. This problem, however, will be discussed in more detail in Chapter VI.

Pragmatic Relations

Quite another line of interpretation of Hare would be to take him to hold that the structure exhibited by (2)–(9) is a *pragmatic* one. The idea would now be that the steps of the argument are not to be conceived of as logical deductions, at least not the ones from (2) to (4) and from (6) to (8) but as steps that are *actually* taken by people who argue in ethical contexts. The point would be that the acceptance of (2) in some way contributed to, or even necessitated, the acceptance of (4). Here the role of (u) may be conceived of in two ways. Either (u) may simply be taken to *assert* that anyone who accepts (2) will also accept (4), or it may be taken to be such that anyone who accepts (2) *and* (u) will also accept (4). But why should this be the case if (4) does not follow logically from (2) or from (2) and (u)? This is not a question that is easy to answer categorically. There are, however, certain suggestions made by Hare and I will mention all the ones I think I have understood him to make. In the next section I will discuss the reasonableness of these views.

First of all Hare's universalistic thesis (u) may be taken as a thesis about the word "ought". The idea seems to be that anyone who uses this word to form a sentence expresses a statement which is universalizable in a way which precludes that nominal, numerical, and nonnatural properties are ethically relevant. Hare writes:

I have been maintaining that the meaning of the word 'ought' and other moral words is such that a person who uses them commits himself thereby to a universal rule. (p. 30)

But some premiss seems to be missing here. For (1)–(9) are *statements* and nothing has been said about how they are (usually) expressed. If (u) is to guarantee that anyone who accepts (2) will also accept (4) because of some peculiarities of the word "ought" (and other ethical words) it must also be taken for granted that the word "ought", or some other ethical words, must be used in accepting (2). But is this true? Do you need to use *any* words at all in order to accept (2)? I will discuss this in more detail in the sequel.

Secondly, the following passage may also be taken as a point of departure for an interpretation of (u):

... in this argument nothing whatever hangs upon our *actual* use of words in common speech ... There is, however, something which I, at any rate, customarily express by the sound 'ought' ... (p. 96)

It is rather that there is this concept 'ought', which we have all learnt the use of (though perhaps less-developed cultures have not); and, having it, we are able to distinguish it from other concepts ... (p. 201)

Here the stress is, not on language, but on what is *expressed* by language in certain contexts. Let us now concede the claim that (2) really uses the concept Hare is referring to (for the sake of the argument). The point then is that whoever accepts a statement which contains a certain concept of ought as its predicate, will also accept a universalized version where *no* stress is put on nominal, numerical, or nonnatural properties. Since (4) does not follow logically from (2) the metaethical principle (u) will now be a statement to the effect that people actually do pass from a certain sort of norm to universalized versions of these in their ethical deliberation and argumentation.

Thirdly, a *group* of interpretations could be obtained if (u) were taken to assert that in *moral* reasoning the step from (2) to (4) is taken. Unless this step in the argument is taken the argument is, simply, not a moral argument.

In *one* interpretation of this group of interpretations the thesis (u) is taken to be a *definition* of the concept 'moral argument'. Hare writes about one who does not universalize his ethical statements that he "... has to abandon the claim that he is justifying the action morally, as we understand the word 'morally'". (p. 99)

But on the other hand Hare also writes:

The word 'moral' plays here a far smaller role than I was at one time tempted to assign to it (p. 37)

so perhaps this interpretation should be avoided?

Another way of developing the idea that those who do not universalize their statements are not making any ethical statements would be to take this to be a synthetic thesis about a certain group of arguments, which are independently identified as moral arguments. The following passage is at least consistent with this interpretation. Hare writes about the man who makes an 'ought'-judgment that he

... must either produce ... some principle or else admit that the judgements he is making are not moral ones. (p. 102)

132

But there is also possibly a third version of this last line of interpretation of Hare's views of ethical argumentation. Hare may also be taken to recommend that the step be taken from (2) to (4) in the argument. This may be the point in saying that an argument is not ethical or moral unless it is universalized. Here (u) is taken to be a norm about which norms to accept. Hare writes:

The kind of argument which I have been *recommending* is rather a form of exploration ... (p. 193; italized by me)

and one may, I think, recognize a certain moral ring in the following passage:

... if a person were to say 'Let's have an argument about this grave moral question which faces us, but let's not think of any conclusion we may come to as requiring anybody to *do* one thing rather than another', we should be likely to accuse him of flippancy, or worse (p. 20)

The last quotation is about the prescriptivity of ethical statements but I think Hare takes the universalizability and the prescriptivity of ethical statements to have similar grounds.

The Relevance to Ethics of Hare's Theory of Ethical Argumentation

The theory of argumentation which Hare holds to follow from his metaethical theses precludes, or is inconsistent with, certain ethical positions. *If* Hare's theory of argumentation really "follows" from his theory of metaethics, in one way or the other, then his theory of metaethics is at least of *prima facie* relevance to ethics. But does it follow? And in what way does it "follow"?

First of all Hare has been taken to assert that (4) follows from (2) and (u) and that (u) is a purely logical thesis (a truth of second-order predicate logic). But then Hare is simply wrong. The *exceptions* made in (4) cannot be granted in this interpretation. And if these are dropped (4) will not say anything that is not said in (2). Moreover (u) is "redundant" in this deduction.

Secondly, (u) has been taken to be a synthetic statement "about the meanings of words, or dependent solely upon them", to use Hare's own phrase. Now (4) has been taken, according to Hare, to follow from (2) and (u). But again this makes Hare's view of the relation false. No statement about the meaning of words imply that certain differences are not ethically relevant. The same is true of the interpretation where (u) is taken to assert something about *which* statements are made (which con-

133

cepts are used) in certain contexts. From such *interpretations* of *what* people say in certain situations no moral conclusions may be deduced. At least Hare has himself said nothing that would make me inclined to rebut this tentative conclusion (which I think as a matter of fact is *shared* by Hare) arrived at in Chapter II. This problem will, however, be taken up again in Chapter VI.

Thirdly, and this is perhaps the most promising line of interpretation, Hare has been taken to assert that the relation between (2) and (4) is of a *pragmatic* sort. Anyone who accepts (2) will also, as a matter of fact, accept (4). This is asserted by (u)—or it happens because (u) is accepted. Now, there are various ways of conceiving of this pragmatic relation, as we have seen. (a) Hare may be taken to hold that one cannot accept an ethical statement without using certain words, tacitly or aloud, and that these words are such that one cannot use them to formulate an ethical statement that is not universal. The idea seems to be that if one does not accept (4) one cannot express (2) without misusing language. This is an extremely awkward theory of language and I am doubtful whether it should be taken at all seriously. At least it seems rather to be of interest for linguistics than for normative ethics. For at most it is shown here that certain moral positions cannot be expressed. It is *not* shown that they are untenable, invalid, or anything of the sort. (b) Hare has been taken to hold that the concept 'moral argument' is so defined (by Hare himself?) that no argument is moral unless it is consistent with the structure exhibited by (2)–(9). But again this is of little importance from the point of view of normative ethics. It is hardly of any importance to anyone besides the reader of Hare's book. (c) Hare has been taken to assert that moral arguments *actually* have the form described by Hare. And in particular, anyone who accepts (2) actually also accepts (4). It is hard rationally to assess the relevance to normative ethics of this thesis. The importance of it seems to depend on *why* this step in the argument is taken. If there are any *good reasons* for it this finding will have some *prima facie* relevance to ethics, otherwise it will be of sociological importance rather. This brings us to the last kind of pragmatic connection, (d), where (u) was taken to be a recommendation that one universalize one's ethical statements. If there are good reasons for such a recommendation the fact that people do, actually, accept (4) if they have accepted (2), because they realize that they have good reasons for this, *will* be of interest to normative ethics. But are there any good such reasons for this recommendation? Hare says that he recommends that the step from (2) to (4) is taken, and he indicates a kind of reason for this recommendation, but he is never ex-

134

plicit on this point. And I do not think that the reasons he indicates are very good ones. Hare seems to believe that in using ethical words we "commit" ourselves to universal rules; this is a phrase he constantly repeats. And this at least indicates that he sees the use of ethical language, in at least some contexts, as a sort of "ritualized", or "institutionalized" activity, where certain responsibilities are "created" as one takes part in it. To use ethical language, in some contexts, is like making a promise. And I suppose the idea is that since one uses *ethical* language there is something about ethical argumentation one thereby "announces" that one will abide by.

This argument is very much my free construction and Hare should perhaps not be held responsible for it. It is however suggested by Hare's talk about "commitments" to universal rules and it is also well in accordance with Hare's talk about "the 'rules' of the moral 'game'" (p. 89). And it is the best argument *I* can think of in support of the idea that, for example, those who have accepted (2) *should* also accept (4). But again there are gaps to be filled in in the argument. Can one not accept (2) without using *any* words at all?

The metaethical thesis (u) is here interpreted somewhat differently from what has been the rule before. It is seen as a recommendation of a kind of reasoning. And the important part of the theory now seems to be *the reasons* set forth in support of this recommendation, viz. the statements to the effect that there is a "moral game" where expectations and duties are "created", "commitments" are made, and so forth. What we must query is whether these reasons are ethically relevant and also whether they are sound. Two critical comments must here be made.

First of all, I think it doubtful whether the reasons for the recommendation are "relevant" to ethics in a sense that they satisfy my condition of specificity of this concept set forth in chapter I. For is not the point made here only on a par with the observation that the use of ethical language, like all kinds of human activity, may be of great importance, in certain situations, to human welfare, or of such a kind that some ethical principle that is not clearly unreasonable applies to it. When you use ethical words in certain contexts, it is possibly true that responsibilities and duties are "created", that some persons' welfare is affected, and so forth, but this is not anything peculiar to the use of *ethical* language. The same is true of all sorts of verbal bahavior. And it could have been shown by ordinary sociological methods, at least as well as by metaethical ones, that you have the obligations and duties you have in the situations considered.

Secondly, I think it doubtful whether the type of context in which the commitment to universal rules is made is very "typical" of normative ethics. I doubt whether we really have to use ethical language in such a way as to commit us to any kind of view in the act of accepting the statement (2). It seems to me as if the contexts where (2) is accepted are not typically of the "public" sort where commitments are made and duties are created. On the contrary, if I wish really to *know* what is right or wrong, or at least reach a well-founded and rational opinion about it, I should rather *avoid* the "institutionalized" use of ethical language where *irrelevant* considerations about the effects of my public assent to one ethical system rather than to another, must be gone into.

It should be noticed that *if* the kind of relevance here discussed *were to* obtain (which I think I have shown is not likely) this would partly be a "moral fact". For it is in relation to some ethical system that duties are "created" by speech-acts. There must be some valid ethical principle to the effect that if such and such is said, then such and such an ethical opinion should be held. So my negative conclusion on this point is not ethically "neutral".

5. A Brief Summary of the Chapter

My conclusions have, once more, turned out to be mainly negative. When I approached the theory of universal prescriptivism from three different points of view, in order to examine its relevance to ethics, I felt some hope that the theory would give valuable insights into the question of whether "ought" implies "can", the question of whether there is any difference between act-utilitarianism and rule-utilitarianism, and the question of how ethical argumentation is to be conceived. But my hopes were all thwarted and the appearance of ethical relevance in universal prescriptivism proved deceptive. What we learned about "ought" and "can" turned out to be a part of linguistics rather than of ethics and the reasons for Hare's view were in any case rather dubious. What we learned about act- and rule-utilitarianism turned out to be highly interest- ing, for example that rule-utilitarianism in a descriptively reasonable interpretation is not acceptable; but this conclusion could not be deduced from Hare's metaethic alone. So his metaethical theory did not hereby turn out to be relevant to ethics. The theory of ethical argumentation which, Hare claimed, followed from his metaethic, appeared after all *not* to follow from his metaethic or, in an alternative interpretation, followed only as a "pragmatic" consequence of it. Those who would accept Hare's metaethical view (u) would also reason in accordance with the structure of ethical argumentation described by him. But the pragmatic relevance here in question appeared to be neither very rational nor specific enough to be interesting from the point of view adopted in this study.

On the whole the formulations of the theory of universal prescriptivism showed themselves to be open to a great variety of interpretations, not only metaethical ones, but also normatively ethical ones. This increased, of course, my difficulties in rationally assessing the relevance to ethics of the theory. My conclusions are relative to my interpretations.

CHAPTER SIX

GENERAL CONCLUSIONS

1. Background

The fruits of my efforts to find some metaethical statement that is relevant to ethics have been meagre. No definite positive instance has been found. Does this indicate that metaethics is really not an interesting field of investigation? Perhaps metaethical studies have been altogether abandoned by those whose interest in moral philosophy stems from an interest for normatively ethical problems? No, this is not the case. Metaethics is still a flourishing discipline. All the "traditional" views still find their advocates.[1] If one only glances at the most influential philosophical periodicals for analytic philosophy one will find naturalists —perhaps Punzo, Brandt, etc.,—nonnaturalists of the objectivistic sort —Zink, Mc Closky, etc.,—and non-cognitivists of various sorts—Urmson, Frankena, etc. And quite a few of them maintain that their results have some ethical relevance. This situation makes me uneasy. Does not this indicate that I must have made a non-representative "sample"? Or is there something wrong with my analytical tools? Is my conception of relevance too narrow? I will try to dispose of the grounds for uneasiness by generalizing my findings. I will proceed in the following manner.

First of all I will define my concept of metaethics more clearly. I will classify the various sorts of metaethical theories in an exhaustive manner so that it will be possible to assess the relevance to ethics of these various *sorts* of theories. I will here broadly distinguish between four kinds of metaethical theories and statements.

Secondly, I will examine whether metaethics has any *logical* relevance to ethics. I will try to find out whether there is any kind of metaethical statement which implies by itself or together with some empirical statement any ethical statement.

Thirdly, I will examine whether metaethics has any *moral* relevance to ethics. I will try to find out whether there is any kind of metaethical theories which imply together with some ethical principle any ethical statement that is not implied by the ethical principle itself.

---

[1] Cf. Andrén et al., *Meta-Ethics 1960–1970*.

Fourthly, I will examine whether metaethics has any *pragmatic* relevance to ethics. The concept of therapeutic relevance will be more clearly defined; in particular I will distinguish between two kinds of pragmatic relevance to ethics, viz. *rational* and *non-rational* pragmatic relevance.

Fifthly, I will examine whether metaethics has any *therapeutic* relevance to ethics. The concept of therapeutic relevance will be more clearly defined. I will distinguish between one kind of therapy whereby we are saved from confusion in our ethical reasoning and another kind of therapy by means of which we are in a positive way improving our ethical reasoning.

In this way four main kinds of metaethical studies are confronted with seven main kinds of relevance to ethics. The 28 theses that result from this confrontation are briefly summarized in the concluding section of this chapter.

2. What is Metaethics?

When in Chapter I, I outlined the scope of this study I restricted the question of whether metaethics is relevant to ethics to a question about the relevance of theories of the meaning and function of ethical language, speech and concepts. I explicitly dismissed theories concerning ethical knowledge, objectivity, ethical argumentation, deliberation and vindication and so forth as not "metaethical", in my sense of the word. These restrictions are I think well in accordance with my conditions of adequacy for the concept of metaethics, i.e. what I denote by "metaethics" it is descriptively reasonable so to denote. The theories I discuss are representative of a good deal of the moral philosophy produced at universities dominated by analytical philosophy. And the question whether metaethics is relevant to ethics is an important and controversial question. But at the same time these restrictions are rather vague. I will therefore try to set forth more clearly two fundamental questions: 1. What are metaethical theories about? 2. What do metaethical theories assert about "metaethical objects", which is the name I will use for that which metaethical theories are about?

What are Metaethical Theories about?

Metaethical statements may be predications of qualities or properties or they may be to the effect that some relation holds between certain entities. What interests me here is what kinds of entities these predications are about and what kinds of entities they are that enter into the relations held to obtain by metaethicists. What kind of entities are metaethical objects?

I will distinguish the following possibilities. Most of them we have encountered when I suggested various interpretations of the theories of Brandt, Stevenson, and Hare.

Word-types. Some metaethical theories assert something about the meaning of some word, say the English word "good". The theories are not about any particular utterance of this word or about some particular inscription of it but about some *generic* entity, which has *instances.* I hold no particular view of the ontological status of word-types and I do not presuppose any particular definition of any particular word-type. I leave it open whether, for example, the English word-type "good" is the same as or different from the German word-type "gut". It is up to the metaethicist to make a definition which suits his purposes. The important thing for me is only that word-types are abstract and generic entities.

Word-tokens. In contradistinction to theories of word-types a theory about words may be about particular, concrete instances, about word-tokens. A metaethical theory may for example be about those utterances or inscriptions of "good" where it has been used with an intention to commend something.

Sentences (types). It goes without saying that generic types of sentences, as well as of words, may be metaethical objects.

Sentences (tokens). Also particular instances of sentence-types may be metaethical objects.

Word-uses (types). Not all metaethical theories are about language. If a theory is about those word-tokens of "good" where the speaker intends to commend something it is probably not, in most cases, primarily the *words* that interest the analyst but *the commending use* made of them in these contexts. It is the "speech-act" itself which interests the metaethical analyst.

Word-uses (tokens). Also word-uses may be conceived of as particular and concrete. *His use of "good" as he said that it was a good car* describes a *particular* speech-act and it is a possible metaethical object.

Speech-acts in general (types). Most speech-acts are, of course, word-uses. But perhaps it is at least conceivable that someone assents, com-

140

mends, expresses his approval, and so forth, without using words. And perhaps these acts could also be called "speech-acts" in a wide sense. And whatever these kinds of acts are called they seem to be possible metaethical objects.

Speech-acts in general (tokens). Speech-acts in general, of course, may also be conceived of as particular.

Sentence-uses (types). It has been held that only words and not sentences are *used* to make speech-acts. But why not say, for example, that there are descriptive and interrogative uses of the sentence "the water is warm". Perhaps these are not speech-acts? But this is a terminological question without importance for my purposes. I think sentence-uses are possible metaethical objects, no matter whether they are called "speech-acts" or not.

Sentence-uses (tokens). My use on a certain occasion of the sentence "the water is warm" describes a particular act which is a possible candidate for being a metaethical object.

Concepts. An important group of metaethical theories are about concepts. The important thing here is not language or speech but what is expressed by language or what is communicated by speech. Concepts, however, may be conceived of in various ways and I will have more to say about metaethical theories about concepts when I discuss their logical relevance to ethics. The concept 'about' will turn out to be problematic in this connection. Theories "about" concepts will turn out to be only apparently so in some cases.

Propositions. The last group of metaethical theories I will mention is about propositions; I use "proposition" in a wide and inclusive sense to cover anything that is expressed in a semantical sense by sentences i.e. even *imperatives* are called "propositions", as well as ethical statements. I will discuss in more detail what it is for a theory to be "about" propositions when I try to assess the logical relevance to ethics of such theories.

My tentative thesis in Chapter I was that no metaethical statements imply ethical conclusions. For metaethical statements and ethical statements are not about the same kind of things. But this thesis is not quite unproblematic. For even if it is true if metaethics is conceived of as theories about language (word-types, word-tokens, sentence-types, sentence-tokens) it is more doubtful whether it is true if metaethics is conceived of as including theories about speech as well. Furthermore it is not at all clear what theories "about" concepts and propositions are really theories about and, hence, it is not at all clear that such theories are not about the same thing as some ethical statements are about. So the question whether metaethics is logically relevant to ethics must be raised once more.

I will, however, investigate a more general problem in this context viz. the problem whether metaethics is relevant to ethics in an empirical system. And a definite treatment of this problem presupposes a discussion of *what* it is that metaethical theories assert about metaethical objects. For even without considering pragmatic and therapeutic relevance to ethics yet we can see that logical relevance in my weaker sense calls for an examination of what is asserted about metaethical objects. Even if a metaethical statement is about something which no ethical statement is about, it might still be the case that the metaethical statement together with some empirical statement implies an ethical conclusion. This may happen for example if the metaethical statement is about a hypothetical fact, say, to the effect that if "ought" is universalizable, then what is right for one person must also be right for anyone similar to him. Then an empirical statement, say, that "ought" is universalizable, may imply a categorical ethical conclusion viz. the ethical conclusion that what is right for one person must also be right for anyone similar to him, if it is taken in conjunction with the metaethical statement.

What is Asserted about the Metaethical Objects?

There are several distinctions between metaethical theories that should be made at this point. One important difference seems to be between metaethical statements that are descriptive and those that are normative (reformative). Perhaps one kind has ethical implications and the other not. The difference here is between theories that are to the effect that the meaning, function etc. of ethical terms, sentences, etc., *is* so and so and theories that are to the effect that the meaning, function, etc. of ethical terms, sentences, etc. *should* be so and so.

Another difference is between theories that *predicate* something about some metaethical object and those that assert that some *relation* holds between metaethical objects. *Prima facie* the former kind of theory might seem more promising from the point of view adopted in this study, because of the kind of predicates and relations involved. While the information that two words have *the same* meaning seems to be irrelevant to the problem of ethical argumentation, say, the information about *what* meaning a certain ethical term has is of *prima facie* relevance to the question how ethical statements may be supported by reasons, and so forth.

What, then, is predicated of metaethical objects by metaethical theories. Typically, I think, something about the referent, or the meaning, or the function, or the logical properties, or the pragmatic causes or effects of the metaethical object. All these terms have to be left vague but I wish to take them in a very wide and inclusive sense; my interest is here rather to exemplify the possibilities than to restrict them by any sharp definition.

The relations asserted to hold are of various kinds. One important kind of relation in this context is what I shall call "synonymity relations". Synonymity relations are all those relations where it is asserted that ethical terms have the same or similar referent, or meaning, or function, or logical properties, or pragmatic cause, or pragmatic effect. The relations may have more than two places. It may for example be asserted that some ethical term in some contexts, to some persons, has the same meaning as some other term in some other contexts to some other person.

Another kind of relational metaethical statement is to the effect that certain metaethical objects are *identical*. It may for example be asserted that the concepts 'good' and 'desired' are identical.

Relational statements may of course, like predications, be denied by metaethicists and they may be quantified over; it may for example be asserted that no term is synonymous with any ethical term unless it is itself an ethical term, that no combination of concepts is identical with the concept 'good', and so forth. These statements are metaethical statements.

A third kind of relational statements I shall call "explications". These function as proposals for convenient conceptual frameworks, although not quite freely chosen. The point of departure is some familiar term with a vague meaning. It is suggested that this term should rather be used with a slightly different, sharper and more fruitful, meaning, than the usual vague one. The relation here between what is explicated and the "explicans" is not quite determinate in this characterization; I think it possible to explicate the concept of explication in various ways that are slightly different.

Synonymity statements and predications may take either a descriptive or a normative (reformative) form. Identity statements are descriptive, or at least not normative. Explications seem to have both a descriptive and a normative aspect.

Some Examples

C. L. Stevenson's "working models" in *Ethics and Language* were in this study interpreted in various ways. One way of taking them was as synonymity statements to the effect that two words or, rather, open sentences, are synonymous. Another way of interpreting them was as predications about metaethical objects. The working models were taken to interpret certain open sentences, i.e. the meaning of these sentences was specified. The metaethical objects in the latter case seemed to be a certain class of *tokens* of the open sentences, not the types themselves. Sentences like "This is good" were analysed as they appeared in certain contexts typical of normative ethics. This discussion I pursued in Chapter IV.

Richard Brandt and R. M. Hare also seemed to analyse linguistic metaethical objects in some interpretations, objects like word-types, word-tokens, sentence-types, and sentence-tokens. In this the theories inaugurated a recent "trend" in moral philosophy, exemplified in the work of Urmson, Ziff, and Katz, among others.

There is an obvious interdependence here between what metaethical theories are about and what they assert about their objects. Theories about linguistic objects, linguistic theories, assert things about meaning, referent, or function of metaethical objects, or assert that a relation of synonymity holds between such objects. On the other hand, all meta-ethical synonymity statements are about linguistic objects.

In Urmson's book *The Emotive Theory of Ethics* Stevenson is interpreted as holding a view about speech-acts, or, as Urmson puts it, about ". . . the use we make of language in speech". This theory is not even *relevant* to questions about the meaning of ethical language, according to Urmson. I am not altogether convinced of the descriptive reasonableness of this interpretation but it yields a theory which is an example of a non-linguistic metaethical theory. The metaethical objects here are *uses* of linguistic entities like words and sentences. What is asserted about these objects is something about pragmatic causes and effects, Urmson himself uses the term "force". In the last of my suggested interpretations of Hare's theory of ethical argumentation, in Chapter V, I took him to hold a view of speech, not of language, as I took him to hold that the point made in the universalistic thesis was that when certain utterances are made, certain responsibilities are "created".

G. E. Moore, in *Principia Ethica,* according to one from the descriptive point of view very reasonable interpretation holds a view about ethical concepts. A characteristic line reads: "My business is solely with that object or idea, which I hold, rightly or wrongly, that the word "good" is generally used to stand for. What I want to discover is the nature of that object or idea, and about this I am extremely anxious to arrive at an agreement" (p. 6)

My wide and inclusive sense of "concept" includes what Moore speaks of as "ideas" and "objects" in this context.

Conceptual analyses are, typically, identity statements. In Moore's case the thesis is a negative generalization to the effect that no combination of concepts is identical with the concept 'good'.

Identity statements can be made about all generic metaethical objects, i.e. about word- and sentence-types, types of word-uses, and speech-acts in general. But not all these kinds of statements yield interesting metaethical theories. To assert or deny that the wordtypes "good" and "gut" are the same or are not the same, seems for example to be of little use to moral philosophy.

When Stevenson in *Facts and Values* speculates about his own method, he represents his own metaethical writings as a kind of *explication*. He writes about philosophical definitions in general that ". . . we are not describing the world but are preparing the way for subsequent description. A growth of concepts is in question, rather than a use of old concepts in forming new beliefs". And this growth of concepts is not quite arbitrary. Stevenson recommends that the point of departure be some well-known term with a vague meaning. The meaning is made clearer by the explication.

From explications, it is not perhaps a big step to reformative theories. I am very much in doubt, however, about what the exact import of these theories is and also about whether there are any such theories actually given in the literature. R. Brandt, who uses the term "reformative" theory, invents an example of such a theory when he writes, in *Ethical Theory,* that such a theory could be to the effect "that it would be *better* if everybody used words like 'wrong' and 'desirable' in a certain way". (p. 156) The reason for this use of the words could, of course, be that the "new" concepts would be more adequate to certain practical or theoretical purposes and more sharply defined than the "old" ones. In that case the reformative theory would be an explication. But what puzzles me about Brandt's example are the reasons he is willing to give for this reform viz. for example, that "if everybody did use them in this way, then what would be meant by ethical statements would be confirmable by observation". (p. 156) This seems to me to be to "reform away" serious ethical problems.

From this comprehensive view of various types of metaethical theory it should be clear that it is not at all inconceivable that one kind of metaethical theory is relevant to ethics while another is not. Hence the investigation will have to take into account all the possible variations in order to yield a definite conclusion.

Since I discuss the "relevance to ethics", in various senses, of metaethics I will for the sake of argument usually (but not always) operate with the following grouping of metaethical theories: (a) *linguistic and descriptive theories,* i.e. all the theories where the object is a word or a sentence and where the form of the statement is descriptive, (b) *theories about speech,* (c) *theories about concepts or propositions,* and (d) *explications.* Normative or reformative theories about language will be subsumed under explications in most cases; I will say more about them in the next section.

The classification exhausts all possible "metaethical" theories in *my* (restricted) sense of the term.

3. Conclusions about the Logical Relevance to Ethics of Metaethics

I have found, I think, good reasons to conclude that the mere fact that linguistic metaethical statements are about something different from what ethical statements are about guarantees that no linguistic metaethical theory imply ethical conclusions.[2] This thesis, however, left the question open whether theories about speech, concepts, and propositions, as well as normative theories, are relevant to ethics in the sense that they imply ethical conclusions. Since my conclusions in the following will be negative I will not say anything more specific about this very "strong" concept of logical relevance (cast in terms of a weaker concept my negative conclusions will gain in strength) but will directly

---

[2] There is, of course, a problem here as to how the relation of implication is to be taken. For since the second argument of it is an ethical statement there are philosophers, I think, that would maintain that trivially metaethical statements lack logical relevance to ethics. There are no logical relations whatever that take ethical statements as their arguments. No statement, metaethical or not, is logically relevant to ethics. About this line of argument I shall only make the following comments. First of all I think it far from clear that ethical statements lack truth-values; and if they may be true or false I cannot see why they cannot also imply or contradict one another. Secondly, even if ethical statements lack truth values they may most probably contradict one another or at least be "inconsistent"; and the concept 'inconsistency' may just as well as the concept 'truth' be taken as primitive in a definition of 'logical consequence'—if *that* concept cannot be left primitive. Thirdly, as I refrain from using the idea that ethical statements lack logical relations nothing is lost with regard to the strength of my conclusions, for these are critical all the same, i.e. to the effect that metaethical theories lack logical relevance to ethics.

proceed to a weaker concept which I have called "the concept of relevance to ethics in an empirical system"; I made some suggestions about this concept in Chapter I and I used it in Chapter III when I discussed R. Brandt's naturalistic theory. The definition of the concept which I made in Chapter III is to the following effect:

Definition. The metaethical theory m is relevant in an empirical system to ethics if, and only if, there is a set of empirical premisses e_1, e_2, ... e_n, such that

(i) e_1, e_2, ... e_n are true and consistent together with m,
(ii) there is some ethical statement which follows logically from the conjunction of e_1, e_2, ..., e_n, and m and
(iii) this ethical statement does not follow logically from the conjunction of e_1, e_2, ..., e_n alone.

When I apply this concept of logical relevance to ethics to concepts of metaethics of various sorts I will deviate a bit from what would be a more usual way of grouping metaethical theories. I will discuss theories about language and theories about speech together and I will give some special consideration to normative metaethical theories, besides what will be said about them when I discuss explications.

*The Logical Relevance of Metaethical Theories
about Language or Speech*

The theories of the type here discussed assert something about the referent, function, or meaning of some ethical words or sentences, or about synonymity between these kinds of objects, or about the pragmatic causes or effects of certain speech-acts. How can such findings be logically relevant to ethics, even in an empirical system?

I think the usual line of argument is to the effect that findings about language or speech in some way settle certain ethical problems. If it is shown that ethical statements lack truth values it is shown that a search for the truth in normative ethics will be a search in vain. Or, if it is shown that ethical statements describe of some supernatural facts, then we are forced to take supernaturalistic facts into account in normative ethics. These ideas are here only vaguely indicated. I do not think they are sound and I shall try to show both exactly what is involved in them and how they fall short, by means of a dialogue between two persons, A and B.

Should A have Interfered?—a Dialogue

A: Yesterday morning I was faced with a serious moral problem. I saw my neighbour, a young unemployed gipsy, giving his child a heavy beating. What should I do about it? Would it be right for me to interfere? Or would it be better not to? Would my interference be misunderstood? Would I be acting racialistically if I interfered? Or would I be acting racialistically if I did *not* interfere?

B: I can see your situation. But I am not yet clear about exactly what your problem was. The situation gives rise to a lot of questions. How will the man interpret your interference? What is your motive? Is the child really suffering from the treatment? I am not clear about which of these problems you are referring to, with the phrase "a serious moral problem".

A: My problem was whether I ought to interfere or not to interfere or whether both acts were equally right.

B: Yes, I think you said so at first. But as you know the case is a bit complicated nowadays. For ever since the emotive theory of ethics was established we have been forced to, in a way, "reinterpret" situations like this. Your problem was not really what you thought it was.

A: I am no expert on the emotive theory so I will not try do dispute its validity. But in what way does the emotive theory show that my problem was different from what I believed it to be?

B: The reason is simply that the emotive theory shows that ethical terms like "right" and "ought" and so forth, used in typical ethical contexts, express nothing but the feelings of the speaker. When you use these terms you "express" nothing at all in an ordinary semantic sense. Your "statements" are without logical content. So when you said that your problem was what you "ought" to do or what was "right" to do, you did not express anything the answer to which could be contradicted or reasonably declared true or false and so forth.

A: I am not quite sure that I follow you now. I know that the emotive theory asserts that ethical terms in ethical contexts express nothing but the feelings of the speaker and that the relation here of "expression" is not an ordinary semantic relation. But what has this to do with my problem?

B: But the emotive theory is about the terms you used to express your problem.

A: How do you know that? I have not told you how I *expressed* my problem. As a matter of fact I never expressed it at all. Or do you refer to my description *now* of my problem yesterday? But if the emotive theory shows that what I really expressed when I today told you that my problem was what it was right to do, is that my problem was to find out what my attitudes were, then I will have to conclude that I have not made myself clear. For that was *not* my problem yesterday and it was *not* my intention to *say* that it was my problem yesterday.

B: I am not referring to your use today of the terms "right" and "ought". And the important thing is that *if* you had tried to express your problem, no matter what terms you had used, you *would* have expressed only a doubt about what were your most serious and profound attitudes about the case.

A: I had thought that the emotive theory said something about the English words "ought" and "right" and perhaps also about their counterparts in other languages. But now it seems as though the theory says something about *speech* rather, i.e. about the use of language in certain situations.

B: That is correct, although the theory is about language as well. The most important thing in your case seems to be that the theory says something about what you express when you use language in a certain context in a certain way. When you use language in ethical contexts to express something which is not only an empirical problem but what has been called a "moral" problem you only express a certain uncertainty about your own attitudes. "Reveal" is perhaps even a better word in this context than "express", for it has nothing to do with logic.

A: But how do you know that the emotive theory is about *my* situation? Was the context I described "ethical"? And is it not a normative problem to say which situations are ethical?

B: These are complications we need not enter into. The emotive theory uses a naturalistic definition of "ethical" and a very wide and inclusive one, so your problem is most certainly covered.

A: I'll concede that for the sake of argument. But I am all the same not quite certain that the theory is true of my case. For isn't the theory really a kind of empirical generalization, a statistical statement? How do you know that it is true also of *my* case?

B: According to the latest information the theory has been confirmed as a scientific law. We have reasons to believe that it is true also of "counterfactual", hypothetical situations.

A: But it is a law of behaviour. And is it not possible to break such laws if one chooses to? Is this not a distinguishing feature of laws of behaviour? And if it is *possible* to express my problem, no matter whether this is actually done, then the problem really *exists*.

B: I do not agree with your conception of laws of behaviour. And

149

this law is in any case stronger than such a law. You may no more "break" it than you may "break" the law of gravitation.

A: You surprise me. But, of course, life is full of surprises. So perhaps you are right. This does not change much, however, for I am still uncertain what the correct solution to my problem is.

B: You have not yet understood the emotivist's point. What I have shown you is not only that you cannot express your problem but that there *is* no problem of the kind you thought. And this is why I hold that the emotive theory is of relevance not only to metaethics but also to normative ethics.

A: I do not understand this. I see now that the emotive theory has very interesting and strong implications—there are things that I cannot say. But what has this to do with normative ethics. My problem is what it is, no matter whether I can express it or not, and it demands a solution.

B: I disagree. When you are trying to solve your problem you are hunting a ghost. Your problem does not exist. The emotivist has shown that the statement that you ought to have interfered, that you ought not to have interfered as well as the statement that both alternatives are equally right, do not exist.

A: What do you mean by that? How is it important?

B: Well I am afraid it is a bit complicated to show this. Let me try however. Let us grant the ordinary semantic axioms that '*p*' is true if, and only if, *p* and that '*p*' is false if, and only if, not-*p*. Suppose hypothetically that I ought to have interered. Then according to the semantic rules 'I ought to have interfered' is true. But when I say that this statement being an ethical statement, does not exist, I mean that it lacks truth-values, it is neither true nor false. This, however, implies that it is not true. And I have arrived at the conclusion that the statement that I ought to have interfered is both true and not true. Hence, emotivism seems to be inconsistent with any solution to your would-be problem.

A: But is not this strange, that as you say, emotivism seems to be inconsistent with any solution to my problem, indeed with any ethical statement.

B: Yes, so it seems. And is not this what has been suspected? Is not this argument the rationale of the common saying that emotivism undermines morality?

A: But the argument is confused. For *if* we apply semantic predicates to "statements" which lack truth values as well as to "ordinary" statements, if we take our semantic axioms to be true also of, say, imperatives, we have to change the axioms accordingly. We have to weaken the axioms so that '*p*' is true only if (but not if) *p* and so that '*p*' is false only if (but not if) not-*p*. We must do this as well as give up the idea that any statement is either true or false. And in that case you cannot derive that it is true that you should have interfered from the statement that you should have interfered as you did a moment ago.

B: I can see your point. My argument a moment ago was a bit rash. All the same I think the emotivist has shown that your problem does not "exist" though this does not mean that any solution to it is inconsistent with emotivism. I must confess that I am not for the moment sure how to argue most convincingly in defense of this thesis. Perhaps you would be somewhat more willing to agree with me if I could prove that *some* metaethical theories *do* "force" you to accept certain ethical statements?

A: That sounds plausible.

B: The emotive theory seems at least to be inconsistent with meta-ethical theories that do imply ethical conclusions. Take for example a theory to the effect that when people use ethical language in contexts typical of normative ethics they express statements about the approval of the majority. It does not matter how you try to "avoid" this would-be finding for it is assumed to be a *law*. It is true, for example, of the situation you just described. It has been shown, if the theory is correct, that what you were wondering about, was really what the majority would think of your interfering. Now, even if the statement that 'you should have interfered' is neither true nor false, has no ethical implications it seems clear that already the statement that this statement is empirical *has* ethical implications and even more obviously so the statement that this statement is a statement about the approval of the majority. For if you take for granted the hypothesis that there are no empirical facts you may deduce that this statement, if empirical in the way that it makes a positive assertion about an empirical object, is false. And granted the plausible empirical hypothesis that the majority would approve of your interference you may deduce that you should have interfered.

A: But even if proved *inconsistent* with theories *with* ethical implications, the emotive theory has not been proved relevant to ethics.

B: I think you are right there.

A: But the argument is confused for another reason too. Not even naturalism or supernaturalism is relevant to ethics, no matter what empirical presuppositions you make. And the reasons are the following. When the metaethicist asserts that my problem does not exist, or is so or so, he is not really making a statement about a statement in the same way as you do, when you say that it is true that the grass is green. His talk about statements is not a means of stating facts. When I say that it is true that the grass is green this may be conceived of as a statement of fact—that the grass is green. But the metaethical case is not parallel. What the metaethicist is saying is rather something about language or speech. He says that when you use language in a way typical of normative ethics, and so on, you are not expressing anything at all, or you are expressing something about the approval of the majority, and so forth. He does *not* say that certain statements, which we are acquainted with, independently of this description of them, are neither true nor false or are expressions about the approval of the majority. If he says "what is expressed in ethical contexts" is so or so, this expression is used to describe, it is not merely an identifying expression.

B: Really? Yes, I think this sounds plausible. But I must give it a second thought. By the way, how do you know that the metaethicist isn't after all "talking about statements" in the sense required in my argument? Perhaps he is not talking about either language or speech at all?

A: This would be contrary to your description of the emotive theory at the beginning of this dialogue. Furthermore it would be contrary to the assumptions in this section of this chapter of the book.

B: Book?

A: Yes, didn't you know? We are acting in a book of philosophy as an illustration of a line of reasoning.

B: I had no suspicion of that. But I must say I am not surprised that *you* know. You seem to be much closer to the author than I am.

The Moral of this Dialogue

This dialogue was designed to show that no metaethical theories about language or speech have ethical implications, whether alone or within an empirical system. Various objections to this conclusion are discussed.

First of all the idea is discussed that if a metaethical theory makes very strong causal claims one cannot but abide by what it concludes. If the theory is to the effect that what is expressed in ethical contexts is and *must* be (because of some empirical *law*), say, statements about the will of God, then ethical problems *are* theological problems. The idea of causal necessity has been introduced to cope with the objection A makes in the dialogue that perhaps the emotive theory is not true of *his* utterances yesterday. I think, however, that the strengthening of the causal claims makes this line of argument fare no better. For, as A points out, no matter how strong the causal claims are, the theory is of only linguistic import. It says something about what A would have expressed, had he tried to formulate his problem. The metaethicist's finding is only one about language or speech. A's problem is what it is and not another thing, no matter whether it can be expressed or not.

Now B tries another move. He tries to show that A's problem dissolves, or appears to be very different from how A himself conceived it, if emotivism is true. Here B at first uses an argument which is not very good. He argues that since ethical statements are neither true nor false according to emotivism, the emotive theory according to ordinary semantic principles contradicts any ethical statement. So emotivism produces chaos in morality and, B concludes, there are not really any ethical problems. This argument, however, is scholastic. If semantic theory is to be true also of statements that lack truthvalues, a radical change of the semantic axioms must be made.

Forced to admit the shortcomings of his argument about truth-values, B tries to depart from the thesis that ethical statements according to emotivism are of a peculiar, non-empirical, kind. Here B tries to show that this view *contradicts* a view *with* ethical implications. He holds that if we were to find out that ethical statements were empirical statements, as the naturalists have claimed, or even that they were of a very particular empirical sort, say, about the approval of the majority, we would be able to derive ethical conclusions from metaethics provided we may take certain empirical statements for granted. If we knew that the majority approved of X we could deduce from the naturalistic theory that X was good, and so forth. Now it is obvious that the emotive theory contradicts any naturalistic theory of metaethics.

Here A makes the very natural comment that even if the emotive theory contradicts a metaethical theory *with* ethical implications *this* does not guarantee that the emotive theory itself has ethical implications. But A makes his argument more general. He tries to show that natualistic theories do not imply any ethical conclusions either.

In order to question B's assumption that naturalistic theories imply ethical conclusions, A examines in what way metaethical theories are held to have implications about the nature of ethical statements. A here notices a certain ambiguity which is important. Sentences of the kind "Statements expressed in contexts typical of normative ethics are empirical" may either be to the effect that what is expressed in contexts typical of normative ethics are empirical statements, or it may be to the effect that certain statements that we are acquainted with and recognize as ethical statements, are empirical statements. In the former case this statement about statements appears to be a statement about language or speech. Something is said about what is expressed in certain contexts, by certain uses of ethical language. In the latter case the statement is not about language or speech at all but about certain statements. It is not so easy to grasp the real import of the latter kind of statement. In *this* section, however, I am only discussing metaethical statements about language or speech, as A points out, so the latter case has to be (and will be) discussed in another section. But when one understands the distinction here made one also realizes that the former kind of statements about statements—which are really statements about language or speech—lack relevance to ethics for the same reasons as was noticed at the beginning of the dialogue. No matter how strong causal claims are made or may be taken for granted in these statements about language or speech it remains possible that the *problem* A is faced with is *not* an empirical one, no matter what he happens to, or even *must,* say if he tries to *formulate* it.

In a general formulation, my point is that even if it is shown that language or speech is such that some statements cannot be expressed or communicated, this does *not* prove these statements *non-existent* nor that the *questions* they are intended to answer dissolves. But the argument here refuted, that since one *cannot* express certain statements they do not exist, may, of course, take a *logical* form. It may be contended that some statements about language or speech *imply* certain ethical conclusions. This is suggested in the example where naturalistic theories are discussed. I have, in Chapter II, held that since statements about language and statements of ethics are about different kinds of entities, no logical relations hold between them. But is this argument adaptable also to statements about speech? I think not. For statements about speech like some ethical statements are about human *acts.* All the same I think that metaethical statements about speech-acts lack logical relevance to ethics. Consider the following metaethical statement about speech:

(1)   To judge an act as right is to assess the value of its consequences as equal to or higher than the value of the consequences of any alternative to the act in question.

I think that those who want to argue that (1) has ethical implications would hold that (1) implies:

(2)   An act is right only if the consequences of it have not less value than the consequences of any alternative to it.

But even if both (1) and (2) are about actions they are not about *the same* actions. In particular there are some actions that (2) but not (1) is about. For while (2) is about *all* acts (1) is only about a narrow class of speech-acts.

154

I think the negative conclusion about logical relevance in an empirical system is true quite generally of metaethical statements about language and speech. I can only think of one serious objection to this conclusion when I have disposed of the idea that metaethical statements imply ethical conclusions and that it is ethically significant what is *empirically possible to say*. It could be thought that there are hypothetical metaethical statements of some sort where the "antecedent" is empirical and the "consequent" is normative. This is a case where it would be possible to deduce ethical conclusions from metaethical theories together with empirical premises. But no metaethical statement has this form. To see this let us distinguish between various ways of taking the hypothetical character of metaethical statements.

First of all the statement could be conceived of as a material implication. But this would make the metaethical statement as little interesting as the statement that if the world is flat then exploitation is bad. Let us suppose that the statement that if "good" means the same as "desired" then everything desired is good is taken as a material implication then this statement may be true simply because the antecedent happens to be false or because the consequent happens to be true. No *connection* is established between the two "facts". No metaethical statements, of course, are of this kind. Here a metaethical statement has been "expanded" in a non-essential way; it has been combined, simply, with a statement that is *not* metaethical.

Secondly, it could be conceived of as the statement of a logical necessity. It is asserted that, with logical necessity, if "good" means the same as "desired" then everything desired is good. But this would only make the metaethical theory beg another question which I wish to discuss in this study; this means that this kind of metaethical theories must be discounted as not "metaethical" in *my* sense.

Thirdly, the hypothetical statement could be conceived of as a normatively ethical principle, a "pure" norm. I think there are reasons not to take this kind of statement to be metaethical either. But it is an interesting kind of statement, which so to speak, establishes a relation between linguistic facts and "ethical facts". I will discount it as not metaethical, since it is an explicit norm and since it seems to be very close to an answer to one aspect of the problem discussed in this book. Hence, I wish to question its *truth* rather than its *relevance to ethics*.

Analogous arguments may be constructed to cope with ideas that metaethical theories are conjuctions, or disjunctions, of empirical and normative statements.

The Logical Relevance to Ethics of Conceptual
and Propositional Metaethical Theories

In a metaethical theory about concepts, it is asserted that one concept
is identical with another, say, that 'ought' is identical with 'not right to
refrain'. This analysis of a concept is closely linked with a corresponding
analysis of a proposition, or, rather, a propositional function, viz. that
'*x* ought to be done' is identical with 'it is not right to refrain from
doing *x*'.

I shall discuss first, this kind of analysis of concepts and propositional
functions.

But perhaps there are analyses of statements that lack obvious parallels in conceptual analyses. I am thinking of such statements about propositions as those to the effect that ethical propositions lack truth-values,
are neither true nor false, may be verified by empirical methods, and so
forth. I shall discuss these kinds of analyses of ethical statements after
I have concluded my discussion of analyses of concepts.

Conceptual Metaethical Theories and the Paradox of Analysis

Anyone familiar with and in sympathy with some argument leading to the
so called "paradox of analysis", might be tempted to seek an easy way
out of the problem of the relevance to ethics of metaethical analyses of
concepts. If these analyses give rise to paradoxes then why bother any
more about them? And I would concede that *if* these analyses are paradoxical then it is not interesting to examine them here. But are they
really paradoxical? I think not, or at least not in every case. And as one
tries to see *why* it becomes obvious too that conceptual analyses are a
group of rather different theories; these differences may be important
for the problem of whether analyses of ethical concepts imply ethical
conclusions or not.

I am not at all sure how to argue most rationally in support of the
thesis that conceptual analyses (in general) are paradoxical but I think
the following would be a fair account of at least one line of argument.

Let us take as our point of departure the analysis discussed by Moore
and Langford; cast in my terminology in this study, it becomes:

(1)   The concept 'brother' is identical with the concept 'male
        sibling'

From (1) one then "deduces" the statement

(2)   (1) is identical with the statement that the concept 'brother' is
        identical with the concept 'brother'.

Now, since (1), as was seen in (2), is identical with a mere tautology, (1) has been seen to be quite trivial and not really an analysis. And it does certainly not imply any ethical conclusions, we may add, no matter whether the concept analysed is ethical or not.

Here we are confronted with a rather general problem about identity statements. These seem to be necessarily true, if true, it has been held. But even if this problem is quite general, I think there is a particular solution to it for the cases I am discussing. How the solution is obtained depends on the sort of identity statements involved. We will see this as we proceed.

The problem confronting us now is how (2) could be obtained from (1). Does (2) follow logically from (1)? I think not. The most reasonable, although inconclusive, argument to the effect that it does seems to me to be the following.

When (1) is asserted the following statement is asserted as well, being a logical consequence of our assertion:

(3)   The term "'brother'" is synonymous with the term "'male sibling.'"

Now, since "'brother'" and "'male sibling'" are synonymous they also denote the same object. So we deduce the statement

(4)   "'brother'" and "'male sibling'" denote the same object.

But now we realize that what is expressed by the sentence to the right of "(1)" above is a mere tautology; for what is expressed is seen to be merely a statement to the effect that one and the same object is identical with itself. But is this argument really sound?

There is, I think, something fishy about the step from (1) to (3). Some tacit presuppositions must have been made here. For how else could (3), which is a statement about *words,* be obtained from (1), which is a statement about *concepts?* I think the premisses that must be added, are the following:

(5)   (1) is an analysis

(6)   (1) is (most) naturally expressed by the sentence (a): "The concept 'brother' is identical with the concept 'male sibling.'"

Now it follows, since Moore so defines 'analysis' that since (1) is an analysis and since (a) may be used to express (1) then the terms of (a) are synonymous.

Have we now deduced (2) from (1)? And, if so, is this paradoxical? Several comments should be made here.

First of all it must be noted that (2) was not deduced from (1) alone; it was not really deduced at all. It was rather the case that you were given some information about how to read the sentence here expressing (1). And this information forced you to the conclusion that the sentence expressing (1) only expressed a truth of first order predicate logic with identity. This should be the point rather than that (2) follows from (1). Since (1) has been seen to be a logical truth it does not in any interesting way imply any statements. The only statements it implies, are logical truths, which follow from *any* statement.

Secondly, even if (1) and all other analyses are truths of logic it might be wondered whether this means that they are trivial. I am not sure that this is true generally.

Thirdly, even if (1) is a logical truth and perhaps also trivial, there are *other* statements made by the analyst that are *not* trivial. I am thinking of the statements with at least linguistic import that (1) is an analysis and that (a) expresses (1). These statements have the interesting logical consequence that "'brother'" and "'male sibling'" are synonymous. If *this* is taken to be the point of the metaethical analyses of concepts, that certain terms are synonymous, then, however, we need not say anything more about them. Now the discussion of the relevance in a logical system to ethics of these theories may be subsumed under the discussion in the section above, about theories about language and speech. But I think more should be said on this point. There are still ambiguities in the formulation of analyses that must be removed.

Sentences like "The concept 'brother' is identical with the concept 'male sibling'" are open to various interpretations—hence the problem that we never knew *which* statement was denoted by "(1)" above. Who would have expected that it was a mere tautology?

One way of taking this sentence is to take the two phrases "The concept 'brother'" and "the concept 'male sibling'" to be definite descriptions; we take them to denote, respectively, the (unique) concept expressed by "male sibling" and the (unique) concept expressed by "brother". Now the sentence could be taken to express that these terms denote the same concept. This is a statement of linguistic import—it is a kind of statement which I said above, was the real point of one kind of metaethical analyses.

Another way of taking the sentence, is to take the two phrases "The concept 'brother'" and "the concept 'male sibling'" to be proper names, identifying but not describing expressions; it is taken for granted that we are acquainted beforehand with the concepts referred to. This was done above and it yields an interpretation which is a truth of logic with identity. It is asserted only that one and the same concept is identical with itself.

A third way of taking the sentence is to take "The concept 'brother'" to *name* and the phrase "the concept 'male sibling'" to describe. This is rather a line of interpretation and it could be developed into various directions.

Here the concept 'brother' is taken to be an *individual* of some sort. But which sort? It is here taken for granted that we are acquainted with the concept 'brother'. But are we? And even if we are acquainted with the concept 'brother' are we also acquainted with *moral* concepts? An ontological view seems here to be presupposed that there *exist* ethical concepts. But what is it for a concept to exist as an individual? Is it to occupy a place in Plato's heaven? Or are there other possibilities?

What is asserted *about* these individual concepts, may also vary. It could be, again that this concept is identical with the (unique) concept expressed by "male sibling". Then we are told *which* concept is expressed by this phrase. Another possibility would be to take it to be asserted that this individual is identical with a concept with a certain "structure" i.e. with a concept that consists of the two parts 'male' and 'sibling'. Then we are told something about the "nature" of the concepts analysed, to use Moore's phrase.

The important thing with some of the variations of this third line of interpretation of sentences like "The concept 'brother' is identical with the concept 'male sibling'", is that they yield statements that are not about either language or speech. Whatever is to be said about them must be said about them on their own. It is a fact that the conclusions from the previous section can not simply be adapted to them.

Linguistic analyses I have already dealt with. Those analyses that are tautological I need not, of course, discuss. So I will concentrate on analyses of concepts considered as individuals.

Ethical Concepts Conceived of as Individuals

Those who take ethical concepts as individuals may proceed in either of two ways. The concepts may, on the one hand, be taken to be *abstract* entities; then a kind of "Platonism" will result. These abstract "objects" exist, but not in time or space. The concepts may, on the other hand, be taken to be parts of people's "consciousness"; they must be taken, then, as *concrete* entities. In the latter case two persons cannot have *the same* conception of anything.

I shall altogether disregard the former possibility. I do not know whether it could be made at all conceivable. Even if this could be done, however, I will not pay any attention to it in this study. I take these theories, about these kinds of objects, to belong rather to metaphysics than metaethics, and I have no intention of assessing the relevance to ethics of metaphysics. My reasons for this are two. On the one hand I do not feel competent to judge about theories that seem to me so abstruse. On the other hand I think a discussion of these metaphysical theories would lead outside the tradition to which most of the theories I discuss belong. I will have something to say, however, about theories about "phenomenologically given" concepts provided these concepts are ethical concepts.

If the "existence" of concepts is taken to mean that concepts are "immediately given" to your sense or intuition or something like that I am not at all sure whether there are any ethical concepts. Do we directly "apprehend" goodness? Are there any ethical concepts that are directly sensed or intuited or which are innate? And if there are, what is the relevance to ethics of descriptions of such entities?

These questions cannot be satisfactorily answered unless the distinction between concepts that are directly "given" (to your senses, your intuition and so forth) and concepts that are more or less "theoretical", is made quite sharp. And this cannot be done in this study. I am here touching on problems that require full-length studies in themselves for their solution. I shall here only try to make the following two points clear.

First of all I think it very doubtful whether there are any concepts of the sort here presupposed to exist. I cannot offer any definite argument to prove that my doubts are rational, but in order to make them somewhat more intelligible, and in order to clarify somewhat more what it is for a concept to be "given", I wish to recall a disctinction between concepts that are "given" and concepts that are "primitive". I think much of the credibility of the claim that there are concepts that are directly "given" derives from a failure to see this distinction clearly. There are in every context some concepts that must remain undefined, primitive. To ask in every case for a definition is like asking in every case for a more profound explanation. But this does not mean that the primitive concepts are also "given"; the adoption of primitive concepts may be highly conventional. While some set theories, for example, take the concept of set as primitive it is defined in others. In order to be "given", in a sense which is an interpretation of what it is for a concept to "exist", a concept must not have this conventional character.

Secondly, even if there *were* ethical concepts that were directly

160

"given" I think descriptions of them would not be logically relevant to ethics in any empirical system. Here it will not do to hold that meta-ethical statements and ethical statements are about very different sorts of things. For now metaethical statements are neither about language nor about speech but about "thought", in a wide and inclusive sense. A moral evaluation may be about motives, intentions, and so forth, i.e. also about human thought. But on the one hand it seems to be very different to *describe* pieces of thought and to *evaluate* them morally. Here my argument rests, of course, on somewhat stronger premises than elsewhere in this study. I take some version of the argument against naturalism for granted. I think all the same that this is rather uncontroversial. From descriptions of human consciousness or thought nothing follows about the normative or ethical status of it. It takes some kind of normative principle to bridge the gap between the "is" and the "ought" here. On the other hand I think some version of the argument about what premises and conclusions are about, may be adapted also in this case. I am not at all sure as to how an argument from a conceptual analysis to an ethical statement is most rationally conceived of, but perhaps someone would suggest the following:

(1)   The concept of goodness directly presented to the intuition of man is naturalistic, hence,

(2)   If two things are equal in all natural respects and one of them is good so is the other.

But this deduction is not valid. For in spite of the fact that both statements are in a way about the same kind of things, (2) being also about thought, there are things which (2) is about but which (1) is not about. While (1) is only about a narrow class of experiences (2) is a general ethical principle.

I will be content with these two considerations. It should be noticed, however, that the question whether analyses of ethical concepts are "relevant to ethics" in *some* sense is not yet answered. It may be thought, quite rationally I think, that *if* there are ethical concepts that are "given", then descriptions of them have at least *prima facie* relevance to ethics *in some sense*. I will return to this question in Section 4 of this chapter.

Statements about Statements

Some statements about statements have no obvious parallels in statements about concepts. While, on the one hand, the statement that a statement referred to in two different ways, say 'This ought to be done' and 'This must not be omitted', is one and the same, may be taken to be identical with the statement that certain concepts are identical, say, 'ought' and 'must not be omitted', the statement on the other hand that certain statements lack truth-values, are empirical and so forth, lacks parallels. Let us consider some such statements to see whether they are metaethical and whether they imply ethical conclusions.

(1) The statement expressed by "Murder is wrong" in contexts typical of normative ethics, is that murder is disapproved of by God.

(2) 'Murder is wrong' is true.

(3) 'Murder is wrong' is neither true nor false.

(4) 'Murder is wrong' is not empirical.

(5) 'Murder is wrong' is empirical.

(6) 'Murder is wrong' is to the effect that God disapproves of murder.

All the statements (1)–(6) seem *prima facie* to be about ethical statements.

The statement (1) is most naturally taken to be only apparently about an ethical statement, however. It is really a statement about language. Something is stated about what is expressed by a certain sentence in certain contexts. This kind of statement and various versions of it obtained by changing what is said about the sentence in question, for example after the fashion of (2)–(6), or by changing the contexts specified, has already been dealt with in a section above about linguistic metaethical theories. This statement about language has not any logical bearing on ethics.

The statement (2), on the other hand, is more naturally taken to be a statement about an ethical statement. Or is it not? The problem is that my formulation which expresses (2) is not quite unambiguous. In one interpretation of my formulation, (2) could be taken, like (1), to be a statement about language. The point would be that the statement expressed by "Murder is wrong" is true.

This, however, is not the statement I intend to refer to, by my formulation of (2). Besides, this kind of statement has already been discussed. Another interpretation of my formulation expressing (2), would be to take (2) not to be about language or speech. Any reference to any speaker, time, situation or language may then be omitted. The point would be that the statement that murder is wrong is true or, perhaps even clearer expressed, that it is true that murder is wrong.

162

Again *two* lines of interpretation of my formulation are open. In neither of these is the apparent statement about an ethical statement a statement about any statement.

To see the point of the first line of interpretation consider a parallel empirical example.

(7) 'The grass is green' is true.

Is not (7) equivalent, or even identical, with 'The grass is green'? According to very common semantic intuitions, yes. This kind of talk about statements is required in some contexts, for example, where you have to quantify over statements, but in most contexts this second order talk about statements may simply be replaced by first order talk about "reality". And is not the ethical case quite analoguous? Is not ''Murder is wrong' is true' equivalent or even identical with 'Murder is wrong'? In this first line of interpretation I take the answer to be, yes. But then (2) is not *really* about statements at all. It is only a more complicated way of saying that murder is wrong. Hence, (2) is not a metaethical statement but an ordinary ethical statement.

The other line of interpretation of my formulation of (2) becomes possible when one realizes that 'truth' may be taken to be a much stronger concept than what was presupposed in the former line of interpretation. Suppose that 'truth' is defined to require, in order to apply, some sort of objectivity, or the existence of certain facts, as well. Then p is only a necessary but not a sufficient condition for the truth of 'p.' Now (2) may be taken as a kind of combination of an ontological statement (that there are ethical facts) and an ethical statement (that murder is wrong). The statement (2) would now be to the effect that there is an objective fact which makes it true that murder is wrong, or, simply, it is because of some objective fact that murder is wrong. Of course (2) now implies ethical conclusions viz. that murder is wrong. But is (2) really about ethical statements? Not at all. I would rather say that (2) is about (ethical) "realities" (that murder is wrong) and about some kind of ontological or metaphysical fact (that an objective reality makes murder wrong). Is (2) a metaethical statement? I would say, no. My criteria for distinguishing between metaethical and non-metaethical statements in cases like this are perhaps not very sharp. If this kind of statement were included then metaethical statements would be logically relevant to ethics. But since (2) is not after all about what I have called "metaethical objects" I think it reasonable to exclude it. Furthermore, (2) seems simply to be a conjunction between *two* statements, one ethical and the other ontological.

And the relation between these two statements seems to be altogether superfluous. Hence, I think there is nothing typically metaethical about their conjunction.

The statement (3) seems to be a more promising candidate. It seems to be a contention made by some non-cognitivistic metaethicists. As far as I can see, as was noted in a previous section, (3) is ethically neutral, it does not have any ethical implications, nor does it bring chaos into morality. The reason why it may be thought to have ethical implications is, I think, the apparent reasonableness of the following argument: (3), hence 'Murder is wrong' is not true. But suppose murder is wrong. Then, according to ordinary semantic intuitions, 'Murder is wrong' is true. This contradicts the conclusion from (3) that 'Murder is wrong' is not true. Hence it must be rejected that murder is wrong.

I have already rejected this kind of argument. If 'Murder is wrong' really lacks truth-values and if semantic principles are still taken to apply to it, these principles must be revised in some suitable manner. I cannot go into details here, but compare what has to be said of imperatives if semantic principles are taken to be true of them. 'Shut the door!' is neither true nor false, hence not true. In spite of this 'Shut the door!' may not be rejected because it implies that 'Shut the door!' is true. For it does not imply this. The semantic principle, that 'p' is true, if, and only if, p must be rejected if "p" takes imperatives as values as well as factual statements. This principle states only a necessary but not a sufficient condition. Or, you might perhaps even say that p does not state any condition at all, if imperative. Then the whole semantic principle becomes nonsensical.

Even (4) seems to be a typical metaethical statement. I have elsewhere admitted that such statements contradict statements that *seem* to have ethical implications. But this does not indicate that (4) itself has ethical implications. In fact I know of no good argument in support of the view that it has ethical implications. All the same I think it far from clear to what exact effect (4) really is. This problematic character (4) shares with (5) and (6). The statements (5) and (6), which are contradicted by (4) *seem* to have ethical implications. For does not (5), together with the statement that there is nothing empirical at all, "la vida es sueño", imply that all ethical statements are false and, hence, for example, that murder is not wrong? I think this is the case if "is empirical" in my formulation is taken to express *is a positive empirical assertion*. But I do not think that "la vida es sueño" is *empirical*, though it may so seem. It is rather a kind of ontological principle. So this kind of apparent relevance is not relevance to ethics in an empirical system. Furthermore I think it false that "la vida es sueño". Hence, this kind of relevance, whatever you call it, does not obtain. This thesis of mine I do not know how to prove. But does not (6), then, together with the statement that God disapproves of murder imply that murder is wrong? It is hard to tell unless we get quite clear about to what effect (4), (5), and (6) are. *Prima facie* it appears to be possible to construct *some* metaethical principles of this kind which imply ethical conclusions, if conjoined with true empirical premisses. But perhaps also these appearances are deceptive.

My formulations expressing (4), (5), and (6) may be interpreted in various ways.

First of all (4), (5), and (6) may be taken to be statements about language, i.e. about what kind of statements are expressed by certain sentences. This interpretation I dismiss, since I have elsewhere dealt with such statements.

Secondly, (4), (5), and (6) may be taken to be at least apparently about a certain *already identified* statement viz. the statement that murder is wrong. In all the statements (4), (5), and (6) something is taken to be said about this statement. But here it is important to make a certain distinction. When I assert that the statement '– – –' is so and so I take it for granted that we know *what* statement I refer to. But granted this, *some* statements about '– – –' will turn out to be either trivially true or trivially false, viz. statements to the effect that '– – –' is the statement that ... For either the statement I express by "'...'" is the same as the statement I refer to by "'–––'" or it is not. And this identity-statement is, if true, trivially true and, if false, trivially false. We are here confronted with a sort of "paradox of identity". The statement (6) seems to be of this paradoxical sort. It strikes me as obviously false. To me, at least, to say "'Murder is wrong'" is not to refer to the same statement as is expressed by "God disapproves of murder". And these were the words I used to express (6).

This trivial character of statements like (6) is the main reason why such statements are never made by metaethicists, as I think they are not. Should a formulation similar to the one expressing (6) appear in an essay in metaethics it would without doubt express instead something of the same sort that (1) does, viz. that "Murder is wrong", in contexts typical of normative ethics, expresses the statement that God disapproves of murder. This is a statement of linguistic import and it is of course very different from (6). Statements like (6) are not only avoided by metaethicists. They are also, because of their trivial nature (truths of predicate logic with identity), void of ethical implications. Or, they are

165

not relevant to ethics because they are trivially false and hence consistent with no premisses whatever.

But there are other statements about an identified statement '– – –' which are not in this obvious way trivial. I think (4) and (5), as well as (3), *may* be taken to exemplify this, although they are not relevant to ethics in any empirical system, for reasons already mentioned. These statements classify a certain ethical statement; in (3) we are told that it is neither true nor false, in (4) that it is not among empirical statements and in (5) that it *is* among empirical statements. At least in (3) this seems to be information of some sort, not really about a statement but about *semantics*. When we learn that 'Murder is wrong' is not among statements that are true or false we learn something about a semantic classification. And perhaps (4) and (5) in some parallel manner teach us something about ontology? This I am not so sure about, however, for what kind of classification is it to distinguish between empirical and non-empirical statements? Perhaps (4) and (5) are more naturally conceived of as statements to the effect that it is true that murder is wrong only if certain empirical facts obtain and to the effect that murder is wrong regardless of any empirical facts respectively. These statements are, more simply expressed, to the effect that what makes murder wrong are certain empirical facts and that murder is wrong irrespective of any empirical facts.

The point here is that a classification of a *known* statement ("known" in the sense that we know *what* statement it is) may teach us something about a classification; we learn something about the criteria and above all about the extension of it. But this kind of knowledge is, of course, highly *conventional* and it is of no *ethical* importance, as far as I can see.

If not taken to be classifications of this sort (to take them to be so is not very natural in relation to (4) and (5) while it is the most natural way of taking (3)) the statements (4) and (5) could be taken, as has been noticed above, as statements of ontology. Then they are not about statements at all i.e. not about any metaethical objects. And I think it reasonable, then, to discount them as not metaethical.

Statements about Statements—Concluded

To conclude, then, the statement (4) does not have any ethical implications. What makes it appear relevant to ethics is that it *contradicts* (5), which appears to be relevant; but even if inconsistent with a statement *with* ethical implications it does not itself have any ethical implications.

The statement (5), which *seems* relevant to ethics in an empirical system, on closer examination appears to lack such relevance. For even if "empirical" is taken as *about positive empirical facts* (otherwise it must be presupposed that 'in the deduction of ethical conclusion' *all* empirical statements are false, i.e. also negative generalizations of empirical statements), no *empirical* principle implies ethical conclusions together with (5). For the idea that "la vida es sueño" is not an empirical idea but a typical example of an *ontological* principle. Moreover it is probably false.

The statement (6), lastly, has been found to be trivially false. Hence it cannot be relevant to ethics in any empirical system. It cannot be consistent with any premises at all.

There is a striking fact about this discussion of the statements (1)–(6) which I think, deserves special attention. It appears as though all apparent statements about ethical statements dissolve into statements about other things. What appeared to be statements about a certain ethical statement has turned out to be statements about language, ontology, ethical facts, semantics, or else trivially true or false. I think this is no coincidence. As a matter of fact I think it altogether *impossible* to make statements about statements in any *other* manner. Statements, if they "exist" at all, are not things such that you can know *what* they are but at the same time be ignorant about their properties. This is a general characteristic of abstract "entities". You may define or "construct" them, but then you have said all there is to be said about their nature. They have no "hidden aspect", no "deep structure" and so forth. You may of course learn something about their "external relations". You may learn that a certain statement is true (which is knowledge about facts) or that it is neither true nor false (which is knowledge about semantics) but you cannot "discover" any "internal" properties. Abstract entities have no internal properties besides the defining ones.

This is the reason why statements about concepts or propositions dissolve into statements about other entities or turn out to be paradoxical. This is also the reason why such statements do not really present any problems of their own, for someone examining the relation between metaethics and ethics, besides the kind of analytical problems I have dealt with in this section.

The Logical Relevance to Ethics of Explications

The point of departure for explications is a concept that is vague and which plays an important role in some context that is of interest for some practical or theoretical purpose. The concept one starts with

167

may be "given" by some phrase in ordinary language or it may be suggested by some criteria which do not have the definiteness of a definition but all the same vaguely indicate a concept. To make an explication is to *propose* a "new" concept instead of the "old" one. This could be done either so that the term is proposed to be used with a somewhat changed meaning or so that it is proposed that the new concept replace the old vague concept in certain specified contexts. Examples of explications would be suggesting that the term "ought" be used with the sense of "maximize pleasure" in ethical contexts or suggesting that the concept 'ought' in a certain statement of the utilitarian theory be restricted in its application to *particular and concrete* actions (in contradistinction to "abstract" actions like the generic act of stealing).

The proposal of a new concept cannot be made quite at will—it is part of the meaning of "explication" that the new concept suggested is "similar" to the old one in some respect. I will not here try to account for the various ways in which "similar" may here be assigned a meaning. Very crudely this requirement could be specified by saying that the term must not be given "too different a meaning" and the new concept not be "too different" from the old one. It is also natural that the new concept be more *precise* than the one it is meant to replace. But this, I think, is only the consequence of a more important requirement, viz. that it be convenient for some practical or theoretical purposes to use the new concept instead of the old one. An explication is made in order to further some methodological aim, to make more clear and comprehensive some theory or some practical question. It is in relation to some aim of this sort that the fruitfulness of an explication should be assessed.

This characterization of explications is not very precise and indeed there are various ideas about how the concept of explication is itself best explicated but I think enough has been said for an assessment of the logical relevance of explications to be made.

Explications have been seen to have two elements. On the one hand they presuppose that two terms, the "explicandum" and the "explanans" have a similar meaning and, on the other hand, they make a proposal or recommendation that a certain concept be used in certain contexts instead of the concept that has been used in these contexts before. The recommendation is based on considerations of the theoretical or methodological convenience.

I think it clear that the former, descriptive element, lacks ethical implications. It is, like the statements already discussed in this study, only of concern for linguistics. But what about the second element, the recommendation? Does that have ethical implications?

I think the answer is again negative. For this proposal, even if normative, is not a *moral* proposal. It is motivated, and this is crucial, by methodological considerations. The new concept is used in order to make things less confused, in order to facilitate or simplify the formulation of certain theories and so forth. This may be of very great ethical importance—I will return to this problem—and it may also be the case that a certain explication is fruitful in relation to one ethical theory but not in relation to another, but the norms expressed are not *ethical* norms. The purpose of a metaethical explication is to suggest that new and slightly different questions be asked by normative ethicists—not to suggest answers to moral questions.

The Logical Relevance to Ethics of Reformative
Metaethical Theories

The definition of 'reformative metaethical theory', if I have understood those who write about such theories, for example Richard Brandt, can be obtained from the definition of 'explication'—if some conditions are dropped from the definiens.

A reformative theory recommends that some concept be replaced in certain contexts by another. It is not, however, required that the old concept and the new concept be "similar" in any sense. In this respect the recommendation may be made "at will".

But of course there must be some *point* in the reformation of the conceptual framework. One example from R. Brandt's book *Ethical Theory* I have mentioned before, in Section 2 of this chapter. It may be used to illustrate how one could argue in defense of a reformative theory. Those who make reformative metaethical statements

... may be arguing that it would be *better* if everybody used words like 'wrong' and 'desirable' in a certain way. They may be pointing out that, if everybody did use them in this way, then what would be meant by ethical statements would be confirmable by observation. (p. 156)

This may sound strange, however. For could we not now recommend as well that doctors use the word 'ill' to express the concept 'human'. Then it would be less problematic to confirm statements to the effect that people were "ill". But what then about the problem that interests both doctors and patiens, viz. the problem whether the patient needs medical treatment or not? How are we to discuss this problem now that we are deprived of the conceptual framework designed for the purpose of stating *this* problem clearly? Obviously, even reformative metaethical definitions should meet some requirement of "theoretical convenience".

169

Otherwise hardly anyone would bother to make them. And then in most cases it follows both that the concepts proposed to replace some old concepts are similar to these and that the new concepts are more precise than the old ones. Now what has been said about the logical relevance to ethics of explications may be adapted as well to reformative metaethical theories. But perhaps there are also other ways of conceiving of reformative metaethical theories.

To recommend that 'desired' be used instead of 'good' in certain contexts may be to recommend that statements about what is desired be accepted as answers to the question of what is good. This recommendation may be motivated by ethical considerations. Only if this recommendation is obeyed are true or correct ethical statements accepted, it might be thought. This is a fairly reasonable interpretation from a descriptive point of view of utterances like "By 'good' I mean *desired* and you should do so as well". This is an expression of a normative ethical view. This, however, is probably not a common usage among metaethicists who are eager to distinguish between definitions and statements of fact. And of course such "theories" will be excluded from the domain of *my* concept of metaethics—the theories belong to normative ethics.

A recommendation of a concept, which is a disguised recommendation that a certain statement be accepted as the answer to an ethical question, may be motivated also in other ways. Something may be said about the effects of the acceptance of these statements or it may even be held that it is a "moral fact" that one simply *ought* to accept these statements.

I don't know whether this is a reasonable interpretation of any actual metaethical theories. R. Brandt seems to come close to it in the example I cited above. But also in this interpretation reformative metaethical theories lack relevance to ethics. For even if one is morally obliged to accept certain ethical statements, perhaps because of the effects that will ensue, it does not follow that these statements are *valid*.

But are not these "meta-norms" about what kind of statements to accept (cast in the form of recommendations of concepts) really ethical statements? In a way, yes. They are the result of an "application" of an ethical principle to certain facts. When one is advised to accept certain statements this is done either because of the effects or because of some other morally relevant trait in your act of acceptance. Hence, it is doubtful whether these theories are really metaethical theories. But no matter how we classify them they are not very interesting from the point of view of normative ethics; the same recommendation may be made for very different reasons, and it is rather these reasons (the ethical system applied in the actual cases) that is interesting from an ethical point of view, not the recommendation itself. But the ethical system is *not* implied by the recommendation.

Conclusion

In this section I have defined a concept of logical relevance of meta-ethics to ethics.

I have argued that since metaethical theories about language are about something very different from what ethical statements are about the former do not imply the latter. A version of this argument has been used also to refute the idea that theories about speech have ethical implications.

I have also tried to show that theories about language or speech do not in any way show that certain ethical statements are untenable because they are shown to be inexpressible. I have expressed doubts about the idea that metaethical theories show the impossibility of expressing certain views but *even* if it could be shown, say, that ethical language is such that only implicitly universal ethical statements can be communicated by it, this does *not* show that this, or only this kind of ethical statements are valid.

In particular I have tried to disprove an argument in defense of the view that the emotive theory brings chaos into morality. This argument has been seen to stretch semantic ideas in an unreasonable way.

I have outlined the thesis that analyses of ethical concepts lack logical relevance to ethics. I have distinguished between various versions of such analyses. These have been found to be either about language or speech, or to be theories of metaphysics (and hence not of metaethics), or to be theories about human *thought*. Theories about metaphysics I have not examined. No metaethical theory about human thought has been found to imply ethical conclusions. Here, again, a version of the argument that logical relations between two statements presuppose that they are about the same thing, has been used and found effective.

I have discussed in detail various version of metaethical theories about ethical statements. These have all been seen to be, as a matter of fact, about something other than statements (such as facts, language, speech, ontology, semantics) or truths of logic with identity.

I have noted that explications do not imply ethical conclusions. They are designed for quite another purpose. Partly they describe language. Partly they evaluate. But descriptions of language do not imply ethical conclusions. And the evaluations made are not ethical.

I have discussed normative, or reformative metaethical theories and I have noticed that what may be said about explications may equally well be said about them. I have not found any reason to distinguish sharply between explications and reformative metaethical theories.

4. Conclusions about the Relevance to Ethics in an Ethical System of Metaethics

The Concept of Moral Relevance

A very natural conception, from the point of view of descriptive reasonableness, of "relevance to ethics", would be to take an item of information to be ethically relevant if it made possible the application of some ethical principle. It is relevant information, say, that a certain act maximizes welfare if there is an ethical principle to the effect that acts that maximize welfare are right. For this principle implies that if a certain act, h, maximizes pleasure, then h is right. And this statement, together with the statement that *this* act maximizes welfare, implies that this act is right.

It is always possible, however, to invent *some* principle which makes *any* fact relevant to ethics in this way. Hence, this concept will have to be restricted to be interesting: it will be required that the ethical principle is *valid* (or reasonable, or true).

This intuitive conception is a bit too narrow for my purposes. I will not require that the statement which is being tested for its relevance, and the ethical principle, are about the same thing. I will allow, for example, cases where an ethical principle is to the effect that if the term "..." means the same as "---" then so and so is right (this might seem queer but the reasons for this conception will become obvious as I proceed).

There are some further problems about this intuitive concept of relevance to ethics but I shall deal with them in relation to a strict definition. The concept I will use, which I will call the concept of "relevance to ethics in an ethical system" or, for short, the concept of "moral relevance" is defined in the following way.

Definition. The metaethical theory m is relevant in an ethical system to ethics if, and only if, there are ethical statements $e_1, e_2, \ldots, e_n$, such that

      (i) $e_1, e_2, \ldots e_n$ are valid and consistent with m,
      (ii) $e_1, e_2, \ldots, e_n$, if hypothetical, are "law-like",

(iii) there is some ethical statement which follows logically from the conjunction of $e_1, e_2, \ldots e_n m$, and

(iv) this ethical statement does not follow logically from the conjunction of $e_1, e_2, \ldots e_n$ alone.

My reasons for adopting a concept of this kind are rather obvious. This is a descriptively reasonable interpretation of the term "relevance". If metaethics possess this kind of relevance it is probably a discipline worth studying. And instances of this kind of relevance are probably specific of metaethics, if they obtain.

I shall comment on the somewhat obscure condition (ii) in the next section. The requirement that $e_1, e_2, \ldots e_n$ be (together) consistent with m is superfluous if my thesis that no metaethical statements imply ethical conclusions is right. But if this thesis of mine is false the requirement is essential; it is there to prevent *any* false metaethical statement which implies (a false) ethical conclusion from being relevant to ethics for any additional reasons besides that it has this implication. Unless this requirement is stipulated, this false metaethical statement, together with the true negation of its false ethical implication, would imply *any* statement, since it would be an inconsistency. This would altogether prevent my saying that a particular metaethical statement is morally relevant to a particular ethical statement.

It is important to notice that this concept of relevance to ethics is *ethical*. It takes ethical considerations to decide whether it applies. Hence, in one important sense, the question whether metaethics is "relevant" to ethics is a moral question. It cannot be dealt with in a purely "scientific" manner. The problem is not only a semantic, or an empirical, or a logical one, it falls itself partly within normative ethics. Hence my adoption of the term "moral relevance" as short for "relevance to ethics in an ethical system".

In relation to the concept of moral relevance to ethics I will discuss five separate questions. First of all, is there any truth in the dictum that the emotive theory entails that everything is permitted? Secondly, are theories about language or speech morally relevant? Thirdly, does metaethics make it possible to moralize about our ethical practice? Fourthly, are analyses of ethical concepts morally relevant? Fifthly, are explications morally relevant?

If Emotivism is True then Everything is Permitted?

The emotivists have sometimes been accused of weakening peoples' sense of morality. It has been said that if Stevenson, or Ayer, or Hägerström is right, then everything is permitted.

I have discussed this question earlier and then concluded that *one* line of argument, to the effect that emotivism is inconsistent with any ethical statement, is invalid—this was in Section 3 of this chapter. Now I shall deal with this question in a more general manner. I will discuss various interpretations of the dictum that if emotivism is true then everything is permitted and I will try to see how they may be relevant in relation to the concept of moral relevance.

One way of conceiving such hypothetical norms would be to take them to be material implications. Then it could seem as though my concept of moral relevance to ethics would apply. For does not the emotive theory, together with the ethical premiss that if emotivism is true then everything is permitted imply that everything is permitted? But appearances are here deceptive. The condition in the definiens that the "extra" ethical premisses in the deduction be, if hypothetical, "law-like", will exclude the premiss that if emotivism is true then everything is permitted, conceived as a material implication. My reasons for excluding such statements should be obvious. For the reason why this premiss is true, may be that the emotive theory is false, or that everything as a matter of (moral) fact *is* permitted. Since I have not defined clearly the concept of ethical statement, I hesitate to exclude material implications with a factual antecedent and a normative consequent as non-ethical. This necessitates my condition of law-likeness. This concept is, of course, rather vague and there is not much that I can say in this connection to make it more precise. The idea is that the hypothetical statements be true also in hypothetical, counterfactual, cases. It must be implied by the premiss that if the emotive theory *were* true then everything *would* be permitted. Perhaps this may also be taken as a defining characteristic of "pure hypothetical norm". Nothing is a pure hypothetical norm that does not imply any "subjunctive" reformulation? These, however, are problems I need not enter into.

Another way of conceiving the hypothetical statement that if the emotive theory is true then everything is permitted, would be to take it to be a *logical* implication. This case could not and of course should not, be excluded by definition. Such a statement would be allowed as an "extra" premiss in the deduction of ethical conclusions from metaethical statements. But if a metaethical theory is relevant to ethics in this way, it is also "relevant" in a stronger sense: for now the emotive theory is logically relevant to ethics, it implies ethical conclusions itself. And this idea I have already tried to refute.

A third way of conceiving the hypothetical statement that if the emotive theory is true then everything is permitted is to take it as a pure norm, i.e. to take it to imply that if the emotive theory *would* be true then everything *would* be permitted. Now my concept of moral relevance to ethics would apply, if only this norm were true. But is there anyone who is willing to assent to this statement as a moral principle? I think not. It is not a very reasonable moral view. All the same I think there are *other* statements of this *kind* that are, *prima facie,* more reasonable. I shall discuss one such principle which so to speak "connects" linguistic and moral facts.

The Moral Relevance of Theories about Language or Speech

I think statements combining metaethical and ethical "facts" have sometimes been held to be reasonable. Such principles have, I think, been tacitly presupposed to guarantee the ethical relevance of, say, metaethical statements about language or speech. I refer here to principles of the following sort:

If the concept 'ought' which is used in ethical contexts (or which is expressed by ethical terms, or which is expressed by ethical terms in contexts typical of normative ethics) *is universalizable, then only those particular acts which are of such a kind as acts that ought to be done, ought to be done.*

This statement, complicated though it is, is not quite definite. How is the concept 'ought' really to be identified, and what determines whether a certain particular act is of a certain kind or not? Is it reasonable to hold that *kinds* of acts ought to be done? And what is it for a concept to be universalizable? But let us for the sake of the argument suppose that we have answered all these questions in *some* way (the statement is close, I think, to a view held by R. M. Hare) and that we can imagine *some* reasonable ethical system where *kinds* of acts can have a normative status in particular. Now does this statement, together with a metaethical statment to the effect that the concept 'ought' *is* universalizable, imply certain ethical statements? And does not this prove that the metaethical statement is relevant to ethics?

The answer to the former question, I think, is yes, but the answer to the latter one is, no. For there are no *true* principles of this kind.

The question whether the principle here discussed is valid or not cannot be dealt with rationally unless it is made more clear what *sort* of connection is stated in the principle as holding between the metaethical and the ethical "facts". It is important that the principle is really taken to be a *principle.* The connection must not only be *material.* This is required if any of my concepts of relevance is to apply.

On the other hand the implication stated in the principle must not be taken to be logical unless we are simply going to *presuppose* that metaethical statements are logically relevant to ethics.

Then I think the principle is most naturally taken to be an *ethical* principle of a rather peculiar kind. It is asserted that it is "morally necessary" that if 'ought' is so and so then so and so ought to be done. The principle, then, is ethical for two reasons. First of all because it has ethical implications, at least together with a metaethical principle to the effect that 'ought' is universalizable, and, secondly, because there are no other methods than the methods of normative ethics to decide about its reasonableness.

I do not hold that there *are* some methods to decide whether this principle is valid. This question I leave open.

I think this principle is analogous to principles of epistemology where it is asserted that if so and so is perceived then there is a such and such. The difference is only that the antecedent is about language rather than about mental processes or entities and that it is also a moral concept or piece of language that the antecedent is about. This principle about ethical language has ethical content just like an "ordinary" epistemological principle about perception has empirical content. Just as the principle that if someone thinks he perceives a cat on the mat then there is a cat on the mat (to be even *prima facie* reasonable such principles must, of course, be qualified further) implies, together with a statement to the effect that someone thinks he perceives a cat on the mat, that there is a cat on the mat, so the principle above about 'ought' implies, together with the statement that 'ought' is universalizable, at least that certain acts are *not* obligatory.

I do not hold that this is the only reasonable way of conceiving of principles of epistemology. I *think* it is a reasonable view but alternative views have their advocates; some prefer to regard principles of epistemology as a kind of norm about which statements to accept, for example, and I will not pursue any argument on this point. It is this very conception of epistemological principles that is interesting for my purposes and not, say, the one where these principles are taken to be norms about which statements to accept.

But are there any true or valid or reasonable principles of moral epistemology which "combine" metaethical facts (about language or speech) and ethical "facts"? My thesis is that there are none whatsoever. This is a moral view of mine. I see no way of proving it, but I shall invoke two arguments in support of it.

Firstly, I think that to accept principles of moral epistemology which

176

are founded on linguistic facts or facts about speech would be to allow for moral relativity. Different concepts are used in different cultures, there is not *one* concept, not one way of using ethical language but many. The truths of ethics are, however, absolute.

Secondly, I think it clear that other, competing and alternative principles of moral epistemology, are more reasonable. Language or speech is no source of ethical knowledge. According to my moral intuitions, at least, morality is rather a question of solidarity, sympathy, understanding, and identification with other people; and it is rather from statements about such attitudes of ours that morality must begin, if there is any truth at all in the idea of a kind of "prior" epistemological ethical principles.

I do not pretend that this is altogether clear and comprehensible. I only wish to indicate a line of thought which is quite different from the one that takes facts about language or speech as fundamentals of moral epistemology.

Does a Theory about Language or Speech Allow us to Moralize Rationally about our "Ethical Practice"?

In the foregoing, attempts have been made to deduce ethical conclusions from metaethical statements together with statements to the effect that if a certain metaethical fact obtains then something of a *general* ethical sort is the case. What is derived is an ethical *principle*. A positive finding of *this* kind would, of course, have been of the utmost importance. But none has been found. So perhaps I had better weaken my expectations and search for a case where the ethical statement deduced is about some fact explicitly mentioned in the antecedent of the hypothetical "extra" premiss of the deduction. An example would be if some metaethical statement were, say, to the effect that the concept expressed by "ought" in ethical contexts is 'satisfies the interests of the ruling class' and the "extra" premiss in the deduction of a moral conclusion would be that if the concept expressed by "ought" in moral contexts is 'satisfies the interests of the ruling class' then people ought to think anew about their conception of moral problems and their use of ethical language.

The general idea now is that metaethics may teach one something about the "ethical practice" of people, i.e. about how they conceive of moral problems, what they make the object of their morality and even about what statements they accept, whom they morally blame, whom they morally praise, and so forth. And such information may be taken as the point of departure for a moral evaluation of people's ethical practice. Some of this information does yield ethical conclusions together with very reasonable ethical principles. The principles are *applied* to a reality described by the metaethicist. But this finding, very natural as it is, must not be overestimated.

First of all, ethical conclusions derived in this way give us no "new" or "principal" ethical information. We are only told the results of a simple application of an ethical system to certain facts.

Secondly, the findings here that make possible the deduction of ethical conclusions could in most cases have been obtained by *other* methods than metaethical ones. Metaethics is here one kind of means out of several, by which knowledge about a person's habits, beliefs, activities, and so forth may be gained. And it is probably not the best or the most rational one to use.

Thirdly, I think it hard to think of any *actual* metaethical theory which does bring forward facts of this kind. In which situations would it be a relevant information that the concept 'ought' is prescriptive, that ethical language has a guiding function, and so forth? In order to obtain this kind of relevance one must presuppose that metaethics is practised in a much more *empirical* way than has been usual. Also the domain of application of the theories must be more clearly specified and it must be much more restricted. Perhaps the science here suggested should rather be named "content analysis" than "metaethics".

The Moral Relevance of Analyses of Ethical Concepts

I have distinguished between various sorts of metaethical statements about ethical concepts. Some of them have appeared to be really about ethical language or speech, others about metaphysical, abstract entities (I doubt whether these are at all comprehensible and I have discounted them as not metaethical). Possibly there are also metaethical theories about concepts that are paradoxical since they are trivially true or trivially false. But I have also noticed that one possible sort of metaethical statement about concepts is really about *mental* entities, a kind of "phenomenologically given", entities of individual sort. These are of interest in this section.

G. E. Moore in *Principia Ethica* is perhaps an example of a metaethicist who examines phenomenologically given concepts. At least this is one possible interpretation of him. It is clear that it is not language that interests Moore. What interests him are "definitions which describe the real nature of the object or notion denoted by a word, and which do not merely tell us what the word is used to mean" (p. 7). He also writes:

My business is solely with that object or idea, which I hold, rightly or wrongly, that the word "good" is generally used to stand for. What I want to discover is the nature of that object or idea ... (p. 6)

178

But what kind of entities are "the object or notion denoted by a word" and "that object or idea ... that the word is generally used to stand for"? Are "notions" and "ideas" *mental* entities, according to Moore, or are they abstract, "Platonic" entities? At least I think *some* reasons tell in support of the view that they are mental. I think the following quotation weakly indicates this:

Every one does in fact understand the question 'Is this good'? When he thinks of it, *his state of mind* is different from what it would be, were he asked 'Is this pleasant, or desired, or approved'? It has a distinct meaning for him, even though he may not recognise in what respect it is distinct. Whenever he thinks of 'intrinsic value', or 'intrinsic worth', or says that a thing 'ought to exist', he has *before his mind* the unique object—the unique property of things—which I mean by 'good'. Everybody is *constantly aware of this notion,* although he may never become aware at all that it is different from other notions of which he is also aware. (p. 17, italicized by me)

Of course this may also be interpreted in a "Platonistic" manner. I chose the "mentalistic" interpretation because I think it as reasonable as the "Platonic" one and more fruitful than the "Platonic" one for my purpose in this investigation.

According to some empiricistically minded philosophers, among whom I count G. E. Moore, there are certain concepts, properties or notions that are simple and immediately "given;" you "apprehend" them through your senses.

The concept 'yellow' is taken by Moore to be of this kind. These properties cannot be learned otherwise than by ostension. While you can be taught what a unicorn is by a definition you must be confronted with something yellow to learn what yellow is. Such properties, according to Moore, "are simply something which you think of or perceive, and to anyone who cannot think of or perceive them, you can never, by any definition, make their nature known". (p. 7)

G. E. Moore holds a similar view of the notion 'good'. He writes:

My point is that 'good' is a simple notion, just as 'yellow' is a simple notion ... (p. 7)

The parallel is not, however, exact. The concept 'good' is not given to you through your *senses*. It is, in Moore's terminology, "non-natural". All the same it is directly presented to you, you apprehend the goodness in a direct manner. Moore sometimes uses the word "intuition" for this apprehension. It is not at all clear in Moore's philosophy what exactly it is to intuit goodness. Is it a *rational* procedure (an act of thinking?) Or is it due to a peculiar "extra" sensory capacity? These are problems into which I will not enter and need not enter since the act of *appre-*

hension, according to Moore, is always one and the same. If a notion is presented to you through your senses or through intuition the act of apprehending this notion is one and the same (cf. Moore's "The Status of Sense-Data" in *Philosophical Studies,* pp. 172–4 about this.)

From the point of view of a philosophy like G. E. Moore's in *Principia Ethica* I think it could be tempting to take the following argument to be valid and also to assert that the premisses are true:

(1)   The notion 'yellow' is simple and directly apprehended

(2)   If a notion G is simple and directly apprehended there is something that is G

(3)   Hence, there is something yellow.

But if the argument (1) and (2), hence (3) is sound and the premisses true, is not also the following "parallel" argument valid as well and based on true premisses?

(1:1)   The notion 'good' is simple and directly apprehended

(2)   If a notion G is simple and directly apprehended there is something that is G

(3:1)   Hence, there is something good.

My argument here is rather speculative but my point is not so much that my interpretation is the only possible one from a descriptive point of view but that it is a fruitful one. A sceptic philosopher like Hume does not, for example, accept (2), or, at least, he does not know of any way of *showing* (2) valid. In spite of this he accepts the distinction between simple and complex ideas, or notions. He also holds a view which, if true, makes (2) somewhat more plausible than it might seem elsewhere. He holds, in his *Treatise of Human Nature,* that:

... every simple idea has a simple impression, which resembles it; and every simple impression a correspondent idea. That idea of red, which we form in the dark, and that impression, which strikes our eyes in sun-shine, differ only in degree, not in nature. (p. 51)

Impressions, according to Hume, arise "in the soul originally, from unknown causes" (p. 55) and are those "perceptions, which enter with most force and violence" (p. 49). Ideas, on the other hand, are "faint images" of impressions in thinking and reasonings (p. 49).

The point in (2) is that if a notion, X, is simple it must be presented to the mind through sensory or intuitive contact with something that is

X or else it is a replica of a notion that was originally presented to the mind in either of these direct ways. Hume himself hesitates to assent to (2). The "cause" of simple impressions is always concealed from the point of view of a philosophy like Hume's. A philosopher who is more bold about ontology and epistemological matters is R. M. Chisholm. In his *Theory of Knowledge* he assents to a principle which is similar to (2) in certain respects. This principle does not make the qualifications (2) makes that a notion must be simple. But instead something must be believed to be perceived to possess the quality in question:

If there is a certain sensible characteristic F such that S believes that he perceives something to be F, then it is *evident* to S that he is perceiving something to have that characteristic F, and also that there is something that is F (p. 47)

I think (2) is as reasonable as the view of Chisholm's and closer to the spirit of the realism of G. E. Moore. For while Moore does not accept Hume's sceptical views about the external world he *does* use his distinction between simple and complex notions.

Now two questions arise. If the latter line of argument is valid and if (2) is true does this show, then, that any metaethical statement is morally relevant? And is (2) true?

The premiss (1:1) seems to be metaethical, hence I will not question its truth. It is asserted about a mental individual entity that it is simple and that it is directly presented to the mind. There is a certain ambiguity here, however, for what does it mean that a mental entity is "directly apprehended"? One could think that this means that *as* a certain "idea" (which is mental) is present in the consciousness of a person he is (or must have been) directly aware *that* something possesses the "corresponding" (abstract) property. It is here not easy to tell what "corresponding" means to any degree of exactness. But it is also possible to take (2) to imply a sense-data theory where the mental idea itself is the *object* of the awareness. In the latter case (1:1) really is a metaethical principle. Here something is asserted about a mental individual entity and not about anything else. In the former case I hesitate to use the word "metaethics". For even if the thesis that 'good' is simple here seems to be metaethical (about a mental entity) the thesis that it may be directly presented to the mind, "apprehended", is not. This statement is to the effect that *when* I have a certain experience there exists something which I am aware *of*. And this is a statement of ontology, not of metaethics.

The premiss (2) allows of two directions of interpretation corresponding to the two interpretations of (1:1). It is the sense-data interpretation

181

that interests me here. The point, then, is that if a notion is simple and directly presented to the mind, "apprehended", then there is something of the same sort as my experience, whatever "same sort" may mean here. This is a principle which, I think, to some extent belongs to ethics. If adapted to ethical concepts it is a principle of "ethical epistemology". And together with the metaethical view that there are ethical concepts that are simple and directly apprehended it implies that there is something ethical. There are no methods besides the ones of normative ethics to decide about its reasonableness. So I will accept it as an ethical system in which the deduction from (1:1) to (3:1) is made.

I think it clear, now, that (3:1) does really follow from (1:1) and (2), if these premises are consistently taken to be of a sense-data sort. But does this show that (1:1) is morally relevant. I think not. And the reason for this is that (2) is not valid.

I think the whole idea of simple notions suspect. It is hard to see what it really amounts to. But whatever it is one is presented with when one becomes aware of such a mental individual entity I think there is no good reason why *it* should have properties such that something in the (non-natural or natural) world would have to be of a certain (or even "similar") kind. This view of the process of knowledge is both outdated (like the sense-data theory on the whole) and false. And this goes for Chisholm's theory too, which only stresses another quality of the sense-data instead of their simplicity and takes this quality (that the mental experience is thought to be a perception) to guarantee that the world possesses a certain (and similar) property. Our correct ideas are not "marked" in any special manner.

I cannot offer any definite argument on this point. The complications are of course immense. A discussion of all the relevant problems would need a work on its own. Here my conclusion is to be based on a certain general epistemological *presupposition*. This presupposition has also, if I am right, an *ethical* aspect.

What has here been discussed is but *one* possible instance of a general type of argument. The moral conclusion was here very weak, that there is *something* good. But the argument could of course be designed to show metaethical statements morally relevant to much stronger ethical statements. That I intuit X to be good could, for example, in the fashion of Chisholm, be taken as a ground for the statement that X is good.

But since already the argument discussed with its *weak* conclusion turned out to be based on false premisses this is even more obviously the case with these other arguments.

The Moral Relevance of Explications

For the sake of completeness I will also in this connection mention the explicative metaethical theories. I think it however clear that these theories lack moral relevance to ethics; they are simply not designed for such relevance.

Explications have a descriptive aspect; they imply or presuppose something about language or speech. A certain term is assigned a meaning that is not "too far" from the meaning it "ordinarily" possesses. This descriptive aspect shares the lack of moral relevance with other theories about language or speech. Since explications are not based on empirical investigations about the word-use of explicitly mentioned, restricted groups of persons, they do not at all make possible a moral evaluation of the ethical practice of anyone.

Explications have also a normative aspect; a "new" concept is proposed to take the place of an "old" concept in certain contexts. These proposals, however, are not based on *ethical* considerations but on considerations of methodological (theoretical or practical) convenience. I will have more to say about this later. For the moment it must suffice to conclude that since these recommendations are about language or conceptual frameworks—as ethical statements are normally not—and since what is said about these metaethical objects is not ethical, these recommendations do not imply any ethical conclusions, either alone or together with any ethical principles.

Conclusion

My conclusions about the moral relevance of metaethics or, to be more exact, the relevance to ethics in an ethical system of metaethics, may be summarized in five points.

First of all I have held that the question whether metaethics is "relevant" to ethics, in one reasonable interpretation, is an *ethical* question. This I think is an important finding of its own. This means that to solve my problem is not a purely "scientific" matter.

Secondly, I have concluded that metaethical statements about language or speech lack moral relevance in all specific manners. There is no "bridge" between linguistic facts and "ethical facts". The opposite view implies moral relativism and misrepresents the nature of the sources of ethical "knowledge".

Thirdly, I have held that a metaethical science *is* conceivable, which analyses speech, and which *is* morally relevant, though not in any specific manner. Such a metaethic would analyse speech in such a manner that information relevant to a moral evaluation of someone's ethical "practice" could be gained from it. Conclusions relevant to a moral assessment would be gained about which statements certain moral agents accepted and so forth. But no actual metaethical theories have this form. And the knowledge about people's ethical practice that may be gained from them, could probably as well or better be gained from sociological and psychological studies.

Fourthly, I have asserted that metaethical theories about ethical concepts, conceived of as mental individual entities, lack moral relevance. The premises required in the deduction from metaethical theories about mentally given notions or concepts of ethical conclusions, are false. Our correct impressions are not marked in any special way, like this line of thought presupposes. If I am right in my contention that principles of ethical epistemology are ethical my conclusion here is also ethical.

Fifthly, I have concluded that explications lack moral relevance to ethics. They are designed to have relevance to ethics in quite another way.

5. Conclusions about the Pragmatic Relevance to Ethics of Metaethics

My attempts to find out about the relevance to ethics of metaethics have hitherto been concentrated on *logical* relations between metaethical and ethical statements. But as we saw, for example when discussing F. A. Olafson's view of the problem, relations between on the one hand acceptances, or ways of accepting and on the other hand attitudes towards statements, may also be of interest for my purposes. These sorts of relations I have called "pragmatic" relations.

I shall now in various ways try to make precise the concept of pragmatic relevance to ethics by giving various specifications of it and by defining certain crucial terms. Here, as before, I intend my construction of concepts to satisfy my conditions of descriptive reasonableness, specificity, and fruitfulness.

Perhaps the most natural way to take the concept of pragmatic relevance is to have the concept apply when, and only when, the acceptance of some metaethical statement contributes to, or necessitates, in some way, the acceptance of some ethical statement. This, however, is only a rough *line* of interpretation, a line that may be developed in various possible ways. Furthermore, this line is not the only possible one.

One gets different "versions" of this interpretation if one gives different meanings to "necessitates" (or "contributes"). Even the term "acceptance" allows for different, alternative, interpretations. And the strength of the concept can be varied, in ways similar to those tried in relation to the logical concept of relevance.

The concept of pragmatic relevance to ethics is taken to apply when one acceptance necessitates, or contributes to, another. But how are we to identify acceptances? I think a too narrow conception of relevance will be the result if we only identify them by specifying which statement is accepted. I think sometimes it could be the case that even if one is not made to accept any particular ethical statement as one accepts a metaethical theory the *change* of metaethical views may have this effect, or a particular change, say, from supernaturalism to some sort of emotivism, may have effects on your acceptance of ethical statements. But again the *effects* need not necessarily be that you accept certain statements and not any others. The effects may rather be, more generally, a change of your ethical beliefs, or even of your *attitudes* towards your own favored ethical views. The result may be, for example, that you are less serious about which statements of ethics to accept, according as you accept a certain metaethical view.

The Strength of the Concept

The strength of the relation between the acceptance of a metaethical statement and the acceptance of an ethical statement may vary in ways similar to the ones discussed in relation to logical relevance to ethics. The *necessity* or *contribution* may be taken to be conditional. The conditions upon which it depends may be some true empirical statements in general, or it may be required that the person involved accept certain statements *besides* the metaethical ones.

There is also another way of weakening the concept of pragmatic relevance. For where is one to search for the acceptances in question? Are *all* acceptances relevant to the inquiry, or only those made by not-too-special people in not-too-special situations? Different answers to this question yield different concepts of varying strength.

What Kind of Necessity or Contribution?

The concepts of necessity or contribution could be taken to refer to some sort of logical, empirical, statistical, moral, rational, or some other type of relation. But this is perhaps a bit "metaphorical". What is intended is that, if the concept is to apply there must be some true or correct "law" to the effect that if the metaethical statement is accepted then also the ethical statement is, or should be accepted, or, at least, that the acceptance of the metaethical statement contributes to this result. This "law" may for example be a moral principle, an empirical law, a statistical statement, or a principle of rationality. Here the list could be continued with some imagination, and I see no reason not to define the concept inclusively on this point.

The Concept of Acceptance

The interpretation of "acceptance" is problematical and, since such an interpretation should be applicable to ethical statements as well as to factual ones, it cannot be achieved without taking a stand on some highly controversial metaethical problems.

One interpretation of the term "acceptance" is indicated by the following contextual definition. A person p accepts the statement s at the time t if, and only if, p at t holds s to be true. This line of interpretation seems natural in relation to factual statements but will it also hold for normative statements? And how do you decide whether a person really holds a certain statement to be true?

Since the nature of acceptance of ethical statements is a matter of dispute among metaethicists I will concentrate for a moment on acceptance of empirical statements and then see what may be generalized to ethical statements. By what "test" are we to decide whether a person at some time holds a certain statement to be true?

A natural but perhaps rather a naive answer is: just ask him. Of course this method must not be handled uncritically. You must, for example, take every care to ensure that the testee has really understood what you mean by your question, that he is not trying to cheat you and so forth. These are practical problems, however, and I think they could be adequately handled with ordinary scientific methods. But there is a more theoretical problem here too.

Let us suppose that we wish to know whether the Swedish Prime Minister Olof Palme in 1972 held the statement that close relations between Sweden and the Common Market would increase unemployment in Sweden to be true. Let us furthermore suppose that we asked him and he said, no. We then took every care to ascertain that he was not trying for opportunistic reasons to cheat us and that he had really understood our question. Let us also, hypothetically, assume that we found out that all precautions of this sort had been taken. Would we then have ascertained that Olof Palme did not accept the statement in question?

I can imagine a kind of objection to this conclusion. The rationale of it

186

would be the following argument: To be sure Mr. Palme *believes* that he does not accept the statement in question. But this cannot be the very last word about this matter. For did he not accept the statements $p_1, \ldots, p_n$ as well? And did he not accept the empirical laws $l_1, \ldots, l_n$ as well? And do not $l_1, \ldots, l_n$ in conjunction with $p_1, \ldots, p_n$ imply that close relations to the Common Market would increase unemployment? Suppose that the correct answers to these questions is, yes, as I think, as a matter of fact, that it is for some choices of $p_{i:s}$ and $l_{i:s}$. Then did not Mr Palme all the same accept the statement?

There seems to be three ways out of the dilemma set by this objection.

First of all you may withdraw the first conclusion and insist that Palme *did* accept the statement considered. The test is then supplied by the device that also all statements implied by the statements the testee has accepted are accepted by him.

Secondly, you may keep to your original conclusion that Mr Palme does not accept the statement. You must then note that Mr Palme here has appeared to be inconsistent in the sense that he refuses to accept all the implications of his favored views.

Thirdly, you may not only withdraw your original conclusion but also conclude that not only does Mr Palme accept the statement under consideration but he is also accepting its negation. For if you ask him about *it* he would certainly say that he does hold it to be true.

The third possibility is obviously not very fruitful to my purposes. For as soon as a person is "inconsistent" in his views he will, according to this test, accept *every* statement. The second possibility seems to be fruitful. This test really singles out a definite class of sentences or statements in relation to any person and it leads to no strange results. The first possibility is not quite clear. It is here presupposed that there is some means to guarantee that no inconsistencies are accepted. But how could this be guaranteed when one uses two independent criteria, viz. the questionnaire and the logical deduction procedure? Only if one has a method to decide which statement to dismiss when one arrives at inconsistencies could this be guaranteed. But any such criterion seems to be somewhat arbitrary. So I will also dismiss this line of interpretation.

I must now say something about the difficult problem of defining "acceptance" of *ethical* statements. Will the "operationalization" I have just sketched be adequate here too? Objectivistically minded philosophers would answer this question affirmatively, but others would hold that my test could not be used at all. They would hold that people would not at all understand what was meant by sentences like "Is it *true* that one ought not to boil one's wife in oil"?

I am not quite sure how these objections should be rationally assessed but I am inclined to think they are unsound. Because of my uncertainty, however, and in order to make my position as strong as possible, I shall suggest an alternative test for acceptances of ethical statements. My test is meant to explicate and "paraphrase" some ideas by non-cognitivistically minded metaethicists such as R. M. Hare[3] and P. L. Gardiner.[4] I suppose that the statement to be tested is to the effect that the action A ought to be performed whenever the situation S arises. Then a person p accepts at the time t the ethical statement that A ought to be performed whenever the situation S arises if, and only if, p is at t in such a state of mind that should the situation S arise at t, p would see to it that A were performed or he would feel remorse for not doing so or think he is unable to see this or lack knowledge about the fact that S had arisen at t and so forth but would see to this if it were not for this belief that it is impossible or for this lack of knowledge and so forth. The list of "excuses" may be continued somewhat with a little imagination.

But even this concept has its difficulties and obvious drawbacks. First of all it may seem unacceptable to an objectivistically minded philosopher, for what have these *attitudes* and dispositions to *act* of the testee to do with his *acceptances,* they would ask. Secondly, the concept is not adaptable to evaluative ethical statements. But perhaps the latter difficulty could be met by putting the stress, in these cases, not on what the testee is prepared to *do* but on what he is prepared to *feel*?

The Adoption of a Concept

I have now indicated quite a few concepts of acceptance. As for the latest discussed lines of interpretation I can see no need for a choice of one to the exclusion of the other. If it can be proved that metaethics is relevant to ethics in the sense that if you accept certain metaethical statements you must also hold certain ethical views to be true then this is of no little ethical interest. If, on the other hand, it can be proved that if you accept certain metaethical statements you must also, in the way described, "conform" to certain ethical statements, then this too is of some ethical importance. My examination will include both kinds of possible relations.

I am only going to be restrictive over the matter of tests complementing the questionnaire method. I shall *not* count as accepted all the im-

---

[3] Cf. *The Language of Morals* pp. 1, 13, 18–20, 141–4, 168–72.
[4] Cf. "On Assenting to a Moral Principle".

plications of the statements that have been found to be accepted by the method of the questionnaire.

This latter choice brings with it the consequence that the *pragmatic* concept of relevance is not comparable with the logical one in regard to logical strength. The fact that q follows logically from p does not guarantee that p is pragmatically relevant to q. We are here confronted with a concept of a different *kind* from the logical concepts.

Are there any Metaethical Theories that are Empirically Pragmatically Relevant to Ethics?

Metaethical statements may be "pragmatically" relevant to ethics in the sense that, as a statistical or empirical fact, or in conformity with some empirical law, people who accept the metaethical statement also accept some ethical statement (or this relation may hold between *changes* of metaethical views and certain attitudes towards ethical statements, and so forth). These effects of acceptances of metaethical statements I will call "empirical". They may be produced either in a *rational* or in a *non-rational* way; this is a distinction I drew when I discussed the views of F. A. Olafson, in Chapter IV. An effect is rationally produced if it obtains because of the recognition of some good reason; otherwise it is non-rational.

The discussion of rational empirical relevance to ethics is very closely linked to a discussion of moral, prudential, etc. pragmatic relevance. For rational empirical effects are effects of the realization of the "fact" that, if one has accepted p, then one ought, for moral, prudential, aesthetic, purely rational, or other reasons, also accept q.

Empirical Rational Pragmatic Effects

The reasons why those who accept a certain metaethical statement, say that "good" means *desired,* should also accept a moral statement, say that whatever is desired is good, is not that the latter statement is *implied* (logically, or in an empirical or ethical system) by the metaethical statement. If this had been the case there would be some good rational reasons for accepting the latter if one had accepted the former statement. But the foregoing discussion has shown that there are no logical relations of this sort between metaethics and ethics. The reasons then, if there are any good ones, must say something not about the statement you have accepted (about its logical properties) but about your accepting it. Are there any reasons of this sort that are good reasons? This, again, is not a purely scientific question, but partly a question of normative ethics. I think all the same that it is possible to answer it in a manner conformable with all actual moral positions that I know of, at least.

There *are* contexts, I think, where acceptance of statements has a kind of moral significance; the very fact that you have accepted certain statements brings you into a kind of ethical "power-field". I have, for example, often been confronted with arguments to the following effect:

—You who wish to smash the "bourgeois state", imprison the capitalists and establish the dictatorship of the proletariat, you have indeed no right to complain when the "bourgeois democracy" is limited a little by your having to pay a fine for having arranged illegal political meetings.

The idea underlying such reasoning seems to be that whoever accepts *p* and *q* and *r,* where these statements are, in some sense, "part" of a system of statements, must also accept all the other statements of the system. Not because these are implied by *p* and *q* and *r* but because the public assent to *p* and *q* and *r,* because of some conventions, gives the hearers to understand, or gives to them the right to infer, that you embrace all the statements of the system these statements are "part" of. By accepting *p* and *q* and *r* you publicly announce that you are of a certain *kind,* belongs to a certain *group* of persons. Not to take the consequences of this is very much like lying. "Those who support the dictatorship of the proletariat *are* not *really* interested in democracy".

If one disregards the fact that the "system" of which the statement about the bourgeois state and so on are "parts" is polemically misconceived then I think this idea to some extent sound. There are situations where acceptance *oblige*—especially, perhaps, in political contexts. But could anything similar be the case in metaethics? I think not. There are no "systems" containing metaethical *and* normative views of this sort. And, more important, the "act" of accepting metaethical statements is not of a, necessarily public character. The same holds, obviously, for other kinds of normative reasons, like prudential, aesthetic, juridical, and so forth. A sort of insitutionalization and perhaps also "ritualization" of the use of language is needed if these kinds of reasons are to apply—in any *reasonable* theory of ethics, prudence, aesthetics, and so forth. This is a normative conclusion of mine but not, I think, a very controversial one.

I can think of only one, rather indirect exception to this negative conclusion. If one accepts, say, that among the group one belongs to oneself no one has ever been called "good" unless he has white skin and blue eyes, then the acceptance of this statement could perhaps create a ground for one's thinking twice about one's favored ethical views. But this exception is rather indirect and not specific to metaethics. It is not really the fact *that* one knows a bit more about one's ethical convictions that is important. It is the content of the statements one has accepted that is important. The metaethical result suggests that something has gone wrong with your ethical deliberation. Metaethics is here a source of knowledge of ethical sociology. But this knowledge could as well, or perhaps even better, have been achieved by ordinary and more "direct" sociological methods.

Empirical Non-Rational Pragmatic Relevance

There are, however, quite a few testimonies to the effect that metaethics *has* had empirical pragmatic effects. Let us consider some examples which I have taken from discussions with colleagues describing their intellectual development.

There is one, whom we have met in Chapter I when discussing the concept of ethical relevance, who used to be a supernaturalist. What was right was determined by the will of God. As she read Hägerström she, all of a sudden, became an emotivist. This was a moment of liberation. Not that different norms were accepted now. But the attitude was quite different. Ethical statements were not any more held to be true or false, descriptive of any reality. Acceptance of them were held to be only the result of emotive, partly subconscious, processes. A detached view of morality resulted; a feeling of irresponsibility seemed to dominate ethical argumentation and deliberation. A moral stand seemed not any longer to be taken by the subject; it was rather the self that was taken by a moral view; it became stabilized in a moral position. Very soon the sense of liberty degenerated into moral chaos.

There is another who used to be an emotivist but, gradually, began to find universal prescriptivism of Hare's sort more reasonable. This did not change his moral views. He remained a utilitarian. But the way he accepted utilitarianism was changed. Utilitarianism was not only something that "happened" to him—he had deliberately to *choose* it and *argue* in defense of it. This made him take morality more seriously, he says, so that his moral views became more of an integrated part of his very character.

There is a third one who used to be an emotivist too, but slowly began to realize, as she puts it, that non-naturalism, of an objectivist kind similar to the theory of Moore, was correct. This was somewhat of

191

a shock. She suddenly realized that she had never been in earnest in moral affairs. This had resulted in a lack of clarity and comprehensiveness in her ethical beliefs. She did not really have a morality before. Now all this was changed. Her view of morality now is the view of a scientist. She has begun to study normative ethics systematically and she has made, she assures me, improvements. These improvements have been possible, she says, because she has systematically kept her feelings and attitudes clearly apart from her moral studies. She tries not to be motivated by anything but a desire to find the truth.

What should be said about these examples?

First of all, these effects here described, are not only non-rational but *irrational*. For they result from a mistaken belief that they are founded on good reasons. Metaethical statements lack the kind of relevance they are supposed to possess in the examples. Statements about language or speech are not relevant to the question whether arguments could be given for ethical positions or whether there are any moral facts or a possibility of finding the truth about moral questions. It is because of a mistaken belief in such connections that the pragmatic effects have ensued.

Secondly, I think it very probable that such effects really are, as a matter of fact, produced by acceptances of metaethical theories. But I think also that these effects do not exhibit any clear pattern. If one person takes emotivism as liberating him another takes it as binding him even harder. If one person becomes interested in ethics when he accepts a non-naturalist objectivist metaethics, another loses his interest in it for the same reason. Being the results of confused thinking all these effects lack consistency.

All the same I think something should be added on this point. My conclusion may seem more hard to accept than it should really seem because there is a crucial distinction that has not been made quite clearly, viz. the distinction between metaethics and ethical epistemology. I shall now say something about this distinction.

Metaethics and Ethical Epistemology

Metaethics, as it is conceived of in this book, is somewhat of an "abstraction". I have interpreted metaethicists as if they were doing what they *say* they are doing. Their own conception of what they do is of course not altogether incorrect. But it is obviously too narrow in many cases. When metaethical theses are put forward they are, almost in every case, supplemented by normative statements and, above all, statements of "moral epistemology". My discussion of statements about ethical statements has shown that the distinction between metaethics and moral epistemology is hard to make precise. The epistemological aspect and the ethical aspect of the theories are perhaps explicitly denied by the theorists, or they are at least not present in explicit formulations. But they are all the same there to be discovered, as presuppositions, or as implicit in certain arguments, or in some other way. Metaethical theory is seldom "pure"—a reason for this, I think, is that it actually lacks relevance to ethics.

When I deny that metaethics is logically or pragmatically relevant to ethics I do not deny that other "aspects" of the theories suggested by the metaethicists are relevant to ethics. On the contrary, I think in particular that the problem of where to find the "sources" of ethical "knowledge", the problem of "principles of evidence" in ethics, and so forth, are of the utmost importance for ethics. Solutions to these problems are relevant to ethics in a strict logical way. I have discussed such statements before when I discussed whether they constitute a system in which metaethics is relevant to ethics. I have concluded that principles of ethical epistemology, viz. statements to the effect that something is evidence for ethical statements, *are* normative. They imply negative or hypothetical norms and together with empirical statements, they imply positive, categorical normative statements. I have also held that there is no other method besides the methods of ethics to decide about the reasonableness of these principles. Here I think there is a field of investigation that is much more fruitful from the point of view of normative ethics than is metaethics.

I think it is because metaethical statements are confused with statements of moral or ethical epistemology that many might protest against my conclusion that metaethical statements lack pragmatic relevance to ethics. If the emotive theory, universal prescriptivism and intuitionism are taken, not to assert anything about ethical language, speech, or thought, but about where to find evidence in support of ethical statements, then these theories *are* relevant to ethics. The crucial distinction here is between (metaethical) theories that assert that *what* is expressed (ethical statements) by ethical language in ethical contexts, is so and so, and (epistemological or ontological) theories about ethical statements identified independently, i.e. where the "statements about statements" are only a way of talking indirectly about "moral realities themselves".

The problems moral epistemology is intended to solve, cannot be divorced from the study of ethical problems themselves. Here I agree with those who hold that something has gone wrong with modern ethical theory in so far as it is pursued in isolation from normatively ethical problems. But the point should not be so much that metaethics should be studied in closer contact with normative ethics—although this is true too and I will say more about this later—but that something which *is* closer to normative ethics should be studied *rather* than metaethics.

Conclusion

I have in this section put forward the thesis that metaethical theories lack empirical rational pragmatic relevance to ethics. This I have argued for by trying to demonstrate that there are no good reasons for changing one's ethical beliefs when one changes one's metaethical ones. And since there are no good reasons for such a change there cannot be any change which has taken place because of the realization of any good reasons.

My conclusion on this point is not normatively neutral. I have, I think, not made any *controversial* normative claims, however. The acceptance of metaethical statements does not "create" any obligations in any normative system that I know of.

This result includes also the thesis that there are no metaethical theories that are morally, esthetically, or prudentially pragmatically relevant to ethics. For if some metaethical statements *were* relevant in this way, there *would* be reasons for a change of one's ethical views if one had accepted such statements.

As for non-rational effects of the acceptance of metaethical statements, I have admitted that they obtain. But these effects are not only non-rational, but also irrational. They exhibit no consistent pattern. This instance of the idea of pragmatic relevance does not satisfy my requirement of fruitfulness for concepts of relevance to ethics. It is of no importance for the decision whether metaethics is worth pursuing whether such pragmatic effects obtain or not.

In this context I have recalled a distinction between metaethics and ethical epistemology. I have made the conjecture that it is because these two kinds of theories are confused that my conclusion about the lack of rational pragmatic relevance to ethics of metaethics seems odd. In passing I made the political statement about research that ethical epistemology is a more fruitful field of investigation than is metaethics.

6. Is Metaethics Therapeutically Relevant to Ethics?

My conclusions, based on an examination of various actual metaethical theories and possible types of metaethics with regard to their relevance to ethics has been almost exclusively negative. What has gone wrong? Is metaethics after all no "prolegomenon" or no "propaedeutic" to the study of normative problems, to use Sumner's terms in "Normative Ethics and Metaethics?"

Before drawing that rather drastic, and perhaps also counterintuitive, conclusion we had better once more try to weaken the concept of ethical relevance. Are my conclusions hitherto perhaps the result of the application of too strong concepts? Perhaps there are more "indirect" but still interesting (for my purpose) connections between metaethics and normative ethics? I think there are at least some moral philosophers who are willing to concede the statement that there are. For example Stevenson, who denies the possibility of deriving ethical conclusions from his metaethical theory (even if not quite consistently), states in *Ethics and Language,* that

The purpose of an analytical or methodological study, whether of science or of ethics, is always indirect. It hopes to send others to their tasks with clearer heads and less wasteful habits of investigation. (p. 1)

Also Hare seems to recognize some kind of weak or indirect relation between metaethics and ethics; he writes in *Freedom and Reason,* just to mention one relevant passage:

The function of moral philosophy—or at any rate the hope with which I study it—is that of helping us to think better about moral questions by exposing the logical structure of the language in which this thought is expressed. (p. v)

I will call these vaguely characterized types of relevance to ethics "therapeutic".

A natural way, in this context, of taking the concept of therapy is to let it apply whenever an "influence" on a person's character or manners in ethical contexts, i.e. on his "ethical practice", is taking place and this influence is a means to (or a hindrance[5] to!) the realization of some end. This end may be conceived of in two ways. Either the aim of the meta-ethical investigations is to facilitate the solving of practical, moral (I here for a moment depart from my habit of using "moral" and "ethical" synonymously) problems, i.e. to facilitate the answering of particular questions of the sort 'What ought to be done in this particular situation?' or 'What shall I do now?,' or the aim is to make easier the answering of properly ethical questions, i.e. to facilitate the answering of questions of the sort 'What ethical principles are valid?' or 'What kind of states of

---

[5] Karl Popper writes, for example, in *The Open Society and Its Enemies II:* "... not only does this concentration on the problem of meaning fail to establish precision, it is itself the main source of vagueness, ambiguity, and confusion". (p. 19)

affairs ought to be brought into existence?' Consequently we can distinguish between two sorts of therapeutic relevance to "ethics" (in my ordinary sense) i.e. one which takes as its aim the facilitation of the solving of "moral" problems and the other which takes as its aim the facilitation of the solving of "ethical" problems—in my now adopted sense of the terms "moral" and "ethical".

More has to be said to clarify by what means these ends are thought to be furthered but already at this point I wish to defend the thesis that metaethics is *not* therapeutically relevant to ethics in the sense that it facilitates in any direct way the solving of moral problems. The reasons for this are, I think, rather obvious from the following example. I have myself some years ago solved a moral problem in the sense that I have reached a preliminary conclusion about what to do; after years of deliberation I have made a decision whether to join the Communist Party or not. During the earlier part of this process of deliberation—the first five years—I had not any contact with metaethics. The next four years I deliberated in an ever more intimate contact with and was much more conscious of various metaethical theories. In which way did this facilitate my decision? Or was the decision made harder to make? Then, in what way? As far as I can see, in no way. For what has been problematic has never, I think, had anything to do with "typical ethical terms", or something of the sort. I even doubt whether I have to any considerable degree been using such terms. What has been problematic has rather been how to get access to relevant knowledge about the Party, its degree of bureaucratization, contact with the working masses, ideological and theoretical line, and so forth, how to get access to relevant knowledge about the consequences of various alternative choices that are possible, how to give to strictly personal inclinations their due weight, how to foresee what would be the most probable effects on my character of alternative decisions and so forth. But ethical terms or ethical concepts—never. And I think this example typical. What it shows, I think, is that even in cases of very important decisions there is something fundamentally wrong with the usual analogy where the relation of the methodology of empirical sciences to these sciences themselves is taken to be reflected or mirrored in the relation of metaethics to ethics, where "ethics" is now interpreted as *morals* (c.f. the quoted passage from Stevenson's *Ethics and Language* above). This analogy is not correct. While sciences like physics are always very highly specialized and conceptually complicated, morals is of direct concern for anyone who has some sensibility and is capable of feeling solidarity. Conceptual confusion may attach to scientific statements and problems but hardly to moral ones. I

196

am even willing to venture upon the hypothesis that most moral problems are solved without any use of moral language at all, perhaps even without any attempt at linguistic formulation. This conclusion gains credibility from the fact that even *ethics* seems to be to a great extent *not scientific*. I see no evidence for the idea that our ethical knowledge grows by advances in terminology or conceptual framework. Is there even such a thing as a growth of ethical or moral knowledge? Can moral insights be accumulated? In a way, yes—and in another way, no. Each person may accumulate moral knowledge from his own practical experiences, I believe, and as his experience grows he can to some extent "share" the experiences of others. But this knowledge is never cast in a scientific structure, his insights never get that kind of order. His knowledge does not allow for communication to any great extent.

The conclusion about therapeutic relevance to morals is valid, I think, no matter how we conceive of metaethics, whether as an activity of some sort or as a mere acceptance of certain statements as true. At the same time this may be thought to be rather insignificant, since the example is a bit artificial. In most cases—and in the exemplified one too, to be sure —it is practically impossible to distinguish or separate the moral problem from the ethical ones. This is because one's ethical system is never completed. One's ethical knowledge, no matter how private, grows (to put it optimistically) with every practical decision. And, of course, this growth to *some* extent takes the form of explicitly formulated ethical "systems" or "rules". Ethical and moral deliberation take place together. Thus ethical therapy, the possibility of which I do not wish now to question, would have some practical significance if it would obtain. (I am not at all sure *how* significant, for the reasons mentioned above. Perhaps it is only a cultural idiosyncracy that makes us overestimate normative, "systematic", ethics. As one realizes the ultimate lack of precision and definiteness of even the most reasonable ethical systems, one sometimes wonders whether there is much gained by them. It seems to me as though the more "closed" a theory is in *one* respect—like ideal utilitarianism in some versions with respect to the criteria of rightness—the more "open" the theories are in others—like ideal utilitarianism with respect to its axiology.)

Let us now concentrate on the problem of whether metaethics ever has a "therapeutic relevance" to ethics—and hence also indirectly to morals. There are, I think, various lines of thought about this question suggested in the literature. There are various notions of the kind of therapy alleged to obtain relative to the specified aim of improvement of our ethical practice. Take for example the passage quoted from Ste-

197

venson above. There it seems as though the idea was that common sense suffers from conceptual and semantic confusion. The metaethicist saves common sense from this confusion and, hence, gives to common sense "less wasteful habits of investigation" in relation to ethics or morals. This line of thought may appear in various forms and I shall deal with some of them presently. A somewhat different view of the kind of therapy in question seems to be implicit in the passage quoted from Hare above. There metaethics is taken as improving your ethical practice, not by saving you from confusion but in a more "positive" way, by providing *instruments* for a more effective ethical thought. I shall deal with forms of this line of thought in the section after the next one.

It should be noticed that what has here been considered as two different lines of thought are rather complementary than alternative views of the relation between metaethics and ethics. Furthermore the distinction between them is rather vague. Hence, no contradiction is revealed when one finds that Stevenson in some places seems to be inclined towards accepting an "instrumentalistic" view and Hare towards accepting a "salvatory" one. This is the case with Hare at least when he writes in *The Language of Morals* that "our moral language leads ... to needless practical perplexities" and points to metaethics as one way out of these. It is also the case with Stevenson in many places in *Facts and Values*.

I shall now deal with the questions, one at a time, of whether metaethics has a therapeutic effect of a "salvatory" sort and whether metaethics has a therapeutic effect of an instrumental sort, for our ethical practice.

Does Metaethics Save Us from Confusion?

I shall briefly consider three kinds of ways in which metaethics may be held to save us from needless ethical confusion. The first way takes metaethics to eliminate apparent, though not real, ethical disagreement which is based on semantical confusion. The second way takes metaethics to prevent a vain search for a certain sort of justification of ethical statements. The third way takes metaethics to dispose of certain problems in one of the following three ways: either the problem is shown to require no solution, or it is shown to have a trivial solution, or the problem is even shown not to "exist".

Does Metaethics Make Possible the Elimination of Disagreement?

We have already encountered an argument to the effect that metaethicists show certain sorts of disagreement to be merely apparent. This was when in Chapter V discussed Hare's thesis that act-utilitarianism (AU) and rule-utilitarianism (RU) could by metaethical means be shown to be extensionally equivalent and, hence, that adherents of the two views could be shown to disagree only apparently.

This argument is fairly generally accepted; for example it is used by Frankena in *Ethics* to refute not only (AU) but also what he calls "act-deontologism". Both theories are "shown", with reference to Hare, to be "disguised" forms of their general counterparts or else altogether inconceivable. All the same I have found, if my argument in Chapter V is sound, that Hare's argument is wanting. And I think it possible to generalize my negative conclusion to all cases where a metaethicist "proves" to warring parties that the theses over which they are disputing are really equivalent. Let us see why.

I distinguished, in relation to Hare's argument, three directions of interpretation of the metaethical analysis. Either it was a theory about the word-type "ought", or it was a theory about certain tokens of "ought", or it was a theory about certain speech-acts, i.e. ways of using language, no matter which words were used. But in none of these cases is it possible to draw any conclusions about any particular ethical principles. If one person believes that (RU) is correct and another that (AU) is correct the metaethicist can say nothing whatever to resolve this disagreement. For he is not at all making statements about the subjects of these propositional attitudes. The metaethicist is not talking about (RU) and (AU). But suppose the two persons tend to express their ethical convictions by the use of the word "ought", or suppose their ethical utterances are among the analysed ones, and so forth, would not this make the metaethicist's theory apply to them? Would it not then be possible to show that they were not disagreeing after all? This depends upon whether the metaethicist is making law-like statements or merely statistical ones and upon how he defines the field of application of his theory. In most cases we do *not* know whether his theory applies to the actual example, but let us suppose that it does, since such cases are at least conceivable. Now, can one reasonably conclude that the two conflicting parties are, after all, in agreement? Yes, but for very peculiar reasons. It is only because no one is really accepting—contrary to the suppositions in the example—the moral principle (AU) (or, according to some of Hare's arguments, (RU)). This finding about language, speech etc., is, of course, of the utmost importance, fantastic as it seems, not perhaps for normative ethics, but all the same for some practical purposes. We must now admit, for example, that I have failed to express (AU), though I tried to do so in Chapter V, and that no one is able to express it. There is something about the word "ought", or about certain uses of it, or about certain ways of using language, which prevents the expression of (AU).

This, of course, is not an interesting case of ethical relevance of metaethics. All these results, that existentialism is untenable, that act-utilitarianism is really rule-utilitarianism, that egoism is inconceivable, and so forth, are of sociological importance but they have no ethical compulsion whatever. The *validity* of these theories is not affected by these results.

This is not a very specific kind of relevance to ethics either. Probably there are other sciences that could have produced these results as well, say a general linguistic theory.

Moreover, the actual examples here discussed are most probably examples of false theories. This is only a passing remark, I do not wish to draw on it in any way in my conclusions, but I think it should be noticed all the same. It is quite possible to interpret Hare's universalistic theory (u) in such a way that it "allows" for (RU) as well as for (AU). Nothing is said by Hare about which properties are to count as relevant or irrelevant in the universalization. So when I hold that a particular act h ought to be done the class of acts I imply are obligatory may very well be those that, like h, fullfil the conditions of (AU), while the classes of acts moralized about in (RU) may be abstracted by very different criteria.

But in a less drastic way metaethical theories may resolve certain cases of (apparent) disagreement. It could for example be pointed out that certain words are ambiguous and that two conflicting parties use it in different senses; they are not really contradicting each other. This could be the case, for example, if one person were using the word "good" with a purely autobiographical meaning—"This is good" means *I approve of this*—and another were using it with a supernaturalistic meaning—"This is good" means *God approves of this*—and they both falsely believed that they were disagreeing over the question whether happiness is "good" or not.

This kind of relevance, in order to obtain, would of course call for a radical *change* of metaethical methodology. Metaethics would have to be about certain well-defined utterances by certain particular persons in certain particular situations, and the methods of validation would have to become empirical. It would not be a "prolegomenon" to normative ethics and the relevance would not be very *specific,* but all the same it would be of some practical importance.

Does Metaethics Make it Possible to Put an End to a Vain Search for the Truth, for an Objective Ground or Rational Sanction in Ethics?

Some metaethicists seem to hold that when ordinary people start to think about their ethical conceptual framework or vocabulary they get confused. From this confusion the metaethicist alone is the one to save them. S. Zink writes, to mention one example, in *Concepts of Ethics:*

... the ordinary person ... can express what he thinks with fair readiness and point. But if he comes to compare what he says on different occasions, he can feel puzzled, for he seems to contradict himself ... In an easy-going mood the ordinary man says: 'Good is relative' ... but when speaking of a particular question, say Hitler's persecution of Jews, he will denounce this in the strongest language, as 'Hitler was an evil man' ... I shall attempt to show that these paradoxes arise from overlooking distinctions of meaning in our concepts, an that an analysis of their meanings enables us to resolve the puzzles. (p. xii)

Zink seems to hold that when people have accepted emotivism and other sorts of non-cognitivism they have been faced with paradoxes or puzzles. Hence, if Zink is right, this is a case of *negative* therapeutic relevance of the kind Popper has spoken of. But according to Zink the way out of the puzzles is not to abandon metaethics but to pursue more thorough metaethical reflection.

But is it true that the metaethicist can eliminate confusion in this way? And how in fact is it done in that case?

There are two lines of thought about this matter. The one is sound but not very interesting. The other one indicates a very interesting form of ethical relevance, but is unsound. I have mentioned them both before.

On the one hand it is clear that it is at least conceivable that a metaethical theory informs *you* about *your* linguistic manners or *your* use of certain terms in certain contexts. You could learn, say, from the metaethicist that what you express in "ethical contexts" is something that lacks truth-values, that cannot be rationally justified and so forth, or, to choose an example closer to Zink's intentions, something that *can* be *known* although it does not describe any fact. Here the metaethical analysis of your argumentation informs you about your own "ethical practice" on points where you lack self-knowledge. I think this argument sound. This kind of relevance to ethics *is* possible. But it is not very specific, for this knowledge could probably have been obtained by other scolarly methods equally well, or better, and it requires, to obtain, a reform of the usual metaethical methodology. Metaethics will have to become more empirical, its field of application will have to be more clearly identified.

On the other hand it might be thought that the metaethicist teaches us something about ethical knowledge, ethical validation, or the sources of ethical knowledge. The metaethicist shows that, as a matter of fact, ethical statements *may* be true or false, ethical knowledge *can* be obtained, certain facts *do* constitute evidence for ethical statements and certain experiences *are* sources of ethical knowledge. But this idea, interesting as it is, is false. Metaethics has nothing to do with these subject-matters. This may be concealed because meaethical statements sometimes appear to be about ethical statements, so that when we get some information about these we indirectly get some information about "ethical facts". But here appearances are deceptive, as has been seen in my discussion about statements about ethical statements in Section 3 of this chapter.

But could not the former line of argument be made more interesting if only it is taken to prove not only that *you* acquire knowledge about *your* way of using certain terms but that a whole *society* or *culture* uses ethical language in a certain way? May not one way of making collective decisions rather than another gain credence by such a discovery? And would not this information be highly politically relevant? I think here of arguments of the following sort. 'If emotivism is true there is no truth in ethics, hence the best political system would be a voting system where each person's subjective likes and dislikes are given equal weight'. 'If naturalism is true then much of the power should be given to experts. Only experts can tell which acts are generally approved, maximizing satisfaction and so forth'. 'If intuitionism is true, a democracy with much stress on participation would be the only rational thing to have. For in that case decisions would have to be taken deliberately and only after you have taken part in argumentation and made a disinterested observation of all the relevant facts *yourself*'.

As a matter of fact there *are* pragmatic relations of this kind. I think it is no coincidence that Hare,[6] for example, who is a noncognitivist (prescriptivist) holds the view that the only "liberal" way of making collective decisions is to give to each mans moral ideals an equal weight. But these connections are irrational. Metaethics cannot facilitate our collective decision-making by selecting or suggesting for us a particular method or, even by rejecting any methods. For the *crucial* questions get no answers from the metaethicist: how *should* decisions be made? How *should* people pursue their political deliberation? *Is* there a truth to be searched for in politics? The latter question remains even when it is ascertained that no one whatever bothers about it.

[6] Cf. *Freedom and Reason*, pp. 177–79.

Does the Metaethicist Eliminate Ethical Problems?
Even if metaethics is neutral in the sense that no ethical conclusions can be derived logically from metaethical premises only, perhaps meta-ethics is yet a "propaedeutic" to the solution of ethical *problems?* Since I am now discussing ways in which confusion or misunderstanding may be eliminated the question then is whether metaethics may in any way *eliminate* ethical problems? There are three ways in which this could be thought to happen. A certain problem may be seen to be quite without importance (for some purpose), it can be seen to be *nonexistent,* or it can be seen to have a *trivial* solution.

Again we must distinguish between two ways of conceiving this relevance. One is sound and not very interesting, the other is interesting but unsound.

On the one hand it is conceivable that a metaethical theory shows that what you thought was an important problem, is without importance, that where you thought you were faced with a problem none was to be found, or that what you thought was a very intricate problem was a triviality. Take the following examples. One searches for an answer to a question expressed by the sentence "Which act out of these ought to be done?" and the metaethicist shows that the question that here troubles one, the question expressed by this sentence, is really *which act is favored by the majority?* One had thought that one was faced with a problem of the outmost importance for one's practical life—and one has found that what faced one was only a question of sociology, a question of minor importance. Or one is troubled by a question expressed by the sentence "Which normative system is true?" and one is told that this sentence does not express any question at all, it is a piece of sheer nonsense. Hence, what one thought was a problem did not exist. Or one is troubled with a question expressed by the sentence "Is act-utilitarianism or rule-utilitarianism the most reasonable theory from a normative point of view" and one is shown that "act-utilitarianism" and "rule-utilitarianism" in this context refer to theories that are extensionally equivalent. Hence, the question has a trivial answer: they are equally reasonable.

All these cases are conceivable. To obtain these forms of therapeutic relevance requires only that you can decide whether a metaethical theory applies to this very formulation you are confronted with. It must be noticed that these forms of relevance are not very specific. The results could have been obtained also by ordinary methods of linguistics or sociology. There is also something very unnatural in the situation. What the person discussed is interested in, is not a clearly identified problem—but *that* problem (whatever it is) *which is expressed* by a certain interrogative sentence. Otherwise the answer that there *is no* problem would not be accepted. Otherwise the most rational response to these findings would be to try to give a *new formulation* of the problem one had obviously failed to formulate.

On the other hand it may be thought that what is gained here, by the metaethical theories, is knowledge about ethical problems themselves. But, I need not repeat my argument, nothing of the sort is the case. The distinction between ethical epistemology and metaethics has once more been muddled.

Again, however, my mainly negative conclusions strike me as not the very last thing that can be said about the relation between metaethics and ethics. This brings us to my last sort of relevance to ethics, the instrumentally therapeutic ones.

Does Metaethics Provide Instruments for
a Better Ethical "Practice?"

I have distinguished between various sorts of metaethics but I have said little about "ethics"—except that I wish to have a wide and inclusive concept where norms and evaluations of various sorts are included and except that more theoretical problems (which ethical system is the most reasonable one?) as well as more directly practical problems (what is to be done now?) are to count as ethical. I have also had to exclude material implications with a factual antecedent as being non-ethical. I shall now try to widen my concept of ethics by explicitly allowing that not only *results* (like ethical statements and theories) and *problems* (cast as questions) are included, but also other "aspects" of the ethical "practice". I will investigate whether there are any therapeutic effects on any of these "aspects".

It is also conceivable that the therapeutic effects depend on which ethical system the ethical "practice" is concentrated on. I will indicate with reference to some points that whether certain effects obtain or not depends on which ethical system is investigated. But let me first distinguish between the various aspects of the ethical "practice".

First of all I think it conceivable that metaethical insights might have effects for what could metaphorically be called "ethical observations". There are various ways among metaethicists of conceiving of these. According to some they are only a special sort of empirical observations, according to others they are a kind of intuitions or rational insights, according to yet others they are a sort of feelings. But no matter how they are conceived metaethics could perhaps be of some help for this activity.

204

Secondly, I think it conceivable that other parts of the theoretical ethical "activity" are affected by metaethical insights. The classification of ethical "phenomena", the choice of hypotheses, the adoption of concepts in normative studies, and so forth, may perhaps gain in efficiency or cogency in some way as one realizes certain metaethical facts?

Thirdly, the presentation of the results may perhaps gain in terseness and effectiveness if the normative ethicist uses certain metaethical insights.

Fourthly, ethical decisions, choices, and the adoption in practical life of ethical views may perhaps gain something from a knowledge of metaethical facts.

All these four "aspects" I consider aspects of what I have metaphorically been calling the "ethical practice".

Metaethics, I have shown, may be of various sorts. As far as I can see the most promising sort of studies in *this* context are explications and conceptual analyses (of concepts that are "phenomenologically" or "intuitively" given). The idea is that the metaethicist suggests certain fruitful concepts which can be used in the ethical practice.

There are no systematic discussions in the philosophical literature about this kind of relation but there are a few suggestions that such relations do obtain. It seems to have occurred to some philosophers that the "moulding" or "growing" of new concepts—Stevenson in *Facts and Values*—or the analysis of concepts—MacIntyre in *A Short History of Ethics*—affects ethical reasoning, thinking, and behavior.

Stevenson holds that many philosophical problems are problems of "a clarification of our views rather than an extension of them" (p. 176); the question to be decided is rather *which is* the problem than how is the problem *solved*. And here explications may be of help. "In such a problem we are not describing the world but are preparing the way for subsequent descriptions. A growth of concepts is in question, rather than the use of old concepts in forming new beliefs". (p. 175)

MacIntyre seems to hold that the application of our ethical "knowledge", that our very behavior in ethical contexts, is changed by changed metaethical views (about what is the correct analysis of a certain ethical concept). He writes:

... to analyze a concept philosophically may often be to assist in its transformation by suggesting that it needs revisions, or that it is discredited in some way, or that it has a certain kind of prestige. Philosophy leaves everything as it is—except concepts. And since to possess a concept involves behaving or being able to behave in certain ways in certain circumstances, to alter concepts ... is to alter behavior (p. 3)

But why is this so? In what way may one profit from the meta-ethicists' suggestions of concepts for use in one's ethical practice? In what way does the possession of a new concept alter your behavior? In MacIntyre's case I suspect that this is only a "by-product" of his behavioristic views in general. And I think it is a "product" that is not quite rationally obtained. For it is one thing to manifest the adoption of a concept by being *able* to act differently in certain situations and another thing really to *modify* one's behavior. The former follows perhaps from MacIntyre's psychology according to which to possess a concept *is* to be able to act in certain ways in certain situations, but the latter does not follow. It is not necessary that the actual behavior is changed. And is it not the latter that MacIntyre needs if his argument is to show that there are therapeutic effects on our ethical practice? But perhaps also a new *capacity* of action may have some importance. Let us study more carefully these various possible relations between meta-ethics and normative ethics.

Does Metaethical Knowledge Increase our Sensitivity to Ethical "Facts?"

It has been held that it is difficult or impossible to "see" or, more generally, "perceive", what we have no conception of—or even no terms for. There are no, or only a few, "pure" observations, it has been held. We must possess the concept of a chair before we can see a chair, or see something *as* a chair. And it has also been held, in opposition to various "essentialistic" philosophies that the concepts are not "given" to us, or "innate". As a child learns to see he also learns to conceptualize. We have the concept of a chair because what is denoted by it (what it is true of) is something with a certain practical function in our lives. There are other concepts that we have for more "theoretical" reasons, like the concept of an electron. The point here is not that we need electrons in our daily life but that we need to take them into account in a certain theory. But the point, again, is that the concept is not *given*—we conceptualize to satisfy certain purposes. Another example of this view, in a rather extreme version, is the saying that on Greenland there are a lot of words and concepts for different shades of white that we lack in English, hence, English-speaking people, and people who think like Englishmen, *cannot see* these variations of white! They lack the adequate concepts. And they lack them because they do not need them, as do the nomadic Eskimoes.

The views here suggested are not very precisely formulated. They are not uncontroversial. All the same I think they have at least some advocates. Are they sound? And, if sound, is it possible also to adapt them to *ethical* concepts? And, if true also of ethical concepts, do they make it probable that metaethical proposals of new ethical concepts affect our sensitivity to ethical distinctions?

To me, although I cannot here construct any definite argument to this effect, it seems as though the views here put forward are more reasonable the more "theoretical" the concepts are to which they are applied. The example of the shades of white I find very hard to believe (I think *I* can observe the differences as well, although ordinarily I do not care to look out for them) but the example of the electron seems very probable. The example of the chair seems to lie somewhere in between. I do not really know what to say about it.

If this is true, viz. that the view here put forward is a reasonable view about electrons but not about shades of white then the question whether the same could be true of ethical concepts will be a question of how "theoretical" ethical concepts are (for this I think is the relevant difference between 'electron', 'chair', and 'white'). This is an important problem. As far as I can see the answer must vary from one ethical system to another to be to the point. I shall discuss a few examples where I do believe that this kind of therapeutic effect *may* obtain, i.e. where ethical concepts *have* a kind of theoretical complication.

In an "act-deontological" theory of normative ethics the ethical concepts may be taken to be of a kind which is very similar to that of empirical concepts. And the same is true of a theory of goodness of Moore's kind. Here ethical concepts are taken to be directly apprehended through your intuition. One does not need first to get access to the concept in order to intuit something *as* good. This is immediately clear to one. This is, I think, the most common conception of ethical "observation" provided it is extended to include cases where the "intuition" may have also an *emotive* character and where no knowledge is thought to be acquired by the "observation", but only a kind of subjective opinion. I think it a sound conception of normative ethics provided it is not taken for granted that ethical "observation" is always correct, i.e. provided intuition, moral sense, and so forth, are taken as fallible. I will not here enter into the problem whether these views are correct. I only note that according to one common view of ethical "observation" ethical concepts are not theoretical but of a rather "empirical" sort, to speak metaphorically. Hence, no theoretical complexities may be clarified by the metaethicist. This, of course, is consistent with the fact that theoretical complication pertains to non-ethical concepts which are used in ethical theory, concepts like 'action', 'consequence', 'end', 'means', and so forth.

If my suggestions on this point are sound, it is probable that we have here the rationale of the fact that today some metaethicists seem to abandon metaethical analyses—and instead concentrate on "second-order" ethical terms, like the ones mentioned. *These* theories I think are of the utmost importance for normative ethics—but according to my definitions they are hardly metaethical.

But not all metaethicists and normative ethicists agree with the thesis that ethical concepts are "simple", not "theoretical". One point of disagreement among utilitarians over ethical concepts has been whether these should be taken to apply to *particular and concrete acts* or to *abstract and generic* acts. Or do they apply to *particular but yet abstract* acts? All these three views have had their proponents. This seems to be a theoretical "muddle" and the concept of obligation would probably be very far from our immediate "intuitions" if it were held to apply to things without concrete existence. Perhaps the metaethicist could here assist in the ethical investigations. If the metaethicist would propose a solution to this problem, by explicating a concept of ought which applies, say, only to concrete and particular acts, this may perhaps have important consequences for normative ethics. This would, for example, perhaps solve certain deontic paradoxes; it could perhaps create some new ones; and it would altogether change the way of conceiving normative ethical problems for those who previously used a different concept of ought. Let us consider this example more closely.

Suppose that 'ought' is applied to "abstract particular acts" in the sense that the acts that are obligatory are acts which are made by a particular person in a particular situation but which are of such a sort that they may have *versions*.[7] Now, a utilitarian principle seems to produce paradoxes, as may be seen if one considers the following case:[8]

a = Peter studies philosophy in 1969

$-a$ = Peter does not study philosophy in 1969

a_1 = Peter studies philosophy at Uppsala in 1969

a_2 = Peter studies philosophy at Oxford 1969

---

[7] a_1 is a version of a_2 if, and only if, it is logically necessary that if a_1 is performed then a_2 is also performed, $a_1 \neq a_2$, and a_1 and a_2 have the same agents and are contemporary.

[8] The example and this formulation of the problem is from L. Bergström's *The Formulation and Application of Utilitarianism*.

Suppose now that the consequences of a_1 are better than the consequences of -a but the consequences of a_2 are worse than those of -a. Suppose also that the consequences of -a are better than those of a. Now it seems as though a_1 ought to be done according to most formulations of the utilitarian theory. But does not this imply that a also ought to be done? And is not this paradoxical if -a has better consequences than a?

There are various ways of dealing with this paradox. L. Bergström has suggested that the application of the utilitarian principle be restricted to what he calls "relevant alternative sets". Others have recommended that the deontic logic one needed to show this example paradoxical must be abandoned. My point here is that *one* alternative way of dealing with this paradox would be to define an alternative concept of ought. This paradox could be avoided altogether, it seems, if 'ought' were defined so that it could only apply to *concrete* particular actions. Perhaps this would produce *other* results that are paradoxical—I will not enter into this problem in all its complexity—but the important thing to notice here is that different conceptions of ought give significantly different "content" to certain moral principles. All the three indicated ways out of the dilemma (the construction of another deontic logic, the revision of the field of application of 'ought' to concrete acts only, or the introduction of the idea of relevant alternative sets) are examples of explications of new concepts of ought. Here it seems as though the metaethicist would be able to assist in making the ethical principle precise.

The problem here is much more complicated than I have been able to explain in a few lines. It should be noticed, however, that at least in some utilitarian ethical systems, the ethical concepts *have* a kind of theoretical and complicated character. Hence, at least in these cases, it seems possible that the metaethicist can assist in explicating them; what the metaethicist does in these cases is really to propose a certain field of examination for the normative ethicist. He assists in the formulation of the problems to be dealt with. And he indicates a subject matter for study that was perhaps not thought of before. In this way certain paradoxes may be avoided and others will perhaps face us. A new way of thinking about ethical matters may ensue. Perhaps one even gets other kinds of "intuitions", or "insights", or "feelings", and so forth, than one did before. If the new conception brought about by the metaethicist is a concept of ought that applies to concrete acts this *may* be the result of a description of a concept which is directly "given" (a conceptual analysis). If the new conception, on the other hand, is a concept of ought that applies to abstract entities defined partly by the concept of relevant alternative set it is most probably the result of an explication; this concept is highly theoretical.

An important thing to notice is that it is hard to see how metaethics, conceived of in this way, could be pursued in isolation from normative ethics. At least the explications would require arguments to the effect that they were fruitful. It could be shown, say, that certain ethical deontic paradoxes were eliminated by them. But only a normative reasoning could show this. For it is in relation to certain ethical theories as well as in relation to the theories of deontic logic, that these instances are paradoxical.

But could not this case be generalized? Are there not more radical ways in which the metaethicist may be held to produce results with effects on the very direction of ethical studies? I think there of the differences which will ensue if one takes the advice of the metaethicist who explicates 'ought' naturalistically instead of the advice of him who defines 'ought' supernaturalistically, or if one takes the advice of the metaethicist who explicates 'ought' intuitionistically instead of the advice of him who explicates it emotivistically, and so forth. Here 'ought' is taken to appear in the question of what acts ought to be done. All these suggestions of concepts are at the same time suggestions of problems and questions for normative ethics to deal with.

Again, however, it seems as though the differences are hard to assess with respect to their reasonableness in isolation from normative ethics itself. In the case of *some* of these conceptions there are *some* philosophers who would say that there are no answers to the questions asked; the question is misconceived and the formulation of it does not express anything at all. In other conceptions there are those who would say that there *are* answers to be found but that these questions are not "ethical" questions in *their* sense of the term. In yet other conceptions it seems as though "ethical questions" would altogether lack relevance to practical questions.

The adoption of a conception of moral questions, or a concept of ought in one's ethical investigations, is a complicated procedure which requires, in order to be rationally carried out, considerations of practical need, theoretical complications, descriptive reasonableness and so forth. But provided the metaethicist is willing to back up his explications with such considerations it seems as though his suggestions could be of some help to the normative ethicist. The ethicist will be directed to a certain field of examination that he had perhaps not thought of before. He will have access to a conceptual framework that may perhaps help him to see things he did not see before. His *results* will in no way be determined

210

or anticipated by the metaethicist. But the ethicist will be told which problems to solve.

A radical objection to this very idea would be that the ethical concepts, like the concept of ought, *are* simple and directly apprehended in some way. So we know pretty well what an ethical problem is. At most, the metaethicist may, once and for all, *show* this by indicating this concept of ought (which is simple and cannot be described, only "pointed at").

Another objection, less radical, would be that metaethics, as it is actually practiced, never takes the form here required. It is not the case that explications of ethical concepts, suggestions of new or revised concepts, are accompanied by arguments to the effect that in this way fruitful questions will arise, theoretical perplexities be avoided, and not too vast deviations from ordinary language be made. So at least this kind of relevance to ethics, in order to obtain, would require that a *reform* of the metaethical methods were made.

The second objection I think valid. In most cases the kind of speculation about ethical concepts here described is performed without contact with particular normative systems. It is not discussed in which way various concepts affect the reasonableness of various theories of ethics. But there are a few exeptions too. One example is H. Castañeda's discussion of the compatibility of utilitarianism and deontic logic.[9]

The former objection I do not know how to assess rationally. To be sure *some* alleged metaethical observations, conceived of as *proposals* of concepts, would be quite irrational. A concept of ought that is purely naturalistic I think would be altogether inadequate to our purpose with ethical theory. But on the other hand I think it clear that even if there is a simple concept of ought directly presented to our minds many of us have failed to see this. And perhaps a theoretical discussion of various alternative conceptions may make us see clearer into these matters.

Does Metaethical Knowledge Improve the "Systematization" of our Ethical Views and Insights?

From the above discussion I think it clear that the metaethicist to some extent might assist in the adoption of an *object* of normative ethics; he proposes concepts to replace other concepts in ethical questions which are asked from the point of view of common-sense and the ethical questions themselves are also slightly changed.

I think it is possible to develop this line of thought further. I think the metaethicist may not only suggest a certain object for ethical theory

---

[9] Cf. his article "Ought, Values, and Utilitarianism".

to deal with but may also assist in the systematization of ethical insights and the organization of ethical investigation. One example would be, I think, if ethical concepts were "split up" in the sense that ethical questions would be divided into parts and dealt with step by step. Instead of giving an exhaustive account of obligation one might, for example, deal with *two* questions which are *parts* of the question of what acts ought to be done.

One concept of ought could for example be defined in the following manner:

> h ought$_1$ to be done$=_{df.}$ assessed with regard only to the total amount of value brought into existence (*ceteris paribus*) h ought to be done

and another concept could be defined in the following manner:

> h ought$_2$ to be done$=_{df.}$ assessed with regard only to the distribution of value in the world (*ceteris paribus*) h ought to be done.

Given these concepts of ought, and perhaps also others, it is possible to make ethical "investigations" step by step and it is possible to arrive at conclusions like the one that a certain act ought$_1$ to be done, ought$_2$ to be done but ought$_3$ not to be done, while another act ought to be done in all senses defined. Now ethical "hypotheses" may be set forth without any attempt being made to find the truth, the whole truth, and nothing but the truth, in one single stroke.

Once more it is obvious that metaethics, if it is to be relevant to normative ethics, cannot be undertaken in isolation from normative considerations. The adequacy of the concepts defined, depends on which theory they are to be used in. There is no methodology of metaethics which is not part of a methodology of normative ethics; if metaethics is to have *this* kind of therapeutic relevance to ethics metaethics can *not*, for example, be pursued as a strictly descriptive empirical discipline where certain linguistic phenomena are described and classified. What makes a metaethical proposal fruitful is the use that can be made of it in normative ethics.

Does Metaethical Knowledge Improve the Presentation of Ethical Results?

If certain theoretical ethical concepts are defined and a terminology for these are constructed then, of course, this terminology will also be convenient (though not indispensible) when one presents the results of normative ethics. If, say, the question of which acts ought to be done is investigated from a restricted point of view like that of the distribution of value only, it is convenient to have a term and a concept for those acts that ought to be done from this point of view.

Abbreviations may also be introduced by means of metaethical definitions. Instead of saying that a certain act must not be omitted one may say that it is obligatory, and so forth. This treatment of ethical concepts may be developed into whole systems of deontic logic—and has often been so developed. Mostly it seems, however, as though this highly speculative, though technical, treatment of ethical concepts were rather of interest for the logician than for the normative ethicist. But in some cases such a treatment of ethical concepts *is* made necessary because of certain deontic paradoxes. At least it seems as though a revision of certain deontic principles might be *one* way out of certain problems discussed above where utilitarianism has been seen, in one version, to be incompatible with deontic logic. Another way out of this paradox, as was said above, would be to restrict the field of application of the utilitarian theory, either to concrete acts or to acts that are members of relevant alternative sets. Also in this case it would be convenient to have a clear terminology in this respect when one presents one's normatively ethical results.

Does Metaethical Knowledge Improve the Application of Ethical Insights to Practical Life?

It is more difficult to see any use for metaethics in the application of ethical views or insights to practical life. But indirectly such use is of course possible. In so far as metaethical insights may shed any light on the system one more or less consciously accepts and tries to adopt it could be of some help. Take again the case of the metaethical theory which takes 'ought' to apply only to particular acts. A clear understanding of this restriction of one's favored ethical views would put an end to a vain search for a principle about the obligatoriness of generic actions.

If suitable abbreviations are introduced, or if solutions to ethical problems are worked out "step by step" by means of the introduction of suitable concepts (which allow ethical questions to be "split up") this may also make easier the application of one's ethical insights. Even if no exhaustive ethical system can possibly be reasonably ascertained since it is hard to weight considerations of distribution of value against considerations of the total amount of value, it may still be possible to say of *some* acts that they are right or wrong, since no conflict is here involved.

Conclusion about Metaethics as a Means to a Better Ethical Practice

For the first time in this study I think I have found cases of relevance to ethics of metaethics that are of definite importance. Explications of ethical concepts have been seen, in certain cases, possibly to improve on our sensitivity to ethical distinction, on our systematization of our ethical investigations, on our presentation of ethical results and on the application of ethical views in practical life. Two comments must be made, however, that somewhat lessen the importance of this result.

First of all, it is actually only seldom that metaethics has the form required if this kind of relevance is to obtain. In most ethical systems ethical concepts lack theoretical complications and it is not fruitful to speculate about how they are to be defined or explicated—they have to be taken as primitive. But in some interesting cases there are theoretical problems pertaining to ethical concepts; it is for example not quite clear whether the utilitarian theory applies to concrete actions only or to abstract kinds of actions as well. Here a metaethical explication and the reasons put forward to support the thesis that it is fruitful may be of help to the normative ethicist. Only a few of all the various theories of metaethics set forth could have this kind of relevance.

Secondly, if suggestions of new or revised ethical concepts are to be of interest, the metaethical studies in which they are offered must most certainly not be pursued in isolation from normative ethics. It is even doubtful whether there is any point, analytically, in separating here a part of the studies pursued by the moral philosopher and calling it "metaethical". No definite assessment of the fruitfulness of the explications made is possible unless normative considerations are made. The concepts defined are to be used in a certain ethical theory. The paradoxes the new concepts are designed to dissolve are paradoxes in relation to a certain ethical system. And "metaethics", in this sense, will be a discipline without a methodology of its own.

7. The Chapter Concluded

In this chapter I have tried to generalize and extend views and suggestions set forth when I discussed three metaethical theories in earlier chapters, viz. the theories of Brandt, Stevenson, and Hare. I have distinguished between various sorts of metaethical theories and I have confronted these various sorts of theories with various concepts of relevance to ethics. In this way I have arrived at, roughly, 28 theses about the relation of metaethics to ethics (this is a simplification; many modifications and various versions of these have been discussed). In most cases the answer to the question of whether metaethics is relevant to ethics has been negative. There are some exceptions, however.

If metaethics is developed in the direction of what has been called "content analysis", i.e. if it deals with certain well-defined classes of utterances of some specified persons in some specified situations, then I think it possible that a kind of moral relevance obtains. One could find good reasons for moralizing about, or altering, in some cases, one's ethical reasoning, one's application of one's favored ethical views, and also some political views about collective decision-making would turn out to be the most rational ones. But what is frustrating with this kind of moral relevance is that no *new* ethical knowledge is gained. What is at stake is only the *application* of certain ethical principles to certain concrete cases described by the metaethicist. Furthermore this kind of relevance is probably not very specific, since the knowledge in question could as well or better have been obtained by sociological studies.

It is also possible that therapeutic effects obtain. Some instances of confusion may be eliminated. Apparent disagreement may be shown to be merely apparent. Certain problems may turn out to be rather unimportant. Other problems may turn out to be trivial with respect to their solution.

Some of my conclusions have turned out to be based on certain ethical presuppositions. This is true as well of my negative as of my positive conclusions about *moral* relevance of metaethics.

The most important affirmative answer to the question of whether metaethics is relevant to ethics is the thesis that explications may be in an instrumental way therapeutically relevant to ethics. Certain complicated ethical concepts are clarified, certain theoretical ethical concepts are defined, so that ethical questions are clarified, ethical investigations are made more effective, our sensitivity to ethical distinctions is improved and our presentation of our ethical results is made easier. Again, however, this result has to be interpreted critically. In order to obtain this relevance to ethics it is required that a change of metaethical methodology is made. As a matter of fact a kind of metaethics is required that is very hard to distinguish from normative ethics itself.

My main results, then, could very roughly indeed but perhaps all the same comprehensively and illustratively be summarized in the following "table" (it should be kept in mind that most of the "yes" are due to very trivial instances of the relevance relation; the "yes" about non-rational pragmatic relevance is due to a kind of relevance which is a border-line case. Does it really satisfy my conditions of adequacy for the concept of relevance? The "yes" for moral relevance is due to cases where ethical principles are *applied* but not themselves validated. And the "yes" for relevatory therapeutic relevance is due to cases where no insight into moral problems is gained but only insights into complexities in certain *formulations*. As a matter of fact, the only *interesting* "yes" is for instrumentally therapeutic relevance of metaethical explications):

	Logical relevance	Logical relevance emp. syst.	Moral relevance	Rational pragmatic relevance	Non-rational pragmatic relevance	Revelatory therapeut. relevance	Instrum. therapeut. relevance
Metaethical theories about language (words, sentences, types or tokens)	No	No	Yes	No	Yes	Yes	No
Metaethical theories about speech (uses of words, speech-acts, types or tokens)	No	No	Yes	No	Yes	Yes	No
Metaethical theories about propositions or concepts	No	No	No	No	Yes	No	No
Explications and normative, reformative metaethical theories	No	No	No	No	Yes	No	Yes

ANNOTATED BIBLIOGRAPHY OF LITERATURE
CONCERNING THE RELATION BETWEEN
METAETHICS AND NORMATIVE ETHICS

(1) Adams, E. M., "Classical Moral Philosophy and Metaethics", *Ethics,* Vol. 74, 1963–4, pp. 97–110.

The article makes the provocative claim that not only metaethics, but also classical moral philosophy, are non-normative. The method of argument is to show "how some of the fundamental 'moral principles' proposed by classical moral philosophers which have been taken to be normative, can be translated into metaethical theories". Premises in the argument are, among others, that "metaphysical" claims that "there are no moral values" and that "all values are prudential" are non-normative.

(2) Albert, H., "Ethik und Meta-Ethik, Das Dilemma der analytischen Moralphilosophie" *Archiv für Philosophie,* Vol. 11, 1961, pp. 28–63.

Argues, like (11), (12), (18), and perhaps (5) and (6), in defense of the thesis that the definition of the subject matter of metaethics is non-neutral. Hence, "Auffassung der Philosophie als einer Meta-Disziplin führt ... nicht notwendig zu ihrer Neutralizierung, sonder vielmehr zur Anerkennung ihrer regulativen und kritischen Funktion".

(3) Andrén, G., "Definitions, norms and logical naturalism", *Theoria* Vol. XL, 1974, pp. 138–151.

Argues that "naturalistic analyses of moral notions have normative relevance", assuming that "conceptual analyses are analyses of mental entities, ideas ..."

(4) Bergström, L., "Meaning and Morals", in *Contemporary Philosophy in Scandinavia,* ed. Raymond E. Olson and Anthony M. Paul, Baltimore and London 1972, pp. 185–195.

Bergström defends the thesis that no ethical conclusions follow from metaethical definitions since definitions and principles are not about the same things. A detailed presentation of Bergström's view is found in Chapter II of this study.

(5) Blackstone, W. T., "Are Metaethical Theories Normatively Neutral?", *Australasian Journal of Philosophy,* Vol. 39, 1961–2, pp. 65–74.

Accepts without much argument that there probably are what I have called "pragmatic" effects of the acceptance of metaethical theories. Here Blackstone seems to be in agreement with (11) and (12). He defends the thesis that there may be—and are—metaethical theories that are not implied by the ethical views held by their proponents, but also the thesis that most metaethical theories *are* implied in such a manner. The same is held about the "contraposition" of the thesis. No ethical theories are implied by *some* metaethical theories while some ethical theses are implied by others. Theories about ethical justification and *norms* about what is "cognitively meaningful" are implied. The article is concluded by the thesis that the tenability of metaethical theories depends on the theory of meaning they employ.

(6) Blackstone, W. T., "On Justifying a Metaethical Theory", *Australasian Journal of Philosophy*, Vol. 41, 1963, pp. 57–66.

Deals with the methodological question when a metaethical theory is justified. The adequacy of metaethical theories is naturally assessed, according to Blackstone, by finding out whether they fulfil the aim of providing "an explication or analysis of moral judgments and moral reasoning". So the question arises what it is to provide such an explication or analysis. Here Blackstone claims that it is not enough to assess the truth of the theories *qua* descriptions; the "framework of linguistic categories" which the analysis is cast in must be assessed as well, it must be *evaluated*. The loose and speculative conclusion of the article contains suggestions that this evaluation must be ethically non-neutral.

(7) Brandt, R., *Moral Philosophy and The Analysis of Language,* The University of Kansas, 1963.

Argues that descriptions of ordinary language have no "therapeutic relevance", in my sense of this term, to ethics. Such descriptions do not "set the stage" for normative ethics. The arguments are that "the average person uses 'good' or 'obligatory', in the important contexts, without a definite intended meaning in mind", (p. 16) that "... even if we do not reject the whole concept of 'implicit meanings' as dubious, the implicit meanings of ethical terms cannot function as a source for criticism of a person's ethical reflection or of his ethical principles", (p. 17) that "the meaning of these words ... must surely be supposed to differ from one speaker to another", (p. 18) that "these philosophers aim to use the analysis of ethical language as a device for criticizing ethical reflection, but in fact moral terms as actually used are rather blunt instruments which require to be sharpened for effective use", (p. 20) and that "we are not bound to accept the view that the ultimate aim of normative reasoning ... is to identify the situations in which moral terms in their ordinary senses are properly applied ..." (p. 22).

(8) Corbett, P., "Ethics and Experience" *Proceedings of the Aristotelian Society,* Supplementary Volume 42, 1968, pp. 1–10.

Argues that "moral reflection, ethical analysis and empirical enquiry, so long pursued together, have tended in this country to drift apart". This situation Corbett finds "irrational". His argument proceeds by an examination of the three sets of relations between moral reflection, ethical analysis and empirical enquiry taken in pairs. Concludes that analysis "fortifies" the results of reflection, "at least for people of an intellectual cast of mind". The "presupposition" here seems to be of a causal kind but as regards the "fortification" I have not clearly understood what it is. Perhaps some sort of a logical relation?

(9) Durrant, R. G., "Moral Neutrality and the Analysis of Morality", *Australasian Journal of Philosophy*, Vol. 36, 1958, pp. 169–88.

Discusses whether definitions of "morality" may be neutral, i.e. strictly "formal". Argues that the criteria of prescriptivity and universality, which are taken to define a concept of morality, are neutral and also that they are "sufficient", whatever this may mean.

(10) Fahrenbach, H., "Sprachanalyse und Ethik", in *Das Problem der Sprache VIII*, Munich 1967, ed. H.-G. Gadamer, pp. 369–85.

A survey of current metaethical positions. Makes the claim that most theories "rekurrieren darum in letzter Instanz auf die persönliche Entscheidung der Prinzipien des Handelns, letzlich des 'way of life" and that this Kantian position "... schon ist ein prinzipiell relevantes Antasten der geheiligten Grenze zwischen Meta-Ethik und normativer Ethik ..."

(11) Gewirth, A., "Meta-ethics and Normative Ethics", *Mind*, Vol. 69, 1960, pp. 187–205.

Anticipates the theses which are further developed in (12).

(12) Gewirth, A., "Meta-ethics and Moral Neutrality", *Ethics*, Vol. 78, 1967–68, pp. 214–25.

Discussed in detail in Chapter II of this study. Makes the claim that metaethics is non-neutral to ethics in a logical sense. The argument proceeds by an attempt to show that the definition of the subject-matter of metaethics must be biased.

(13) Gordon, R. M., "Socratic Definitions and Moral Neutrality", *Journal of Philosophy*, Vol. 61, 1964, pp. 433–50.

Defends the thesis that "no amount of evidence decides meaning, for one must decide independently of evidence which usage policies were demanded by language and which were not". The arguments for the thesis are that "there is no empirical criterion by which one can decide whether a usage policy universally observed by the historical speaker of a language L reflects a rule of L or an extralinguistic consensus of the historical speakers of L" and that if "the speakers themselves were unable to decide which usage policies reflect rules and which reflect consensuses, moral discourse would go on practically as it does" In Chapter III of this study I discuss this kind of problems.

(14) Grave, A. A., "Are the Analyses of Moral Concepts Morally Neutral?" *Journal of Philosophy*, Vol. 55, 1958, pp. 455–60.

Argues that metaethics is in some way relevant to ethics. The point of, say, intuitionism is a "moralist's point. It is that the types of theory opposed to it take the authority out of morality".

(15) Handy, R., "Doubts About Ordinary Language in Ethics", *Inquiry*, Vol. 3, 1960, pp. 270–77.

Is there an "ordinary" language? What is the importance of sub-cultural deviations? These and similar questions relevant to the problem of a linguistic reform, discussed on many occasions in this study, are raised. Handy suggests that moral or political views may "affect" the definitions offered for ethical terms. He concludes that "ethical behavior" is a more fruitful source of data for ethics than "linguistic usage", since the latter (in contra-distinction to the former?) contains lots of "built-in prejudices".

(16) Hunt, I., "Value Concepts and Conceptual Truth" *Proceedings of the Aristotelian Society,* New Series, Vol. 63, 1962–3, pp. 23–44.

Examines the "dialectical relationship" between problems of the two "dialectical pools" of "normative ethics" and "epistemological ethics". Interprets Moore, in his discussion of the naturalistic fallacy, as charging naturalists with ethical non-neutrality, and makes the claim that "ethically not neutral", as it is used by Moore, does not imply "not valid".

(17) Lenk, H., "Kann die sprachanalytische Moralphilosophie neutral sein?", *Archiv für Rechts- und Sozialphilosophie,* Vol. 53, 1967, pp. 367–86.

Agrees with (2), (4) and (11) that each "attempt of uniquely characterizing the specific moral is a normative one (at least on a higher level of semantics), and therefore it infringes upon the neutrality of metaethics ..." (quoted from the English summary). Lenk discusses in some detail the "multifunctionalist" conception of ethical language put forward by Nowell-Smith and Wellman.

(18) Lenk, H., "Der 'Ordinary Language Approach' und die Neutralitätsthese der Metaethik", in *Das Problem der Sprache VIII,* Munich 1967, ed. H.-G. Gadamer, pp. 183–206.

Defends a thesis ascribed to Gewirth, Albert and Blackstone to the effect that "Metaethiker selbst normativ urteilen, wenn sie eine bestimmte Art von Sätzer als spezifisch moralische Urteile "auswälhlen" und ihrer Analyse zugrunden legen".

(19) MacClosky, H. J., *Meta-ethics and Normative Ethics,* The Hague, 1969.

In the introductory chapter MacClosky discusses the relation between metaethics and normative ethics—the rest of the book deals with other problems. He claims, without much arguments, that different metaethical theories are related in different ways to normative ethics. While a definition like "'good' functions as a synonym for 'conducive to the greatest happiness'" *ipso facto* is a part of normative ethics the definition "'good' functions as an abbreviation for the expression 'willed by God'" imply ethical conclusions only together with statements about what is willed by God. MacClosky also holds the view that a "possible and reasonable reaction to an acceptance of the truth of a relativist or a subjectivist metatheory could be a rejection of moral standards as unimportant".

(20) MacIntyre, A., *A Short History of Ethics,* New York, 1966.

The introductory chapter discusses the "relativity" of moral concepts, their dependence on historical transformations. But *philosophy* too changes concepts. A "history which takes this point seriously ... cannot but be at odds with the view of all those recent philosophers who have wanted sharply to distinguish philosophical ethics as a second-order activity of comment from the first-order discourse which is a part of the conduct of life ..." According to MacIntyre, "to alter concepts ... is to alter behaviour", a view that I have discussed in Chapter VI of this study.

(21) Mayo, B., *Ethics and the Moral Life,* London, 1958.

Argues, in the introductory chapter, that books on moral philosophy "are not written in order to help people to live better lives . . ." but "by people who are trying to get clear to themselves, and to make clear to others, what morality is". But Mayo himself finds this statement far from clear. And the reason why this *must* be so, he writes, is that a book of philosophy "has no beginning and no end . . . philosophy has no destination". But also *this* statement Mayo recognizes to be problematic since it is a philosophical statement. The main argument in defense of the thesis about the aim of philosophy seems to be that questions of moral philosophy are "speculative" questions, "on the solutions of which . . . nothing that is practical hinges". Yet Mayo seems to recognize the possibility that people trained in moral philosophy might be better moral critics and agents than those unfamiliar with the subject.

(22) Moline, J., "On Philosophical Neutrality", *Metaphilosophy,* Vol. 1, 1970, pp. 20–38.

Sorts out challenges for non-neutrality as they have been advanced against metaethics, to indicate how they apply to other metastudies as well and asks how plausible their grounds are. Criticizes the views of Gordon (13) and argues that there *is* empirical evidence available for metaethical theorists and that one *can* make a distinction between which usage policies are demanded by language and which are not. Proposes an alternative view of objectivity to the one of Durrant (9) and argues against views like the one of Gewirth (12) that this concept may apply to a theory although a demarcation is made between "ethical" and "non-ethical" uses of language.

(23) Mothersill, M., "Moral Philosophy and Meta-ethics", *Journal of Philosophy,* Vol. 49, 1952, pp. 587–94.

Argues that "the distinction between 'normative' and 'metaethical' theories is not at all clear, that by common sense standards contemporary theories *are* normative (specifically, moral) in character, and that a more rigorous distinction is apt to involve circularity . . ." The argument is carried out mainly by examples of metaethicists making ethical judgments in their metaethical writings. Mothersill also sees a possibility of "isolating" the metaethical and normative components of the theories. This, however, would most probably, she claims, yield metaethical theories that are all consistent with one another or at least "non-exhaustive; if this would not be true they would all the same be such that there would be no point in asking which among them is true. For different answers to this question may depend on different basic metaphysical views.

(24) Mothersill, M., "The Use of Normative Language", *Journal of Philosophy,* Vol. 52, 1955, pp. 401–11.

Develops further some points made in (23). Especially the problem of whether metaethical theories have a common subjectmatter is discussed.

(25) Mothersill, M., "Agents, Critics, and Philosophers", *Mind,* Vol. 69, 1960, pp. 433–46.

221

A critical notice of (21). The point made by Mothersill is once again that the distinction between metaethics and normative ethics cannot be made without qualifications. Here the distinction is cast in Mayo's terms of "critics" and "philosophers".

(26) Olafson, F. A., "Metaethics and the Moral Life", *Philosophical Review*, Vol. 65, 1956, pp. 159–78.

Argues that the acceptance of metaethical theories have effects on our moral life. I have discussed the argument in support of this thesis in Chapter IV of this study.

(27) Solomon, R. C., "Sumner on Meta-ethics", *Ethics*, Vol. 78, 1967–68, p. 226.

Argues that (30), in its criticism of (11), is mistaken. Sumner has, according to Solomon, overlooked the fact that Gewirth has given independent reasons for the thesis that no theory can simultaneously be metaethical and ethically neutral. His argument is *not*, according to Solomon, that only *actual* metaethical theories are not neutral, but that in *principle* none could be neutral.

(28) Solomon, R. C., "Normative and Meta-ethics", *Philosophy and Phenomenological Research*, Vol. 31, 1970–71, pp. 97–107.

Argues that "an adequate model of ethical language will be normatively implicative, and that metaethics, characterized as the analysis of the language of ethical discourse, may involve normatively loaded principles". Proceeds by the way of examples, by trying to show that the principle of "universalizability", put forward by Hare, and the principle of "consistency", put forward by Brandt, exclude some ethical statements.

(29) Storheim, E., "Etisk teori og moralsk praksis", *Norsk Filosofisk Tidskrift*, Vol. 4, 1969, pp. 88–103.

Argues that people who hold the same metaethical views may differ in ethics and *vice versa*. But acceptance of theories that constitute "methodologies" for ultimate ethical decisions cannot but put a stamp on the moral life.

(30) Sumner, L. W., "Normative Ethics and Meta-ethics", *Ethics*, Vol. 77, 1966–67, pp. 94–106.

Argues against (10) in an attempt to show "how Gewirth's attack fails to disturb the normative-metaethical distinction itself". Sumner also claims "that this failure is typical of the usual criticisms". He examines the distinction and tries to assess its tenability anew. The point made against Gewirth is that he, contrary to his explicit intentions, tries to prove that no theory is on the same time metaethical and ethically neutral by pointing at *actual* instances only. His method, according to Sumner, is to refuse to "drop" those parts of metaethical theories which are non-neutral simply because they *actually* are parts of the metaethical theories. He does not show that they *cannot* be dropped. (29) is criticized by (26).

(31) Taylor, P. W., "The Normative Function of Meta-ethics", *Philosophical Review*, Vol. 67, 1958, pp. 16–32.

Discusses (26). Argues that the acceptance of emotivism *does* bring about changes in our moral life, no matter whether emotivism is true or not. The reasons why a "performatory analysis of moral statements generates a performatory moral life" are the same as those put forward by (26).

(32) Wheatly, J., "Ethics Does Not Exist", *Ethics,* Vol. 84, 1973–74, pp. 62–69.

Argues "that there is a definite and obvious difference between what we do when we speak and what we say when we speak, and in order to do ethics one must concern oneself with the former ...". The common interest in what we say when we speak has lead modern moral philosophy (metaethics) astray; what modern moral philosophers have taught has been of no help to people interested in ethics.

(33) Wilcox, J. T., "Blackstone on Metaethical Neutrality", *Australasian Journal of Philosophy,* Vol. 41, 1963, pp. 89–91.

Discusses (6). Makes the claim that one's normative ethical beliefs may "suggest" one's metaethical theory; and a normative theory suggests those metaethical theories which entail it. An example is the theory of Bentham. Finally the view that a theory of what is meaningful, evidence, and so on, is "prescriptive", put forward by (6), is criticized. To be true this presupposes so wide and inclusive a concept of prescriptivity that not only emotivism but all theories whatever become prescriptive.

(34) Williamson; J., "Practical Necessity and Truth", *Mind,* Vol. 80, 1971, pp. 379–90.

Metaethical statements are by the positivists held to be "necessary" statements, according to Williamson. So the thesis under discussion may be put: "No substantial principles are necessary, or are derivable from necessary principles alone". Williamson tries to give an "interesting" interpretation of this thesis. At the same time he tries to find an interpretation that makes the thesis tautological!

BIBLIOGRAPHY CONTAINING BOOKS AND ARTICLES
REFERRED TO IN THIS STUDY

Adams, E. M., "Classical Moral Philosophy and Metaethics", *Ethics*, Vol. 74, 1963–4, pp. 97–110.

Albert, H., "Ethik und Meta-Ethik, Das Dilemma der analytischen Moralphilosophie", *Archiv für Philosophie*, Vol. 11, 1961, pp. 28–63.

Andrén, G., Ericsson, L. O., and Tännsjö, T., *Metaethics 1960–1970*, The University of Stockholm, 1973.

Andrén, G., "Definitions, norms and logical naturalism", *Theoria*, Vol. XL, 1974, pp. 138–151.

Bergström, L., "Meaning and Morals", in *Contemporary Philosophy in Scandinavia*, ed. R. E. Olson and Anthony M. Paul, Baltimore and London, 1972.

— *The Formulation and Application of Utilitarianism*, Stockholm, 1974 (mimeographed).

Blackstone, W. T., "Are Metaethical Theories Normatively Neutral?" *Australasian Journal of Philosophy*, Vol. 39, 1961–2, pp. 65–74.

— "On Justifying a Metaethical Theory", *Australasian Journal of Philosophy*, Vol. 41, 1963, pp. 57–66.

Brandt, R., Ethical Theory, Englewood Cliffs, N. J., 1959.

— *Moral Philophy and The Analysis of Language*, The University of Kansas, 1963.

Broad, C. D., *Five Types of Ethical Theory*, London, 1934.

Castañeda, H. N., "Ought, Values, and Utilitarianism", *American Philosophical Quarterly*, Vol. 6, 1969, pp. 257–75.

Chisholm, R. M., *Theory of Knowledge*, Englewood Cliffs, N. J., 1966.

Corbett, P., "Ethics and Experience", *Proceedings of the Aristotelian Society*, Suppl. Vol. 42, 1969, pp. 1–10.

Durrant, R. G., "Moral Neutrality and the Analysis of Morality", *Australasian Journal of Philosophy*, Vol. 36, 1958, pp. 169–88.

Fahrenbach, H., "Sprachanalyse und Ethik", in *Das Problem der Sprache VIII*, Munich, 1967, ed. H.-G. Gadamer.

Frankena, W., *Ethics*, Englewood Cliffs, N. J., 1963.

Gardiner, P. L. "On Assenting to a Moral Principle", *Proceedings of the Aristotelian Society*, Vol. 55, 1954–5, pp. 23–44.

Gewirth, A., "Meta-ethics and Normative Ethics", *Mind*, Vol. 69, 1960, pp. 187–205.

— "Metaethics and Moral Neutrality", *Ethics*, Vol. 78, 1967–8, pp. 214–225.

Gordon, R. M. "Socratic Definitions and Moral Neutrality", *Journal of Philosophy*, Vol. 61, 1964, pp. 433–50.

Grave, A. A., "Are the Analyses of Moral Concepts Morally Neutral?", *Journal of Philosophy*, Vol. 55, 1958, pp. 455–60.

Handy, R., "Doubts About Ordinary Language in Ethics", Inquiry, Vol. 3, 1960, pp. 270–77.

Hare, R. M., *The Language of Morals*, Oxford, 1952.
— "Broad's Approach to Moral Philosophy", in *The Philosophy of C.D. Broad*, Library of Living Philosophers, ed. P. A. Schilpp.
— *Freedom and Reason*, Oxford, 1963.
Harrison, J., "Utilitarianism, Universalization and Our Duty to Be Just," *Proceedings of the Aristotelian Society*, New Series, Vol. 53, 1952-3.
Hedenius, I., *Om rätt och moral*, Stockholm, 1941.
Hume, D., *A Treatise of Human Nature*, ed. E. C. Mossner, Pelican Books, Penguin Books, 1969.
Hunt, I., "Value Concepts and Conceptual Truth", *Proceedings of the Aristotelian Society*, New Series, Vol. 63, 1962-3, pp. 23–44.
Lenk, H., "Kann die sprachanalytische Moralphilosophie neutral sein?", *Archiv für Rechts- und Sozialphilosophie*, Vol. 53, 1967, pp. 367–86.
— "Der 'Ordinary Language Approach' und die Neutralitätsthese der Metaethik", in *Das Problem der Sprache VIII*, ed. H.-G. Gadamer, Munich, 1967.
Lyons, D., *Forms and Limits of Utilitarianism*, Oxford, 1965.
MacCloskey, H. J., *Metaethics and Normative Ethics*, The Hague, 1969.
MacIntyre, A., *A Short History of Ethics*, New York, 1966.
Mayo, B., *Ethics and the Moral Life*, London, 1968.
Moline, J., "On Philosophical Neutrality", *Metaphilosophy*, Vol. 1, 1970, pp. 20–38.
Moore, G. E., *Principia Ethica*, Cambridge, 1903.
— "The Status of Sense Data", *Philosophical Studies*, London, 1922.
Mothersill, M., "Moral Philosophy and Meta-ethics", *Journal of Philosophy*, Vol. 49, 1952, 587–94.
— "The Use of Normative Language", *Journal of Philosophy*, Vol. 52, 1955, pp. 401–11.
— "Agents, Critics, and Philosophers", *Mind*, Vol. 69, 1960, pp. 433–46.
Naess, A., *Empirisk Semantik*, Stockholm, 1961.
Ofstad, H., "Objectivity of Norms and Value Judgments According to Recent Scandinavian Philosophy", *Philosophy and Phenomenological Research*, Vol. 12, 1951, pp. 42–68.
Olafson, F. A., "Meta-ethics and the Moral Life", *Philosophical Review*, Vol. 65, 1956, pp. 159–78.
Popper, K., *The Open Society and Its Enemies*, London, 1962.
Quine, W. v. O., "Two Dogmas of Empiricism", *Philosophical Review*, Vol. 60, 1951, pp. 20–43.
Solomon, R. C., "Sumner on Metaethics", *Ethics*, Vol. 78, 1968–68, p. 226.
— "Normative and Metaethics", *Philosophy and Phenomenological Research*, Vol. 31, 1970–71.
Stevenson, C. L., *Ethics and Language*, New Haven, 1960.
— *Facts and Values*, New Haven, 1963.
Storheim, E., "Etisk teori og moralsk praksis", *Norsk Filsofisk Tidskrift*, Vol. 4, 1969, pp. 88–103.
Sumner, L. W., "Normative Ethics and Metaethics", *Ethics*, Vol. 78, 1967–8, pp. 95–106.
Tarski, A., "The Semantic Conception of Truth", *Philosophy and Phenomenological Research*, Vol. 4, 1943–4.

Taylor, P. W., "The Normative Function of Meta-ethics", *The Philosophical Review*, Vol. 67, 1958, pp. 16–32.

Urmson, J. O., *The Emotive Theory of Ethics*, London, 1968.

Strawson, P. F., "On Referring" *Mind*, Vol. 59, 1950.

Wheatly, J., "Ethics Does Not Exist", *Ethics*, Vol. 84, 1973–74, pp. 62–69.

Wilcox, J. T., "Blackstone on Metaethical Neutrality", *Australasian Journal of Philosophy*, Vol. 41, 1963, pp. 89–91.

Williamson, J., "Practical Necessity and Truth", *Mind*, Vol. 80, 1971, pp. 379–90.

Zink, S., *The Concepts of Ethics*, London, 1962.

9826